GOING

Becoming a Person of Influence

DEEP

GORDON
MACDONALD

THOMAS NELSON
Since 1798

NASHVILLE   DALLAS   MEXICO CITY   RIO DE JANEIRO

Published in Nashville, Tennessee, by Thomas Nelson. Thomas Nelson is a registered trademark of Thomas Nelson, Inc.

Published in association with the literary agency of Wolgemuth & Associates, Inc.

Thomas Nelson, Inc., titles may be purchased in bulk for educational, business, fundraising, or sales promotional use. For information, please e-mail SpecialMarkets@ThomasNelson.com.

All Scripture quotations are taken from the Holy Bible, New International Version®, NIV®. © 1973, 1978, 1984, 2011 by Biblica, Inc.™ Used by permission of Zondervan. All rights reserved worldwide. www.zondervan.com

Library of Congress Cataloging-in-Publication Data

MacDonald, Gordon, 1939–
  Going deep : becoming a person of influence / Gordon MacDonald.
    p. cm.
  Includes bibliographical references.
  ISBN 978-0-7852-2608-6 (trade paper)
  1. Spirituality. 2. Spiritual formation. 3. Spiritual life—Christianity. I. Title.
  BV4501.3.M2285 2011
  248.4—dc23   2011019147

Printed in the United States of America

13 14 15 QG 5 4

The desperate need today is not for a greater number of intelligent people, or gifted people, but for *deep people*.

—Richard Foster

Disciples [*deep people*] are not manufactured wholesale. They are produced one by one, because someone has taken the pains to discipline, to instruct and enlighten, to nurture and train one that is younger.

—Oswald Sanders

PREFACE

MANY YEARS AGO I WAS INVITED TO DELIVER A SUNDAY morning sermon in the Cadet Chapel at the United States Military Academy at West Point, New York. I have no idea whether my visit to the Academy that weekend made a difference in anyone's life. But I do know that being there made an enormous difference in mine.

This is what I saw: young men and women who knew how to present themselves with dignity and excellence. Officers-in-the-making who were inquisitive, thoughtful, and focused. Budding leaders who were being prepared to go anywhere in the world and swing into influential action the minute they arrived.

The mission of the US Military Academy is: "To educate, train, and inspire the Corps of Cadets so that each graduate is a commissioned leader of character committed to the values of Duty, Honor, Country and prepared for a career of professional excellence and service to the Nation as an officer in the United States Army."

My visit to West Point provoked me with a nagging question. What would happen if the church I served became committed to a high-priority leadership training effort that took its inspiration from the mission of West Point?

More than a few seminaries, colleges, and some churches claim to be doing this. They have my applause. Nevertheless, Christians in general do seem to be struggling—at church level anyway—to figure out how to produce men and women who fit the biblical standard of *spiritual maturity* and who know how to inspire others to be faithful to Jesus.

Across the world the Christian movement is going through changes in form and substance that someday may be compared to the changes in the times of Martin Luther or John and Charles Wesley. I don't think I am overly enthusiastic when I say that the church twenty years from now will probably conduct itself and its work in ways that we can hardly imagine today.

It is probable that in these next two decades Christians—in the West, anyway—will have to ready themselves for times we have never seen or experienced before. Suffering, public opposition to faith-based convictions, and pressure in the form of governmental regulation come to mind.

We have just a few hints as to how technology will change the way new generations think and connect. We can only guess at the coming effects of globalization and the ascendant influence of nations like China, India, and others. We are already in the historic "white water" of a world dealing with seemingly insurmountable problems such as debt, climate-energy issues, and burgeoning populations of young, unemployed, very angry people.

Lest I seem gloomy, can I remind you of the seminar Jesus offered his disciples just before he went to the cross? He described to them a world, not unlike ours, that was falling apart, and he appeared to be saying, "The good news amid all this, gentlemen, is that you're going to get to plant a new movement in the middle of this mess. So be wise, alert, faithful, and productive."

Mindful of such tumultuous days ahead, Jesus spent the majority of his time training a small group of men whose message to the world would go viral. If Jesus had followed the ministry strategy that prevails today, he would have spent all of his time preaching. But apart from a few public appearances here and there, Jesus chose to train people. At first he didn't seem to be getting anywhere with his picked ones. Then one day their maturity quotient went through the ceiling.

The takeaway? Great training has exponential results. For those many, many months, the Lord's disciples watched him, listened to him, tried to emulate him with marginal results. Then, overnight, they seemed to get it. The word, the gospel, the message of Jesus, the power of the Holy Spirit finally reached the cores of their souls, and they became changed, powerful apostles.

I imagine something like this happens at West Point. When upper-teen boys or girls come to the Military Academy with petty immaturities, you might wonder about their selection. But, one day, they get it: what upperclassmen have been beating into them, what instructors have been teaching them, what it means to be a part of a great military tradition. And that's when you see what I saw that weekend: soon-to-be-commissioned leaders of character, prepared to serve the nation as officers in the United States Army.

IN THE COURSE OF THIS BOOK I WILL TRY TO EXPRESS THE idea that leadership (a word that romances all of us) is first about character, then about a disciplined charisma and competence. In other words, reshape the spiritual parts of a person, as Jesus did, and a forceful but humble kind of leadership begins to emerge from within.

This seems to have been the way of Moses, for example. If all one needed in order to be a leader was passion, education, and connection, then Moses had it all at the age of forty. Yet the first time out of the box, he failed miserably.

But forty years later, after much soul-scouring in the desert, Moses was a new man. He led less from competency and more from the soul. Watch as he backs down the Egyptian pharaoh, leads a crowd of ex-slaves out of Egypt, and introduces them to the God of Abraham. This is a different man from the one we saw when he was forty.

And how is eighty-year-old Moses different? He's now a *deep* person, purposely *cultivated* by God through direct encounter, through difficult circumstances (humiliation, failure), and through mentoring by resourceful people. Note my use of two significant words—*deep* and *cultivated*—because, from here on out, they will appear again and again in this book. They are what this book is about.

It is admittedly a big leap from the Moses of ancient days to our time. But one might wonder if the present Christian movement, as many of us know it, is capable of cultivating Moses-rated leaders.

When you think about it, we do seem to know how to get unchurched people to visit our buildings and enjoy our programs. We even appear to know how to persuade many to acknowledge personal faith in Jesus. But some are saying that what we do not know is how to produce the deep people who are supposed to emerge after that. We do not produce them, at least, in the quantities that are necessary to the challenges of our times. The result is a growing scarcity in spiritual leadership. And the implication is that without an abundance of deep people—spiritual leaders— tomorrow's organized church could be headed for irrelevance.

So let me ask this question. What might happen if a church made the development of deep people its highest priority? Let me take the question a step further. *What if a church decided that its pastor's greatest responsibility was to lead the effort to produce a continuous flow of deep people?* Unless you're simply a book skimmer, try not to go a sentence farther until you have pondered the implications of these two questions.

When I think about deep people, I am not talking about those who are paid or those who are perpetually selected to serve on the highest governing board of the church because they have money or because they have good business heads. Rather, I have in mind a larger group of people who make up the core of a congregation, a company of spiritually mature folks whose combined influence determines the culture of a congregation.

WHAT MIGHT DEEP PEOPLE IN A TWENTY-FIRST-CENTURY church look like? Here are a few ideas.

- Some live quiet but noticeable lives of devotion to Jesus. We love to be around them because they exude qualities such as grace, peacefulness, joy, wisdom, encouragement, and unconditional love. They motivate us to want to live better, more faithfully.
- Some know how to envision and organize others to do unusual things in alignment with the purposes of God.
- Some possess the capability for praying, caring, and supporting people in times of struggle.
- Some know how to teach and mentor others so that spiritual growth happens across the face of the congregation from children to senior people.
- Some deep people might possess the apostolic (missional) call to project the evangelistic and compassionate work of the church into the surrounding community or to other parts of the world.
- And some love to help.

If a congregation were populated with a goodly number of people possessing strengths like these, it would be a powerful congregation indeed.

In order to explore how a church might go about developing deep people, I want to go back and pick up the story of a New England congregation that I first told about in a book called *Who Stole My Church?*

In the first book, the key issue was intergenerational differences. My role in that book? To be a pastor who helped people who weren't in touch with one another to connect and find ways to serve Jesus together.

In this follow-up book, the new challenge is something I'm calling *cultivation*: how to develop new generations of deepening people who will rise to positions of influence in and beyond their congregation and do it in ways that fit the changing realities of our time.

As in the first book, there are only two characters in this church that really exist. The first one is me, the lead pastor of this fictional congregation. Its people are kind enough to call me Pastor MacDonald, or Pastor Mac, or GMAC (the way I usually sign my correspondence), or just plain Gordon (which I prefer most).

The book's second real character is Gail, my wife of fifty years. Most people usually call her Mrs. Mac or simply Gail. When we are alone together (in real life or in the book), I call her Babe and other private names to which she warmly responds but prefers that I not disclose. I enjoy Gail's presence in this imagined church for many reasons. Among them is my chance, as the author, to put words in her mouth. But always, they are words that are representative of the woman I know in reality, highly respect, and have loved all these years.

The way Gail and I talk and work together in this book is reflective of the way we have lived during our many decades in pastoral ministry. If you have ever wondered how a pastor and spouse conduct the private side of their lives, you may pick up a hint or two in the course of reading. We're fairly typical.

The rest of the people who appear in this book are, like the church itself, fictional; I created them. It's a strange experience to bring characters into being and then hear them take on a life of their own in my head. Sometimes, in the writing, it seems as if I've become merely the group stenographer, recording what they say and what I perceive it to mean.

Who Stole My Church? told the story of a dozen people who formed what came to be known as the Discovery Group. Its purpose? To face the reality of change in our larger world and in the world of the Christian congregation. In *Going Deep* you will meet a few of the old Discovery Group members and pick up on the impact that earlier experience had had on their lives.

An author cannot ignore his past experiences, of course, and there are times when people I have known seep into the mannerisms of those brought to life in the writing of the story. But—and this is offered like a surgeon general's warning—the reader squanders time trying to match the characters in this book with those in churches I have actually led.

The most important thing to remember is this: the church in this book, the city in which it is located, and the people who comprise its congregation can be found almost anywhere. And what they choose to do can be done anywhere.

A reading hint: note the dates and seasons at the head of each chapter. This story is told over the space of two calendar years.

So come along with me and watch these New England people conceive and commit to something initially known as *a great idea*. Then watch them bring it into being.

ACKNOWLEDGMENTS

WRITING THIS BOOK HAS RESURRECTED A HOST OF MEMO-ries about cultivating deepening people.

As we enter life's senior years, Gail and I live with the satisfaction of knowing that our cultivating/mentoring fingerprints are on a modest number of people now in positions of spiritual influence. Some of them have obtained theology degrees and are now ordained pastors and priests in churches. Others have remained a part of the so-called laity, and each day they keep various churches and organizations thriving. Almost all—whatever their vocations—are making a Christian difference somewhere. There have been only a few disappointments, and who knows when some of them—like Simon Peter—will return to feed the lambs.

Often, these sons and daughters in the Lord write us or call us to tell about things going on in their lives, and we are reminded of the words of Jesus, who said, "They will do even greater things than these." They once were deepening people; now they are deep.

MUCH THANKS IS DUE TO MY WIFE AND PARTNER, GAIL, who has hovered near during the effort of writing this book. You can be sure that she has suggested more than a few modifications to what I originally wrote. On a few occasions when she sensed that my imagination was nearly out of control, she said things like, "We would never have said that" or, "That's not the way we really would have done it" or, "Hey wait! I remember a moment similar to that, and it happened differently." When she said such things, I knew I had editing to do.

Our son, Mark, has been helpful to me as he has attempted to interpret for me the ways and thoughts of younger-generational people and the technologies they embrace.

When *Going Deep* began to mature into a book, there was a small group of people who formed about me to help it become a reality. Matt Baugher (vice president and publisher) of Thomas Nelson warmly extended the publisher's hand to me and once again welcomed me as a Nelson author. Jennifer McNeil (senior editor) skillfully coordinated the production process that turns a manuscript into a real live book. I am most grateful to Jennifer Stair on this project for her editorial care of the book and her encouraging words to me. Finally, Robert, Andrew, and Eric Wolgemuth of Wolgemuth and Associates have been there for me from the first day that this project morphed from being merely a dream into an actual book for people to read. Absent them, *Going Deep* would not exist, and I am deeply thankful to them.

Going Deep, which I have loved writing, is dedicated to a man who has been my mentor over most of the years of my life. He is now with Jesus, and I miss him. Many of his mannerisms and perspectives are transfused into me. Many of his chief convictions line my soul, and I hear his encouraging words in my head every day. His name was Dr. Vernon Charles Grounds, the former president, then chancellor, of Denver Seminary. Throughout my life, he was my primary cultivator.

If anyone sees a hint of depth in me, it is in part because of him.

Gordon MacDonald
Concord, New Hampshire

JULY 6

The First Summer

To: Hank Soriano
From: GMAC
Subject: Re: Red Sox

Hank, Gail and I really enjoyed the game yesterday. But most of all I appreciated the chance to spend time with you and Cynthia. Thanks so much for lunch, the game, the conversation. I've thought about your question and here's my first-draft answer. I think it can be read in twelve floors.

IT WAS ON JULY 6, AT AN EVENING BASEBALL GAME IN BOSTON'S Fenway Park, that the great idea first started coming to life.

Gail and I were the guests of our next-door neighbors, Hank and Cynthia Soriano. Hank's company—he's a VP for sales—has season tickets just behind the Red Sox dugout, and that evening we four were the beneficiaries of his boss's largesse.

The game was at the midpoint of the seventh inning and the women were involved in a conversation of their own. Hank and I (typical of most men) had been silent for a few minutes, watching the action on the field. Suddenly, he asked me this question: "Hey, what would you say is your church's elevator story?"

You should know that, except for weddings and funerals,

1

Hank Soriano hadn't gone to church since he was a kid. Cynthia, once a casual church attendee, dropped out completely when she married Hank six years ago. For both of them, this is their second marriage.

If Hank and Cynthia are what some call unchurched, then Gail and I are the opposite: churched up to our eyeballs. I've been a pastor for forty-plus years, before that, the son of a pastor.

Despite our contrasts in church involvement, the Sorianos and the MacDonalds are good friends. Proof? Well, to borrow a biblical comment: "Greater love hath no man than he who provideth his friends with Red Sox tickets." I'm sure Hank and Cynthia know a lot of people, but when it came to sharing an evening at Fenway Park, they chose us.

Being "unchurched" has never prevented Hank Soriano from showing interest in my work. He has always been curious about how various kinds of organizations, even churches, operate and, even more so, how they are led. So when we get together, it's not unusual for him to ask some off-the-wall question about my current activities. I should add that he likes answers couched in business language.

Actually, my neighbor, Hank, does not visualize me as a pastor or priest; rather, I am, in his eyes, something like a company president. Let me illustrate. One day he asked me how my compensation package was structured. Did my contract with the church—he assumed I had one—include a percentage of the offerings? For Hank this was not an unthinkable possibility. "Hey," he said, "I hear the church is growing on your watch. Revenue's got to be up . . . you're due a bigger piece of the pie. Understand what I'm saying?"

When I related Hank's comment to our church leaders (we call them elders) in our next meeting, they thought it was funny . . . and then dropped the subject immediately.

Now, here at Fenway Park, Hank had hit me with another of his wild questions. This one was about our church's "elevator story," which, to be honest, I wasn't sure existed.

I was silent for a moment and then sheepishly confessed to Hank that I couldn't tell him our elevator story. In fact, I further admitted, I didn't even know what an elevator story was.

Did that ever bring Hank Soriano to life! Instantly the ballgame was forgotten.

"You saying that you don't know what an elevator—" Hank got that far, paused, and then started again. He knew a teachable moment when he saw one.

"Well, say you and another guy get on an elevator at the Pru together . . . first floor." Hank was referring to Boston's Prudential Center, a few blocks away. "You've both punched the thirtieth-floor button. Get what I'm saying here?"

I nodded that I did . . . so far.

"So as the doors are closing, the other guy sees your company pin on your jacket's lapel and says, 'So, what's that company of yours do?' Got that? Huh?"

I indicated a second time that I got that. I should mention that sometimes Hank tests your patience with his filler phrases like "Got that?" and "Understand what I'm saying?" It's a verbal habit, part of his Boston brogue, which, if you're short on patience, can drive you nuts.

Hank went on. "Okay, here's the point of an elevator story. You've got the time it takes to reach the thirtieth floor to tell this guy exactly what your company does." Then with a big Soriano smile, he added, with a hint of drama, "And let's just say that if—*if*, I said—your company story is dazzling enough, this guy'll pull out his card and suggest getting together to talk about doing a twenty-mil deal with you. Twenty *million* dollars! Get it?"

I assured Hank that I got it.

"So." Hank sat back and folded his arms as if satisfied that he'd thoroughly instructed me. "What's your church's story? Dazzle me in thirty floors. Pretend there's twenty mil on the line here."

Put yourself in my shoes. You're in sold-out Fenway Park. The score's tied. The Red Sox are coming to bat, and the crowd is singing "Sweet Caroline (Oh, Oh, Oh)," a nightly Fenway Park ritual. And suddenly, the guy who brought you to the game asks to be dazzled by your church's elevator story. And remember that you only learned a minute ago what an elevator story is. *Understand what I'm saying?*

The first thing that came to me as I struggled to respond to Hank was the doctrinal statement on the nature of the church that I'd hammered out years ago in a seminary theology course. But it is hardly a dazzling document, especially for someone like unchurched Hank. Besides, it would have required at least six hundred or more floors to rattle off, and his elevator apparently only went up thirty floors. I also thought about our fifteen-word mission statement—"to point people toward Jesus Christ and his invitation to a full and purposeful life." But that wouldn't have dazzled Hank either.

Here's what Hank Soriano was asking: *What is your church doing today that would cause anyone (maybe even your neighbor, Hank Soriano) to be attracted to it?*

I finally dodged the question by asking for a day or two to think about it. That experience at Fenway was not my finest hour as the "president" of our church.

JULY 6–8

The First Summer

To: Tom O'Donnell
From: GMAC
Subject: Elevator Story

Tom, question for you. What's an elevator story?

To: GMAC
From: Tom O'Donnell
Subject: Re: Elevator Story

Hey, Pastor Mac. Where'd you find that in the Bible? I thought elevator stories were only for business types. An elevator story is a brief description of an organization, its products or services, and how it gets the job done. Some businesses go mad trying to formalize one and get everyone to agree with it.

OVER THE NEXT FEW DAYS, I KEPT THINKING ABOUT WHAT our church's elevator story might sound like. Several times I sat down with my laptop and tried writing one. But when I read some of my drafts to Gail, she was decidedly *undazzled*. I came to realize that Tom O'Donnell was right: thirty-floor elevator stories—the dazzling kind, anyway—are not easy to produce.

5

Finally, determined to get a story written if for no better reason than to redeem myself in Hank Soriano's eyes, I forced one into existence to which Gail reluctantly gave a passing grade. I remember her saying, "It's okay, I guess . . . but don't spend the twenty mil, or whatever, until the cash is in your hand."

Our Church Elevator Story

Our 175-year-old church is composed of people who, through the generations, have shared a common commitment to Jesus Christ. Following his example, we regularly worship God. Studying his life and the lives of those who followed him, we do our best to emulate him in the way we live in our community. Believing that God's central message is about love, we try to assure that our relationships (God, marriage, family, friendships, strangers, even enemies) all reflect what he both taught and did. Finally, aware of his intense compassion for people who lost their way spiritually and physically, we attempt to represent his mission by serving others in the larger world when we become aware of their needs.

Having completed my final version, my imagination went to work. What if my elevator story—despite Gail's lack of enthusiasm—garnered some version of a twenty-mil payday? Exactly what would that payday be? In this case the answer was obvious. The payday would be Hank and Cynthia Soriano visiting our church, deciding to follow Jesus, and wanting to become a part of things. No doubt about it: that would be the equivalent of a twenty-mil deal.

Finally, I pasted my elevator story into an e-mail I'd written to thank Hank and Cynthia for taking Gail and me to the ballgame, then began awaiting his response.

I will confide to you that the dreamer in me anticipated an almost immediate text message that might sound like this: *GMAC,*

Read your ES. Never knew a church could sound so exciting. I'm really dazzled. How quickly can Cynthia and I get involved?

That message never came.

But there was a result of sorts that I would never have anticipated. It came in a conversation Hank and I had when we unexpectedly bumped into each other on the way to our mailboxes the next day to get our morning newspapers.

"Hey, I read your elevator story several times," Hank said. "Not too bad. Never read anything like that before . . . pretty religious . . . but we probably need organizations like yours that do some good in the world. Tell you one thing, though. It's sure different from my store."

Hank often refers to his company as "the store" for reasons I've never understood.

"Well, anyway," I said, "now you know a little bit more about what I do."

"Yeah, I guess so. I can see why you might enjoy your job."

"What makes you say that?"

And then Hank Soriano said something that—now looking back with perspective—began to define the final years of my pastoral life.

"Mac, I'm in marketing and sales. The largest part of my job is training people, which I love doing. I read your story, and I said to myself, *That stuff he writes about can't happen unless somebody's constantly training people.* If you're going to keep that story honest, training, training, training is going to be your most important job. Understand what I'm saying here?

"You may be president of your store, but you should also be the chief training officer. And that combo would come close to being the greatest job there is: discovering who's trainable and teaching them to make that elevator story of yours happen. You know . . ." Here Hank seemed to almost get nostalgic. "I could really love a job like yours."

JULY 9

The First Summer

From my journal

*Fascinating conversation with Soriano this morning.
He actually liked my elevator story. At least he didn't
blow it off. And he had the insight to see that the
key to an organization like a church begins with training
leadership. He said something that amazed me. "Training,
training, training: that's what'll keep your story honest."*

*This morning I'm wondering what Hank would
think if I told him how poor a job we do in training
leaders. Truth is that we do some training in our
church for leaders, but it's optional and is usually
treated in a cavalier way. Anyway, Soriano has managed
to get my mind spinning. Is our elevator story honest?
What does <u>training, training, training</u> mean?*

WRITING THAT ELEVATOR STORY FOR HANK SORIANO ENDED
up dazzling me more than it did him. I say this because it started
me—and ultimately others—on my search for the "great idea."

Let me explain what I mean.

During the several hours I invested in writing my elevator
story, I tried my best to describe what our church did in language

that would enlighten someone who hadn't the vaguest notion of what a church was. In Hank Soriano's case, the challenge was to offer a story that was faithful to the sacred nature of what we sometimes call *the body of Christ* yet comprehensible to a person who could only think in business terms.

Before I started writing my first of many drafts, I tried whittling down the concept of a church to its irreducible minimum. Where could one go in the Bible to see this done? I think I found my answer in these words attributed to Jesus: "Where two or three gather in my name, there am I with them."

I concluded that these words were like the DNA—a building block of sorts—of the church. All that's necessary is for two or more people to come and bond together in a common loyalty to Jesus, the Savior. Result? He becomes present in that gathering. That's all one needs to certify that a church exists for a short or long time: *Christ is here!*

But how would one know that Christ is present? How about these evidences? Lives would begin to change; that's *conversion*. People would begin to love, to care for, to enjoy one another; that's *community*, or *fellowship*. A spirit of generosity would start to fill the air as each person invested his or her energies and resources in the life of the gathering; that's *servanthood*. Children would be instructed; youth mentored; adults of every age would be encouraged; older people might be appreciated, even listened to. That's *love*.

And from there? There might follow an apostolic spirit in those people that would begin to burst outward, beyond the church, into the larger world so that others might experience the redemptive love of Jesus in all sorts of ways. That's being *missional*.

I found it inspiring to imagine this chain of events, and I was refreshed in the thought of how much I have loved the church when it has operated like this over the years. I have enjoyed the friendships, the things people did together, the way we all supported one another when there were difficult times. I thought of those I'd seen come to faith in Jesus and experience a marked renovation of life.

I wondered what the biblical equivalent of an elevator story might sound like. The Ephesian church came to mind because we know as much about that church as any in the New Testament.

If the Ephesian church has an elevator story, this is it: you can read it in just five floors.

When [miracles in the church] became known to the Jews and Greeks living in Ephesus, they were all seized with fear and the name of the Lord Jesus was held in high honor. Many of those who believed now came and openly confessed their evil deeds. A number who had practiced sorcery brought their scrolls together and burned them publicly. . . . In this way the word of the Lord spread widely and grew in power.

Now, there's an impressive story. But did the Ephesian church stay honest? Only a few decades later, this church with its wild beginning became the recipient of one of the sternest judgments a church could imagine. A prophetic angel said to the church: "I hold this against you: You have forsaken the love you had at first. Remember the height from which you have fallen. . . . If you do not repent, I will come to you and remove your lampstand from its place."

It was as if the angel was saying, "You people are just inches from *losing* (losing!) the thing that most marked you in the beginning. In fact, Christ's blessing (your lampstand) is about to be taken from you. Think about that . . . long and hard!"

The angel could have added, "And once the lampstand is gone, you're no longer a church."

I read these lines of Scripture, thought about them several times, and asked myself how this could have happened. How could the Ephesian church have lost so much momentum?

Remember the height, the angel had said. What I called the Ephesian church's elevator story must have described the church's peak moments, its height. But from that point forward, it was downhill all the way. The story lost its honesty.

I thought back over the recent years of our own church's life. Like Ephesus in the days of its elevator story, we were at something of a "height" (to borrow the angel's words). We'd learned how to love and care for one another, how to worship with gusto, and how to get out into the world and serve in the name of Jesus. We were—yes, right now!—at one of those heights.

But if Ephesus had lost its first love and fallen from its height, how long might it be before that could also happen to us? How long might it be before we could lose our elevator story?

These gloomy questions dogged me for days.

Then, a few mornings later when I was sitting out in the sunporch with the day's first cup of coffee, there came a moment when it was almost as if heaven spoke straight at me. And this is what I thought I heard: *You must pray for an idea that will keep your C+ elevator story honest. You mustn't let what happened to the Ephesians happen to you.*

I did as heaven said. I began to pray. Each day at the beginning of my prayer time in the morning (I like to kneel in my home study), I prayed just as I felt I'd been instructed. "Lord, I'm in need of an idea that will have a powerful impact upon our church and, if possible, on me."

Only as I look back now do I see a convergence of insights that were coming together. In my heart I was hearing heaven prompt, *You must pray for an idea.* And with my ears I was hearing Hank Soriano, by no means a Christ-follower, say, "Train, train, train."

11

It was only a matter of time before—again, borrowing from my neighbor's favorite cliché—I would understand what God was saying: that the idea had everything to do with training tomorrow's leaders.

JULY 13

The First Summer

Get-well card to George Huntoon

George,

    I'm so sorry to hear that you're in the hospital. I'm looking forward to visiting you so that I can see for myself how you're doing and pray with you. I've been doing some thinking about a brand of people Paul referred to as shepherds of the flock. It occurred to me that you've been one of those kinds of people for years, George. I don't ever want to stop thanking you for your faithfulness. Many people walk with Jesus today because you were there for them.

                              GMAC

FOR THE NEXT SEVERAL DAYS I KEPT COMING BACK TO THE question: what had gone wrong with the church at Ephesus? What had caused this vibrant congregation to lose what the angel called its *first love*? How had that amazing elevator story lost its credibility?

I believe I found the answer when I reread the words St. Paul spoke to the Ephesian church leaders when he met with them at the seaport town of Miletus. Assuming that it might be the last time he'd ever see them, he offered a piece of fatherly advice: "Keep watch over yourselves and all the flock of which the Holy Spirit has made you overseers. Be shepherds of the church of God, which he bought with his own blood. I know that after I leave, savage wolves will come in among you and will not spare the flock."

Three words, built on a powerful metaphor, fairly jumped off the page at me: *shepherds*, *flock*, and *wolves*.

Shepherds (those at the center of the congregation) were the people who had responsibility for the flock (the larger congregation). Their job description was threefold. They defined the direction in which the flock would move, they assured that the flock was properly fed and rested (you could say nurtured and strengthened), and they guaranteed that the flock was protected from danger and disease at all times.

The wolves were the bad guys. If the shepherds failed to do their jobs, the wolves inevitably showed up and began plundering the flock. They did it with gossip and slander; they did it with off-the-wall teachings; and they did it by exploiting vulnerable people with promises they couldn't keep.

There must have come a time when Paul's fatherly advice to the shepherds at Ephesus was forgotten. Some subsequent generation of leaders must have misunderstood (or resisted) what their shepherding responsibilities were all about. And, just as Paul warned, the wolves appeared. Soon the Ephesian elevator story was plummeting into dishonesty.

As I mused on the debacle at Ephesus, this question blossomed in my mind. *How does a church provide for a continuous supply of shepherd-type people who will sustain the elements of the elevator story and prevent the wolves from messing things up?*

One day I wrote in my journal:

I am excited by an elevator story that accurately describes what God is doing in our church family. No puff words; no superficiality. If it's the right story, it will dazzle.

But what will keep such a story honest? That's the follow-up question.

Humanly speaking, the only thing that can make that happen are people who resemble Paul's shepherds who are committed to keeping the story fresh and operational.

And who would these people be? Visionaries? Communicators? Organizers and managers? Well, it certainly doesn't hurt to have people around with those competencies. But I suspect that we're talking about something more. People—both men and women—who possess a universal spiritual quality that is more important than mere competency. What is that quality I'm looking for?

Lord, you've challenged me to pray for an idea. I'm praying.

JULY 15-AUGUST 15

The First Summer

To: GMAC
From: Rich Fisher
Subject: Your "Idea"

I want you to know that Carly and I have been praying about this idea that you're seeking. Let me be among the first to know when God speaks.

I BEGAN SHARING MY THOUGHTS ABOUT PERPETUATING AN honest elevator story with anyone who would listen. Gail, for example. I must have bored her silly with all of my speculations about sheep and shepherds and wolves. But if she was, in fact, bored, she never let on. As she has always done during our many years together, Gail listened and responded with probing questions of her own. Frequently she suggested that we pray together about this new passion of mine: for greater understanding of the issue, for guidance on how to proceed, for the interest of others who might bring wisdom to the table.

I took small groups of elders and church council members out to breakfast and shared my concern. Everyone expressed great interest in what I was saying and urged me to keep on with my thinking. Before long, everyone was well acquainted with those unfortunate Ephesians who'd lost their first love.

I began to notice that one man, Rich Fisher, chair of our church council, seemed to understand more than anyone else what was on my mind. He took it seriously when I said that I felt compelled to pray and search for a breakthrough idea and promised that he would share the burden of that prayer.

Rich and I began exchanging e-mails and phone calls, trading book titles and scriptures that spoke to how people become shepherds and move to the core of the congregation. Because Rich is a great hockey fan (he loves the Boston Bruins), it didn't surprise me that in one of our conversations he reminded me of the comment attributed to hockey star Wayne Gretzky: "A good hockey player plays where the puck is. A great hockey player plays where the puck is going to be."

Quoting Gretzky was Rich's way of saying that he applauded the fact that I was thinking about tomorrow—where the "puck" was going to be. "Let others worry about today," he added.

On another occasion Rich wrote me:

The world is totally rearranging itself, Gordon: the way it thinks, the way it communicates, the way it organizes itself. I see the evidence every day in my job. Our church has to start envisioning new responses and initiatives to express the Christian way in this new world. We'll be a different kind of Christian community seven years from now, and we're going to need people at the center who will discern what God wants us to be. Don't stop thinking!

I didn't attach any significance to it at the time, but I remember that in one of our phone conversations, Rich asked if I was

familiar with the name General George Marshall. He was reading his biography, he said, and he thought there was a story about
Marshall that would fascinate me. "I'd like to read it to you next
time I see you," he said.

Looking back at those summer weeks when questions about
the future of our church first took root in my heart, I realized that
it all started at the ballgame in Fenway Park when Hank Soriano
brought up the subject of elevator stories.

Soriano! Why had God used him to make me start on my
quest for a new idea?

SEPTEMBER 4

The First Summer

From my journal

> *Saturday. Dump day. Fall is in the air. Slept poorly*
> *last night. Mind racing. Wild week. Meetings, meetings,*
> *meetings: staff, elders, church council. I may*
> *have started something. I smell changes coming.*
> *Many conversations about fresh ideas, some new*
> *approaches. Is the church leadership headed toward*
> *some dramatic turn in the road? How would that*
> *affect me? After talking as much as I have about*
> *flexibility and adaptability, do I really believe it myself*
> *if it threatens to change my life?*

THE SIGN AT THE GATE OF OUR TOWN DUMP SAYS THAT IT IS
open twice a week: Wednesdays (4–7 p.m.) and Saturdays (8
a.m.–5 p.m.). The hours are actually a bit more flexible than that
because Nate, the dump supervisor, usually opens the gate about
an hour earlier on both days. Those of us who try to get an extra-
early start on Saturday mornings appreciate this.

It was one of those Saturday mornings when we—Gail and
I—arrived at the dump in my aging Tundra pickup truck. During
the last two weeks of August, we committed ourselves to our

annual clutter-clearance project, and this morning the truck was full of stuff we no longer needed or no longer used. We were proud of our effort. We told ourselves that we were getting rid of junk our children would never have to worry about if anything ever happened to us.

I backed up the Tundra to the paper-only recycle Dumpster and began to dispose of our week's accumulation of cardboard boxes, junk mail, and wastepaper. Gail busied herself distributing our tin and aluminum cans, plastic bottles, and both clear and colored glass into their appropriate bins. We are recyclers; we call ourselves "creation-care people."

Gail and I had agreed that we'd meet on the other side of the dump at what is known as the Treasure House, where people leave the usable stuff they no longer need. Parents bribe their children to come to the dump and help with the trash by promising ten minutes of rummaging around in the Treasure House. It was at this local landmark where we'd leave the detritus of the clutter-clearance project.

As I was emptying my last container of wastepaper, I heard a voice behind me. "Hey, Pastor Mac." When I turned around, I saw Rich Fisher walking in my direction. He'd come early to the dump too.

THIS MIGHT BE A GOOD TIME TO GIVE YOU MORE DETAIL ABOUT Rich. You'll get to know him quite well before this book ends.

Rich Fisher is near the top of the public school system in our city. He is one of four assistant principals in the high school. Originally a history teacher, Rich made an upward career move when he completed his doctorate in education administration. Everyone at the high school appears to hold him in high esteem.

Rich and his wife, Carly (she's in special education), are also greatly appreciated in our church. They have two boys—Jacob, a middle schooler; and Caleb, a freshman. Carly leads the church's food pantry team, and as I mentioned before, Rich is chair of our church council—a collection of men and women whose responsibility it is to oversee the business side of our church's life.

I WAS SO GLAD TO SEE RICH AT THE DUMP THAT EARLY September Saturday morning because we'd not touched base in the past few days.

There was an awkward moment when Rich got to me and we both extended our hands for a shake. Simultaneously, we both realized that our hands were dump-dirty and pulled them back. I said, "Call it a wireless handshake," and that solved our problem.

After we'd both answered the "How's your week been?" question, Rich said, "I can't believe we're running into each other this morning. Any chance we could get a lunch or breakfast together this next week?"

"Sure," I said. "I'd like that. Council business, or shall we talk more about the Gretzky thing?"

"No council business this time. I want to pick back up on our recent conversations . . . you know, the idea. I've got some things to share with you. I think you'll be interested. Too much for here, so if we could meet next week . . ."

I was glad for Rich's invitation and immediately said, "Time? Place?"

"Well, if you're willing to come in my direction, how about Tuesday at school? I've got a free hour around noon. We could get some healthy institutional food in the school cafeteria and eat in my office."

Rich knows that I generally prefer to meet people, whenever possible, where they work. I like to avoid meeting on church property as much as I can. In Rich's case I'd been to the high school many times when he and I wanted to visit. During the years he'd been a teacher, I even sat in on some of his history classes and loved it. I called it an exchange in expertise.

I reached into the Tundra for my BlackBerry and saw that the time was open. "Tuesday's great," I said.

"Oh, there's one other thing," Rich said. "I have something for you to read. I've been carrying it around in my billfold all week to give you tomorrow morning." He pulled out a small card and handed it to me.

"Don't look at it until you have a moment to really think about what it says."

"I promise," I said, and slipped the card into my jacket pocket.

"Okay. See you tomorrow and Tuesday," Rich said and headed toward his car. A few seconds later he turned and shouted back at me, "Preach well tomorrow. Carly and I will be cheering you on."

That last comment was typical of Dr. Rich Fisher: always the encourager. A pastor can remain strong for a long time with support like his.

When I drove the truck over to the Treasure House, Gail was there to meet me, and she said, "I saw you talking to Rich. What was that about?"

"Oh, he wants to get together next week, so we're going to meet for lunch at the school on Tuesday."

"Something wrong?" Gail asked.

"Of course not. He wants to talk about my current favorite topic . . . you know, the idea."

Together Gail and I removed our "treasures" from the back of the Tundra. A few minutes later we were driving toward the dump gate. When I looked in the rearview mirror, I saw several kids already picking through what we'd left. Now it would clutter their basements for the next few years.

As we drove out the gate, I remembered the card Rich Fisher

had given me. I pulled it from my jacket pocket and handed it to Gail. "Rich handed me this. Could you read it to me?"

Gail took the card, read it to herself, and for a moment remained silent. Wondering what the silence was all about, I said with a hint of impatience, "Hello . . . what does it say?"

"Better listen to this carefully," Gail said quietly. "It's a quote from Richard Foster. 'The desperate need today is not for a greater number of intelligent people, or gifted people, but for deep people.'"

"*Deep people*?" I said. "What a provocative term. It's grabbing."

"Yep. Grabs me too," Gail said.

We drove along in silence for a few more minutes. At one point I broke the silence and asked Gail to reread the Foster quote. She did.

"Read it again," I asked. And she read it a third time.

"Intelligent people, gifted people. You know? Your instincts tell you that those are the kind of people you need to run a church. So those are the kind you look for. You want bright, spiffy people, people who've done well in some career venture. You say to yourself, these are the kind of people that make a church hum. We've had a lot of them in our leadership, and I think I've enjoyed almost every one of them. But Foster says the real need—did he say *desperate*?—is for *deep people*. What's that term mean to you?"

"Oh, I think I know what Richard Foster's saying," Gail said. "I'm not sure I've ever specifically defined a deep person, but I sure know one when I see one."

"Do you see many of them in our church?" I asked.

"I think I see some," Gail said. "Some pretty deep ones, in fact. But you know what? The ones I'm thinking of are beginning to show some gray on top. I wish I could say that I saw more deep people in the younger generations. Maybe the better word for the younger people is *deepening*. Most of them are not there yet."

Deep and *deepening*. What interesting words, I thought. A church needs deep people, and it has to have a way to deepen people. In that moment I knew these words were going to figure greatly in our prayerful search for the breakthrough idea.

SEPTEMBER 6

The First Summer

To: Arlene Lewis
From: GMAC
Subject: Thank you

Hi Arlene,

I've been doing a lot of thinking over the past few weeks about where our church is going to be in a few years. Paul's Acts 20 metaphor of shepherds and flocks has influenced me. Remember when we read that a few years back in the Discovery Group meeting? A healthy flock needs good shepherds. In the last day or two I've started referring to these shepherds as "deep people," and it occurs to me, Arlene, that you're one of them. I just wanted to say thank you.

Oh, there's one thing you might consider doing for me. Tell me how you think we can refresh our supply of "Arlenes." Is there any way to guarantee that there will be more deep people like you tomorrow?

GMAC

To: GMAC
From: Arlene Lewis
Subject: Re: Thank you

Good grief, Pastor Mac. More Arlenes? The thought makes me shudder. But if you're serious with your question about where to find more of those deep people, I only have one answer. Grow them! There were those who grew me when I was young. It isn't any different now.

THIS IS THE START OF MY NINTH YEAR AT OUR CHURCH. IN the earlier book about life in our congregation, I told how I'd come to the church as something of a "compromise" candidate. The compromise was between the younger and the older generations that were embroiled in growing conflicts about how our church was going to live its future life.

The younger generation, mostly people who'd relocated to our area because they loved the New England ethos, wanted a church that was open to all the innovations that were being touted in books, conferences, and satellite seminars. The older generation, mainly those who had been a part of the church since their childhoods, wanted a pastor who'd bring back the organ, the choir, midweek prayer services, and Sunday school. Oh, and hymnals too.

No one got everything they wanted when they settled on me. I was a bit of a disappointment to everyone. But—and this became very important—they discovered that Gail and I had one huge thing to offer. We knew how to love people, and we were confident, then and now, that it's possible to overcome a lot of generational divisiveness if people feel genuinely valued. From the first day Gail and I arrived, we started loving people as best we could, and it paid off handsomely.

The result has been nine really good, even happy, years. Problems? Of course. And you can read about some of the early ones in *Who Stole My Church?* But this second book is not about problems. It's rather about challenges and opportunities.

In the past few years, our church has grown numerically. And it's grown in kinds of "ministries," an oft-used word in the church world. In our church we prefer *ministry* to a word like *program*, which sounds so institutional and organized.

We've also grown in terms of generosity: our people are faithful givers in spite of the fact that few could be considered wealthy.

We've been a generous congregation in terms of serving. Groups of our people have gone to other countries and gotten involved in projects such as home-building, English language instruction, and sports initiatives. Here in our city, we asked our civic leaders where the town needed volunteer service. And they've given us helpful answers that have led to our people serving in hospitals, food pantries, and school tutoring. And that's just the beginning.

Organizationally, our pastoral team has grown in proportion to the size of the congregation. Jason Calder is our youngest and most recent addition to the team, and he is currently leading our worship activities. We call Jason our homegrown guy since he grew up in our church.

We have two other staff members doing pastoral type ministries: Bruce Bartlett (associate pastor and sometime preacher) and Claire Dustin (pastoral care and counseling). Claire, Bruce, Jason, and I have a great relationship, and I feel very comfortable with their partnership.

There's another kind of growth that delights me. We have people moving into our area from other countries and cultures. There are several Hispanic families and singles who are now with us. The standouts among them are Mercedes Perez, a brilliant and

27

vivacious Christ-follower, and a young man, Hugo Padilla. They both come from South Texas. I should mention that Mercedes heads up the Northeast Center for Professional Enhancement, the training school for one of the nation's largest hotel chains. Hugo is with Southwest Airlines.

We also have a Brazilian family: Gilberto and Adriana Silva. Gilberto is a member of our elder board. Both of them have an unusual sensitivity to life in the spiritual realm. I've heard Gilberto express concern to the elders about an attitude or a mood that he discerns in this or that part of church life, and he's always been right on the money. I should add that there are new Christians in our church who are following Jesus because of Gilberto and Adriana. I'd send any person curious about faith in the Silvas' direction.

There is a Haitian couple, Martine and Wilford Jean-Baptiste, who are studying at Franklin Pierce College. They are among the most loving, most optimistic people we've ever met. It seems like every time I meet Haitian Christians, I am newly amazed with their almost effortless ability to find something good in everything that happens. How do they grow up in a suffering nation and generate such joy?

You'd like Hana Tchung, who comes from Korea. She and her daughter, Hyun Jung, are living here for three years while Hyun Jung goes to high school. Hana's husband—his American name is Andy—has remained in Korea, where he is an executive with an auto parts company. He visits his wife and daughter every second or third month.

Hana is an incredible woman of prayer. Soon after she came to our church, Hana approached me and asked if she could come to the church twice a week and spend time praying. I must tell you: we learned the first day that Hana may be a quiet woman, but not when she's praying. When she is praying in the worship center by herself, we can hear her (literally through the walls) shouting out to God in intercession for her family, her country, our church (she talks about revival a lot), and—last but not least—Gail and me. Someday I would like to try to see if there is any correlation between Hana's praying and my best moments in preaching and pastoring people.

I should also mention Samuel and Ramya Anand from India. Ramya loves children and has made a great contribution to our children's ministry. The Anands carry themselves with a dignity—not a haughtiness—that makes us admire them greatly.

Additionally, we have three or four families who came through refugee programs from Sudan and Somalia. Some of our people are assisting them in the study of English, learning American customs and culture, and helping them adjust to new jobs.

Obviously we've received a lot of American-born people into our church. A goodly number of them have discovered Jesus here. In various and different ways, they have made personal decisions to follow Jesus (as we like to put it), and they are growing spiritually.

So all of this—numerical change, financial change, ministry and staff change, cultural change—has been happening to us over the course of the last six years. We've been tested and challenged. In most cases, our staff, elders, and council members have made good ministry decisions. Here and there, of course, there have been a few unwise ones. So we've known lots of blessing and some disappointments.

There's one other kind of change that concerns me. Call it a kind of sociological change. A lot of people are no longer loyal to any one church. We pastors like to think we "own" our people, but the truth is that they are moving back and forth between churches and organizations that sponsor weekend conferences. They watch TV church, sometimes listen to Christian radio. So they get a lot of religious exposure. I'm not sure how to explain my feelings about this new sociology, but my gut tells me that, in the coming years, there are going to be a lot of lonely people who didn't pay their dues when it came to building personal bonds of friendship and community. Maybe a new kind of church needs to be birthed. One that emphasizes community and spiritual development. If so, the need for training, training, training (Hank Soriano's words) is more necessary than ever.

Anyway, we're now into September, and I have intensified my prayers for that breakthrough idea, which is now coming to sound like this: *How can our church enlarge its core congregation with deep people who are prepared to take us into tomorrow exemplifying the Christ-following life and inspiring us to fulfill the mission God has given us?*

Little did I know when Rich Fisher invited me to lunch on Tuesday that our conversation would begin to take this idea-in-process and move it in the direction of greatness.

SEPTEMBER 7

Lunch, the First Summer

Pastor MacDonald,

    God move me pray for you this day. I believe that he speak into your heart, and that you must listen to him. I at church today and pray for you and Mrs. MacDonald.

Hana Tchung

I MEET REGULARLY WITH THE PASTORAL STAFF (BRUCE Bartlett, Claire Dustin, and Jason Calder) from nine to eleven on Tuesday mornings. As we talked our way through ministry issues, the urgent voice of Hana Tchung praying in the worship center could be heard through the wall, and we knew that this humble woman from Korea was praying for each of us.

When I left the church office at 11:30 to go to the high school, Kelly Martin handed me a note in a sealed envelope. I didn't open it until later in the afternoon. It was from Hana Tchung. What she wrote—and wrote well, considering that she's only been speaking English for six months—touched me deeply. How could she have known that, on that very day, I was headed into a conversation that would ultimately impact scores of lives, mine included?

IF YOU'RE A VISITOR, GETTING INTO THE HIGH SCHOOL IS not unlike going through airport security on a high-alert day.

You enter through one door (and only one!), pass through a metal detector supervised by a uniformed guard, and are escorted to a reception area near the principal's office. There you sign in: name, address, date, time, and host. You are given a visitor's pass that clips to your belt or lapel (your choice). And then you wait until your host—in my case, Rich Fisher—comes and escorts you to wherever it is you want to go.

When Rich appeared, we headed to the school cafeteria and selected salads and half sandwiches, each an example of the school's commitment to better nutrition. Then we moved on to Rich's office in the administrative center, where we could eat and talk in privacy.

"You say grace here?" I asked when we were settled. "Or is being thankful illegal in the principal's office?"

"Hm . . . probably okay to do if you don't get down on your knees, shout a lot, or wave your hands in the air," Rich said, feigning seriousness. Then in a dramatic whisper, he said, "I sneak prayers in this office all the time. I haven't been caught by the prayer police yet. See if you can do it without getting caught too."

I heard this as Rich's invitation for me to pray, and I did. "Lord, please make some good things happen in this school today. Bless the young people who have come to learn and the faculty that's come to teach. Even if some don't want you here"—Rich chuckled when I said this—"be present in this place. And I pray this especially for my friend, Rich. Remind him every day of his opportunity to build intellectual and moral quality into the life of this institution. We are both very grateful for this food. Amen."

Following a brief conversation about church this past Sunday—Rich said he liked the sermon—and a bit about his family, we finally got to what was really on Rich Fisher's mind.

"Pastor Mac, it's been a couple of weeks since you and I have talked about your search for a fresh idea. But that doesn't mean that Carly and I haven't been thinking about it. You need to know that both of us are really on your wavelength—"

"And I want you to know," I broke in, "how grateful I am for the Foster quote you gave me at the dump and its term *deep people*. Ever since Gail and I read Foster's words, we've been talking about how much the phrase *deep people* fits our thinking."

"Hey, terrific! When I read that line for the first time, I had a feeling that it might be exactly what you were looking for to better define whatever the breakthrough is going to be. So, let me tell you what Carly and I did on the sly to see if we could hustle this thing along."

"Hustle what along?"

"Yeah, we—well, Carly, actually—got the impulse to have some people over for a barbecue and run a dream session, and it happened last Friday night."

"A dream session," I said. "What's that?"

"Well, actually, it's an exercise we run sometimes here at school. When we do them, we bring people who love to brainstorm together and encourage them to dialogue their way to a solution for a problem we're living with. The people at the table can be teachers, parents, vendors, even students. When dream sessions are done right, they usually produce initiatives we'd never thought of because everyone, for the moment, is on level ground with everyone else.

"Carly and I decided that a dream session with some folks in the church family might be just what was needed to get some thinking churned up. So when everyone arrived, I told them that our purpose for the evening, besides eating, was to imagine what could be done to grow a larger population of spiritual leaders in our congregation. Of course that got people wondering right away about the definition of leadership."

"Man, I would have loved being a bug on the wall. Who was there?"

"Well, you're probably wondering why we didn't invite you." And Rich was right. A bit of me felt overlooked.

"Actually, we thought about asking you and Gail to join us, but you know, when we have dream sessions here at the school, the principal never gets invited because, as I said before, we want people to think out of the box and not worry whether they're pleasing her or not. So we decided not to invite the 'principal' of the church."

(Mental note to myself: Soriano thinks I'm a CEO; Fisher calls me the principal. Does anyone call me a pastor anymore?)

"Makes sense to me," I said. "So now that I know why I was cut from the guest list"—I grinned when I said this—"who were the lucky ones who made it?"

"Carly made up the list. She asked some elders and their spouses, a couple of church council people, and five or six ministry leaders. There were both marrieds and singles. It was a great group, a good mix . . . bright people. About fifteen, I think. The only people who couldn't make it were the Handleys and the O'Donnells."

"And the others . . ."

"Later. I'd rather you hear what they talked about first."

Since meeting Rich at the dump on Saturday, I'd imagined all sorts of things he might want to talk about. But I'd never anticipated this. What Rich and Carly had done on their own, having this "dream session" at their house, was an enormous encouragement to me.

"I was glad to run into you on Saturday," Rich said, "because I wanted to sit with you as soon as possible and tell you what had happened the night before."

"Rich, I'm really stunned. You and Carly are the first people besides Gail to give any indication that you really think that this

34

itch I've got for a breakthrough idea is an important issue. And this dream session you had . . . Man, I'm all ears. Tell me everything that happened."

"Well . . ." Rich leaned forward in his chair as if to underscore what he was about to say. "What surprised me was how much consensus there was. It was clear from the get-go that almost everyone is in sync with your basic concern: that we get serious about building fresh spiritual leadership into the congregation's core. They seemed to understand this."

Rich went on. "You may think you've not been heard, but you'd be wrong. The leadership's hearing you. They just may not fully understand the implications of what you're saying, but they're with you."

"What don't they understand?" I asked.

"Well, if you listen carefully, you hear things that indicate that not everyone is used to hearing the kind of thing you're talking about. If you talk about leadership development, some automatically think about teaching people to fill slots on committees or to head up programs or to serve on the elder board. When we talked the other night, I tried to make sure that they knew you were referring to something far more significant."

I broke into Rich's comments and probably should not have. "Well, that's why I love the term *deep people* that Foster uses because it helps to focus on something more important than just institutional hole-plugging."

"Look!" Rich said. "The kind of leadership you're talking about is a tough thing to define. I know we're talking about it constantly here at the school, and I can tell you that the professionals in my world aren't always in agreement as to how it works. But everyone agrees on one thing: that all organizations need a continuous supply of trained people who know how to bring people together and motivate them to grow to do their best."

35

"So what happened on Friday night? Were there any insights that would move me along in my thinking?"

"Yeah, there were some pretty good thoughts. And by the way, I had to keep reminding everyone that we were just having a discussion among friends and that the only possible action item out of the evening might be to make a few suggestions to you and the elders."

"So . . . how did you get them talking?"

"I kicked off the conversation by reading the Foster quote and then asked this question: 'Name a man and a woman in the Bible who come to your mind when you hear the term *deep people.*' I not only asked them for names but for a reason why they'd picked those people.

"You'd be surprised who they came up with. After we named twenty or thirty people in both Testaments, they picked . . . ready for this?"

"Of course. I'm really curious."

"They elected Barnabas and Mary of Bethany."

I digested this for a moment and then said, "Barnabas makes perfect sense, now that I think about it. Every time he shows up in the early church, everyone is benefited. Yep . . . makes perfect sense. But Mary? Why her?"

"Well, Kathy Cassidy came up with Mary's name. She said that Mary was the only woman we know of who sat at the feet of Jesus—which, and I'd not known this, is a Jewish term that describes what disciples of a rabbi did when they were learning. They sat at the master's feet.

"Then Kathy mentioned the night in Bethany just before Jesus died when Mary was with Jesus and the disciples, and she poured perfume over the Lord's feet. Somehow Mary knew what was coming in the next few days. The men, on the other hand, who should have known what might be coming, were so out of touch that they criticized Mary for squandering the perfume.

"But instead of rebuking Mary, Jesus rebuked the men. He said, 'Mary's the only one that knows what's going on. She was the only one who acted appropriately.' And that, Kathy argued, was an evidence of the woman's incredible depth.

"Funny," Rich went on. "I'd never thought about Mary like that before. But it was clear that she'd made a big impression on Kathy Cassidy."

Rich was absolutely right. And I had to admit that I'd not taken Mary seriously enough before.

Rich continued. "The group talked for a while about what Mary and Barnabas had in common. And the more they talked, the more they began to catch a vision of what depth means. It quickly became the key term of the evening. Soon everyone was talking about deep people."

"I get more and more attached to the term *deep people*," I said. "It excites me. And, besides, I'm so weary of the word *leader*, which has been overused to the point that it's hard to know what it means any longer. I find myself wanting to explore all of its implications."

"The second thing we did," Rich went on, "was to brainstorm on what a deep person might look like today. You know, 'Do we know people around us who strike us as being like Barnabas or Mary—or others like them? Any deep people in our church?' I was encouraged that we could actually come up with some names.

"And that led to asking the question, 'Where do deep people come from? How do they get to a point where others see them as worthy of that term?'

"Everyone agreed that in the good old days—whenever that was—deep people usually came out of solid Christian families and a consistent experience in a church where there was systematic

Bible teaching and exposure to a bevy of deep people from previous generations.

"But that led us to get concerned that this may not be happening as much anymore."

Rich and I talked a bit about why this might be true, and then he said, "Then there was an interesting, kind of special moment in the conversation. Samuel and Ramya Anand were both there, and you may not know this, but Ramya is a very serious gardener."

I mentioned earlier that the Anands are from India. Talk about deep people! They are among the best.

Rich continued. "Ramya described flowers that sometimes grow up in her yard in places where they're not supposed to be. She said that gardeners call them 'volunteers.' Seeds stick to a bird's wing or a dog's paw, for example, and then, when it gets shaken off, it might take root in the new location where it was never intended to be. A short time later, what have you got? You're surprised by a volunteer flower.

"But then, Ramya said, there are the flowers that grow exactly where the gardener meant for them to grow. They're there because they have been planted, watered, protected from weeds. Ramya called them the *cultivated* ones. So you've got two kinds of flowers: cultivated and volunteer. It's nice to have both, but what you really want is more of the cultivated ones.

"So," Rich went on, "Ramya gave us an interesting word picture, and the group glommed on to it immediately. We realized that Ramya was saying that good gardening means cultivating. And spiritual gardening in a church means that you deliberately cultivate deep people."

"Ramya's distinction between volunteer and cultivated flowers is worth the price of this lunch," I said. "That really grabs me. Is there more?"

"Well, yeah, there is," Rich said. "The group talked about

what the cultivation of deep people in a church might imply, how it might have to be distinguished from other programs and activities in the church. We began to realize that this was exactly what Jesus was doing when he selected the Twelve. He wasn't going around picking volunteers; he was a rabbi, and he was in the deep people cultivation business."

Rich unscrewed the top of a fresh bottle of water and took a long drink. He may have done this simply to seize a moment to reflect on what we were saying. Then he spoke again. "It's really interesting to think about what we're saying, because I read a book this summer that has really fascinated me."

"What book was that?" I asked.

"It's the biography of General George Marshall. I think I told you about it a few weeks back at the breakfast. Know anything about Marshall?"

"Sure," I said. "He was general of the army during World War II. After the war he was secretary of state and created the Marshall plan that saved Europe from communism when the war was over. Probably one of the greatest Americans in the twentieth century."

"Good," Rich said. "You get an A."

"That's a first," I quipped.

"Ever heard of Marshall's black book?" Rich asked.

"Black book? No. What about it?"

"Well, back in 1939, a year or two before the war, Marshall was interviewed by a military reporter and asked if the top officers in the US Army were fit to lead our soldiers into battle if another world war broke out.

"Marshall's immediate answer, which he gave in utmost confidence, was no. He said most of the general officers, though excellent people, were not prepared to lead soldiers into a modern war."

With this Rich got up and went over to a bookshelf and found the Marshall biography. He quickly turned to a page that was marked, and he said he wanted to read a paragraph for me.

"Here's what Marshall said to the reporter," Rick said. "'The present general officers of the line have their minds set in out-moded patterns, and can't change to meet the new conditions they may face if we become involved in the war that's started in Europe. I do not propose to send our young citizen-soldiers into action, if they must go into action, under commanders whose minds are no longer adaptable to the making of split-second deci-sions in the fast-moving war of today. . . . They'll have their chance to prove what they can do. But I doubt that many of them will come through satisfactorily. Those that don't will be eliminated.'"

"Those are pretty tough words," I said.

"Absolutely," Rich agreed. "But Gordon, they're the words of a *people cultivator*, not a guy satisfied with volunteers. They're from the heart of a man who thinks the security of his country is pretty serious business. What if we thought that seriously about the spiritual security of our congregation?"

"Whoa!" I said to myself. As Rich spoke about the security of the country, my mind leapt to Paul's concern about the security of the Ephesians, if or when the wolves showed up.

Rich put the book back on the shelf and drank some more water. Then he continued. "The reporter asked Marshall where new generals might come from."

I was now so caught up in Rich's story that I didn't see where it might be leading.

"Well!" Rich raised his voice and pointed his index finger into the air just as a teacher would signal that he was about to give you the point of the story. "Marshall had this little black notebook that he kept with him all the time, and he slid it across the desk so the reporter could see it. He said that the book contained the names of certain younger officers, and that he was spending huge amounts of time studying these men closely. He told the reporter that he was constantly assigning them to projects and tasks that were almost impossible to complete and watching how they handled themselves. And he said something like this to the reporter: 'The ones who meet the challenges of those assignments will be pushed ahead . . . and those who fail will be gone immediately.'"

Rich paused and then went on. "Here's the kicker. When the reporter looked at the list of names, he saw *Devers, Hodges, Patton, Eisenhower, Eichelberger, Patch, Clark, Bradley* before Marshall took the book back.

"Apparently," Rich said, "Marshall kept this black book with him all the time. He often added new names and dropped others as he observed these young officers in action. And when World War II was over, six years later, the reporter realized that the names he had seen in that book back in 1939 were the names of the leaders who led America's army to victory in 1945."

SEPTEMBER 7

Lunch Continues, the First Summer

To: Rich Fisher
From: GMAC
Incredible lunch. Thanks for turning my life upside down.

To: GMAC
From: Rich Fisher
That's what I'm here for.

For a few minutes Rich and I gave our attention to what was left of our lunches, and we were silent. Looking back now, I realize that Rich was getting ready to challenge me to consider a significant shift in my pastoral priorities—a shift that would cause me to stop doing some things I loved to do and turn to some things I'd never really tried before.

"Pastor," Rich finally said, "here's what the Marshall story says to me. Historians tell us that Marshall's supreme desire was to lead the American army in Europe. He thought that would be the ultimate achievement of his military career. But here was his problem: President Roosevelt wouldn't let him leave the country. He was just too valuable to America's overall war effort. He would have to remain in Washington, stay by the president's side, and manage the total war, less the soldier and more the executive.

And the first and most important dimension of that management responsibility was to identify and produce America's new generation of leaders.

"Marshall obeyed that call," Rich went on to say. "It's possible that he had to deal with a lot of personal disappointment because of his desire to smell the gunpowder in the heat of battle. But he accepted the president's command to go out and find other people to do the job. And in part, that's how he won the war for us. He identified the next generation of potential generals, he cultivated them, and he deployed them at the core of the US Army."

"So, Rich," I said, "where are you going with this?"

"Okay. Here goes. When the group talked about the core congregation and how its people are cultivated, they came up with one more insight."

"Which was . . ."

"Which was that the *cultivation* of deep people is not just another generic program in a church. It is something instigated by a small team of people at the beginning who make this effort their number one passion. And then the group came to the conclusion that any serious effort in this direction had to be spearheaded by you . . . and, if she's willing, Gail. That's what we think the idea you've been searching for begins to look like. And you know what? It's not just an idea. It's a great idea."

I started to say something, but Rich literally waved me off as if to say, *Let me finish.* And he repeated himself to make sure I got the point.

"This great idea is a challenge like none other in the church. Cultivating deep people starts small . . . with just one or two people who give it all they've got. We think that's you and Gail. You are the ones to make it happen. If I were to put it in terms that they sometimes use in business, you've got to consider becoming the chief training officer of the church."

43

Again there was silence as I absorbed these words. *Chief training officer!* That's the same term Hank Soriano had used at our mailbox conversation. Could the two have talked, or was the Holy Spirit stapling something to my soul?

I suppose I was trying to think of something appropriate, even noble, to say in response but couldn't. I was kind of overwhelmed, to be frank. All these weeks I'd been flying high with all my thinking centered on the concept of—to use Rich's words—cultivating deep people, and now, for the first time, someone was telling me what the beginning of the process might actually look like. And, to hear Rich talk, it looked like it started with Gail and me.

Since I was silent, Rich spoke again. "I've heard you sometimes wonder out loud how much longer you should keep being the pastor of our church and when it might be time to lay the responsibility down. But here's my word to you—and forgive me if I'm coming on too strong—don't even think of leaving us until you've taken your best shot at doing what pastors all over this country need to be doing."

"Which is . . ."

"Which is to invest yourself in the cultivation of a new layer of deep people. Then if you ever want to get on with something else, you'll have my blessing, even though we'll miss you an awful lot."

I finally found some words to say. "So you think your Marshall plan—if I could call it that—is better than any plan I might have to retire and spend the rest of my life in a kayak."

"Forgive me for my bluntness, Gordon, but I don't call kayaking a successful conclusion to a wonderful pastoral ministry," Rich said. "I call it quitting at the moment when we may need you most. You have some things to teach us . . . to teach me, teach Carly. How to do it? I'm not totally sure yet, but I think you'll have a bunch of learners on your hands if you want to commit yourself to this."

Rich looked me square in the eye when he said this. It seemed as if he had practiced these words many times before he said them.

Any smile that might have been on my face was now gone. I actually felt like crying.

"Better unpack that comment for me," I half-whispered. Down deep, somewhere at the core of my being, was a Voice that seemed to be whispering something like, *Rich is my man. Listen to him.*

Rich drew a deep breath. Then he said, "The group at our house last week dreamed of you coming up with a two- or three-year plan in which you'd help us raise up a whole new generation of deep people at the church. You've done it informally to some extent already. People like Carly and me have been greatly influenced by you and Gail, but in a sense we're like Ramya's volunteers. You probably weren't aware that you were cultivating us, but you were.

"Now we want you to consider doing the same thing for a batch of other people and doing it more deliberately and more vigorously so that it becomes a priority that occupies a large portion of your time."

Rich Fisher was proposing a game-changer in my ministry. Now I was locked in on what this assistant principal at the high school was saying. For the moment this much-younger man was speaking into the life of the older. And I had this sense that any plans—retirement, for example—that I'd been thinking about for the next few years might be in need of revision.

"You and your barbecue guests seem to have mapped out a wonderful plan for Gail's life and mine," I said. "I'm not sure most pastors do what you're describing any longer . . . Maybe a few."

Rich agreed. "Yeah, I know what you're saying. But maybe it's time to find a new way because the old way a lot of pastors do things isn't working that well. You may have to become like a rabbi for some people. A lot of younger people have never seen a mature Christian in motion. They didn't see one in their families when they were kids, and they're not seeing much in our country today."

You may have to become like a rabbi for some people. It was the third time Rich had alluded to the picture of a rabbi. I filed it away in my head to think about at another time.

Rich Fisher spoke again. "The group ended up dreaming about fifty to sixty people, maybe a few more, who'd be cultivated over three or four years by personal association with you and, hopefully, Gail."

"Obviously, you've just upped—I mean really upped—the ante in my thinking, Rich. I think I'm grateful, but I've got a lot of work to do. This . . . this . . . you called it a *great* idea that we've talked about for a while, has suddenly started coming to life."

"Thanks. And I hope you'll think a lot about the General Marshall story. His example suggests to me that there is a way and that you can figure it out. I'd like you to imagine a day when there will be a whole new generation of deep people in place who are envisioned and trained in their desire to serve God and serve people. Dream about that, Pastor Mac. See if you and Gail can make it happen."

Again, there was silence as Rich and I thought about what had just happened in this conversation: what he'd said and what it meant to me.

Then I changed the subject. "So, tell me, who was in this group at your house? You've hardly mentioned a name," I said.

"I didn't want to tell you at the beginning," Rich answered. "I worried that it might somehow prejudice your reactions. One of the most vocal people there was Ben Jacobs."

"Ben Jacobs?" I was astonished. "Vocal? Ben Jacobs, vocal? What a distance he's come. I can remember when . . . You're serious? Jacobs was there?"

"Ben and Catherine Jacobs were both there. We all remember the first time we saw Ben, Gordon, and what you and some others did to bring him to Jesus, and what he's become as a result is astonishing. He's really on his way to becoming a deep person, and it's no accident. You and Ernie Yost and—who else was in on that?—oh, Russ Milner. You guys just loved him into the family and moved him along toward spiritual growth. He's still a bit rough around the edges, but I tell you, he's the kind of guy we need at the heart of the congregation. Talk about influence! Yeah, he was there the other night. And he was in complete agreement with what I've been saying to you. We'd be in great shape as a church if we had a few dozen more Bens."

More Bens! I wanted to laugh out loud at the irony of Rich's words. I remember the first time I met Ben in our church sanctuary. He was sullen, withdrawn, ready to walk at the slightest provocation. He was the product of a dysfunctional family; he had deep psychological scars; he was pretty hostile to any thought of God. But a loving aunt and several wonderful older men had mentored him into Christian maturity. And now! Think of it! Ben Jacobs sitting at a table with other church veterans talking about how Gail and I could redirect our leadership influence and cultivate a few more like him.

"So let's review this wild and crazy version of what you've called a great idea before I have to go," I said to Rich Fisher. "You and Carly, Ben Jacobs, and a few more of our saints whom you still haven't named are suggesting that Gail and I think about scuttling some of our present activities in the church and identifying some promising candidates for the next generation of deep people. We do the Marshall plan with them, and when they're ready, we release them to God's call."

Rich started laughing. "Marshall plan? You're something else! But, yeah, you've got the idea. The Marshall plan. We'll push the elders to get on board. You get started figuring out how you guys might make it happen. And then we'll all go for it."

A few minutes later, after we'd prayed together, Rich Fisher and I headed down the hallway to the visitors' entrance. When we got to the door, I had to squelch the impulse to hug him because somehow it didn't seem appropriate to hug an assistant principal at the doorway of his school.

As I walked away, Rich suddenly called out, "See you, Rabbi."

That's about as close as I can come to relating to you the conversation I had with Rich Fisher that unforgettable Tuesday.

Sometimes I play a crazy mind game in reflective moments. I ask myself, *What are the ten most important conversations you've had in your life?* Each time I do it, I come up with a fresh list. Only a few conversations survive every vetting. There's the first conversation I had with Gail that made me instantly fall in love with her. There's the one that made me a pastor. And now this conversation in Rich Fisher's office at the high school. This one will always be on the list.

SEPTEMBER 7

Midafternoon, the First Summer

Letter to Hana Tchung

> *Dear Hana,*
>
> *I want you to know that God heard your prayers at the church today. I had some meetings with leaders in our church that have begun to open the door to a new vision, a truly great idea. I believe that one of the major reasons that happened was because of your faithfulness in lifting others and me into the presence of the Lord. Thank you, Hana.*
>
> *Pastor MacDonald*

GAIL AND I HAVE A CONDO HOME, ONE OF A DOZEN ON A circular drive on the north side of our small city. A thick stand of trees surrounds our condo, giving us the feeling of country living. As I've already said, the Sorianos live next to us.

I phoned Gail when I'd left Rich Fisher's office to say that I wanted to come home for a short while so that I could relate to her what he and I had talked about. It's not normal for me to suddenly call and say I'm headed home in the early afternoon, and that caused Gail to react with concern.

"Something wrong?" she asked, just as she'd done when she saw Rich and me talking at the dump the previous Saturday.

"No. Not at all," I replied. "We had an incredible conversation. It may provide the answer to one of our most important prayer requests."

"Which one is that?" Gail asked.

"The one about what we're going to do for the rest of our lives."

"Oh, that little request," she joked. I could hear the smile in her voice.

"Yeah. Anyway, I'm really excited, and I want to tell you what Rich had on his mind so we can start thinking about it together."

"Hurry home," Gail said.

WHEN I PULLED INTO THE DRIVEWAY, GAIL WAS WAITING for me, glasses of lemonade on a small tray. We went into our screened-in porch and sat down. I filled her in on everything I remember about the lunch conversation, including a description, as best I recalled it, of the dream session that the Fishers had hosted at their home. I explained what we meant with terms like *deep people* and *cultivation*.

"Sounds like you and Rich had quite a talk," Gail said.

"Well, the most important thing I learned today is that some of our church leaders are beginning to take ownership of my concern about tomorrow's deep people. It's now becoming known as the 'great idea.' And I do think they have a better word than *development*. They're drawn to the word *cultivation*. I really like it too. They also had some thoughts about first steps, and Rich wanted to pass them on to me."

"And . . . ?"

"Some are thinking that I . . . well, really, *we* . . . should consider rearranging our priorities and concentrate heavily on what we could do to raise up this new batch of deep people."

"And they don't think you've been doing that already?"

"Well, sure; they know that. And they know that you've been doing it too. But no one's ever really defined it as a specific task that takes precedence over almost everything else. Training and cultivating people: you know, really, that's not even on the pastor's job description. I get the feeling they want it to be there . . . that they think I should consider moving it up the priority list and make it my—well, really, *our*—first priority."

"More than preaching and managing the staff?"

"I don't hear them downgrading my role as the main preacher. But I get the feeling they'd like me to get out from behind the desk and give myself—again, you with me—to cultivating teachable people. Apparently they think that day-to-day staff management could be turned over to someone else, and you know how much I'd love that. They just don't want anything in the way that would bar me—us—from building in the lives of would-be deep people."

"So what did you say to Rich?"

"Well, there was nothing, really, to say to him except that I'd think about it and talk with you about it. It was just an exploratory conversation. And, of course, we'd have to walk this version of the great idea through all the elders and see if they're aboard."

"Did you think that God was saying something to you during your time with Rich?"

"You know, I do. It probably sounds a bit over-the-top, but I found myself thinking that my time with Rich might rank as one of the most important conversations I've ever had. I sensed that we were on holy ground in his office—burning bush and all of that."

"And how did it make you feel to know that people are talking about changes in what you do?"

"Well, it's exhilarating and scary all at the same time."

"What's the scary part?"

"You know my heart better than anybody. For a minute during the conversation in Rich's office, I had this tinge of fear when I realized that people were suggesting that I stop doing things I've done for years and start doing some things I've never really made that much of a priority before. And you know what happens . . ."

"What happens?" Gail asked.

"Do I have to say it? This great idea might not work, and some might begin to think that I've failed. The next thing you and I know, people in the hallway will start asking each other, 'Isn't it time for Gordon to resign?' That sort of fear flies around in my mind sometimes."

"But you have to admit: they're doing exactly what you've been telling them to do: thinking about a future when you and I will no longer be around."

"Of course. I know that. But that doesn't mean that all the little 'Gordons' inside of me agree with what I've been saying. There's a Gordon down deep inside who keeps insisting that I'm indispensible doing what I'm doing . . . that things would fall apart if I do something different. And there's another Gordon who keeps worrying that if I fail here, there will be no more opportunities coming my way. I don't like these kind of Gordons any more than you do, but sometimes I can't get them to stop bugging me."

Gail put down her glass of lemonade and put her ice-chilled hand over mine. She said, "Those 'Gordons' inside of you need a reminder that God's been taking care of us for fifty years now. Through the years he led us into wonderful places. He led us here. He's not going to quit on us now. This is a great new opportunity to be spiritual father and mother to some of tomorrow's spiritual leaders . . . deep people. You think about that and tell me if there's anything better to do with our older years."

"Yeah, I will. Oh, you'll never imagine who was part of the dinner at Rich and Carly's house last week . . . never in a million years."

"So save time. Tell me."

"No, you guess. Here are some clues. Think back about six years. It's Sunday morning. We walk into church and there's this weird guy sitting off in the back right corner. He sticks out like a sore thumb. The ushers are nervous about even going near him . . . Someone says he may have a gun and be getting ready to shoot up the place."

"Ben? Ben Jacobs? Ben Jacobs was at that dinner?"

"Utterly brilliant! Rich and Carly invited him and Catherine to be part of the group. And Rich said he, well, actually both of them, were just about the most valuable contributors to the conversation."

"I can't believe it," Gail said. "What made Ben and Catherine so special?"

"Somewhere during the evening, apparently, Ben told his story for the first time. He told everyone about coming from Virginia and living at Connie's."

"Well, everyone knows about that."

"True. But apparently, Ben went on and talked about what had happened to him when that pedophile in his church got to him when he was a boy. Then he told them how Ernie Yost had befriended him and introduced him to the men of the church . . . how they'd helped him work through some of his personal issues. He gave them the whole nine yards: how he joined the worship team, came to faith, what caused him to grow spiritually, how he'd met Catherine, and how much he loves our church community."

"I can't imagine what that must mean to you when you hear that Ben said those things."

"Even now, as I'm having a bit of time to process it, I'm saying to myself, maybe God wants you and me to discover and cultivate several dozen more Ben Jacobses?"

"You're sure of that?"

"I'm on my way to being sure. But I know one thing. This great idea, as Rich calls it, I could never do it without you."

SEPTEMBER 7

Evening, the First Summer

To: Ben Jacobs
From: GMAC
Subject: Dream Session

Ben,
Yesterday, Rich Fisher and I were together, and he told me
about your participation (and Catherine's) in the dream session at his house last week. Ben, forgive an old pastor if he
seems to be gushing, but I want you to know how proud I am
of you. Rich feels that many of the things you said were the
key to a very successful evening. According to him, people
were listening intensely to you when you talked about your
own experience and about cultivating deep people. My
opinion? God used you powerfully, Ben. The way you have
grown during the course of your Christian journey in the last
several years is breathtaking.
Gratefully,
Pastor Mac

AFTER MY CONVERSATION WITH GAIL, I HEADED BACK TO
the office. There were a couple of late-afternoon visits on my calendar. Elsie Appleton, eighty-something and a lifetime member

of the church, wanted my promise that I'd preside at her funeral when she died, and I assured her that, if I outlived her, I would.

Then I met with Tom Stephens, who lost his job a year ago and feared he was about to lose his home. The first of these two conversations was easy. All Elsie Appleton needed was to hear my promise that I'd be there for her. But the second, my conversation with Tom Stephens, broke my heart. All I could do was pray for him and offer the name of a guy in banking who I thought might have some counsel for him. When Tom left, I had to sit in quiet for a while and deal with the feeling that I had somehow let him down. Surely, I kept thinking, there is more that I could do for a man with such a problem. But what?

After a while, I wrote Tom a note to assure him that I would not forget our conversation. Then I returned a few phone calls, answered some e-mails, and approved Jason Calder's draft of next Sunday's "scorecard" (my term for our worship bulletin). Finally, after a quick stab at reorganizing the piles of paper on my desk, I headed back home.

That evening after dinner, Gail and I watched the evening news and then (because the Red Sox were rained out in Detroit) picked up the afternoon's conversation about my lunch with Rich Fisher.

We covered a lot of topics in the hour that followed. One of them was about getting more specific about such terms as *deep* and *deepening people* and what we really meant when we spoke of *cultivating* them.

At one point we talked about the issue of selection: What does one look for when searching for potential deep people? Are there obvious indicators? What did Jesus see when he approached men like Simon Peter and Matthew? What did he find in them that he didn't see in some Pharisees in Jerusalem? It was then that one of us (we're not agreed as to who) first used a word we'd never used before: *growable*.

Growable describes a person who is eager that his or her life be continuously reshaped to replicate the redemptive and serving love of Jesus Christ.

We both liked our new word and our definition of it. We agreed that *growable* and *growability* had to be at the top of the list of criteria when we searched for people to be mentored into depth.

I noticed that, as we talked into the evening, both of us subconsciously kept plugging conditional phrases into what we said—phrases such as, "if we did this," or "if God wants," or "assuming the elders approve." It was a recognition that we didn't want to be presumptuous, to get so caught up in the romance of this great idea that we couldn't hand if off to someone else if that was the way things should go.

The conversation even continued after we climbed into bed. Among the last things we talked about were the other words we found we were now using—some old, some used but not easily defined, and some that were being manufactured as we talked. *Deep people* was a fresh term. *Teachable*: an old word. *Growable*: a new one. *Mentoring*: often used but not adequately appreciated or understood. *Cultivation, volunteers*: words that came from Ramya Anand's gardening illustration and Rich and Carly's house last week. And then there was the totally overused word *leadership* and its modifier, *spiritual*, as in spiritual leadership or spiritual leaders.

Finally we embraced and I prayed. "Father, you've been there for us over these many, many years. We could probably come up with a thousand stories of times when we needed guidance, and you gave it. And we remember moments when we had nothing to go on but faith, and you responded. And now, Lord, we face another one of those occasions when the question is bigger than our ability to completely understand it. We feel the stirring of a new idea, an idea from you . . . the chance to be a spiritual mother and a father to younger Christ-followers, to oversee their growth into being deep people of influence in and beyond our church. If this is your purpose for us, please, please make it clear so that we do not walk into something you'd not planned for us . . ."

A moment or two later, Gail was asleep. But I wasn't. In fact, I don't think I ever got to sleep that night. A few hours later (1 a.m., to be exact) I finally left our bed and went to my study. My mind would not turn off.

SEPTEMBER 8

Early Morning, the First Summer

To Do

Make list of every man, woman, couple who played a cultivating role in your life over the years.

☐ Why did they do it?
☐ How did they do it?
☐ How did you react?
☐ What was the result?
☐ Did you ever thank them?

To: Geoff Handley and Monica O'Donnell
From: GMAC
Talked with Rich Fisher today. Need to talk with you about an idea he & some others have. R u open for breakfast Thurs or Fri? I'd like it if Rich could join us.

From my journal

4 a.m. I've not slept much at all. My mind is still racing from yesterday's time with Rich F and my follow-up conversations with Gail. For the last many weeks I've been the guy with the idea who was the pusher, pushing everybody to get serious about this cultivation of deep

people. But suddenly, yesterday, the pusher became the "pushee." At lunch Rich was the one leading me with his questions and his insights. Last night Gail was coming up with thoughts and questions of her own. Now I learn that some others have actually spent an evening discussing the idea and are beginning to believe in it.

Gail and I must begin to define our role in all of this. I am reminded of a powerful moment in the life of W. E. Sangster (an English writer and evangelist) when he struggled to define God's purposes in his life as a leader.

"The church is painfully in need of leaders," he wrote in his journal. "I wait to hear a voice and no voice comes . . . I would rather listen than speak (but there is no voice . . .). Bewildered and unbelieving I hear the voice of God say to me, 'I want to sound the note through you.' God help me . . . God help me. What is the initial task? To call [my church] back to its real work."

I feel that same way here in my little world of central New Hampshire.

So what is our initial task? Apparently, it's to see if there's a way to cultivate deepening people.

So we've got some things to pray about more fervently. Are we in fact the ones to do whatever needs to be done to get this thing going? That's prayer number one. And Fisher thinks he already knows the answer: yes. I get the feeling that Gail agrees.

The second thing to pray about: are we prepared to back off some things we've always enjoyed doing and to focus on a relatively small group of "growable" (another new buzzword?) people?

*Another thing for prayer. Now that conversations
are started, we've got to start thinking about what
it is that we really want to make happen and how
we'd do it. Again, this is not about getting people
on boards and committees. Rather it's first about
raising up a group of deepening people who know how
to hear God speak, how to respond, how to find the
maximum point of service that fits their situation.
My assumption: that such men and women—rightly
cultivated—will give our church all the leadership
it needs both inside the church and far beyond its
organizational borders. Easy to talk about; more
challenging to make happen.*

IT WAS ABOUT 5 A.M. WHEN I FINISHED WRITING MY thoughts. Leaving my desk, I settled into an easy chair with my Bible and a legal pad. I'd gotten the idea when I was still in bed that I should try to identify as many references in Scripture as I could find that spoke to the idea of cultivating deep people. It shouldn't surprise anyone that one of the first places I turned to was the second letter to Timothy, where Paul pushes Timothy to pursue a strategy of multiplication.

Paul wrote, "The things you have heard me say in the presence of many witnesses entrust to reliable [growable] people who will also be qualified to teach others."

There it is, I thought. The challenge to pass on from one generation to another generation what has been learned and experienced.

Was Paul pushing Timothy like Rich Fisher had begun to push me the previous day?

In the next hour I moved forward and backward through both Testaments of the Bible, reviewing familiar verses and paragraphs that highlighted the many themes and principles of people cultivation. Before long I had several pages of notes on what I'd found.

I took quick glances at the stories of Joseph, Gideon, Ezra and Nehemiah, David, Esther, Simon Peter, and Barnabas. There were others, of course. But they all had one obvious thing in common: they possessed a remarkable depth of spirit relative to their times.

The first light of a new morning was beginning to appear in the sky when I flipped through the Gospels, stopping here and there where I had previously marked paragraphs that showed Jesus in action fashioning the Twelve for their apostolic future. I lingered for a few moments in the early chapters of Acts, where Peter and a few of his comrades emerged as remarkable, fearless leaders. Talk about spiritual depth. Is the Simon Peter on Pentecost day the *same* Simon Peter who, in the past, had second-guessed Jesus and made commitments he wasn't able to keep? How had the change come about? Whatever Jesus had done was truly exponential. There was almost no change in Peter for three years. Then in the space of weeks, the man became a true champion. Again, how had that happened?

Closing my Bible, I sat in my chair, squinting my eyes so that I could read the titles of books in the biographical section of my library across the room. There were the names of many deep-spirited leaders down through the centuries of Christianity: Augustine, Benedict, Patrick, Francis, Luther, Calvin, Zinzendorf, Wesley, Whitefield, Jonathan Edwards, William Wilberforce, Charles Simeon (my personal hero), the Booths (Catherine and William), Slessor, Carmichael, Bonhoeffer . . . and the list went on. All of them were people who did what they did out of a depth of soul from which God spoke.

Not all of them were clergy or theologians. Some of them were people in business and in government. That's where we would have to focus our energies: on men and women who went to work in the larger world every day. I was not interested in cultivating people simply for church work. I wanted to invest myself in people who might master the art of spiritual influence seven days a week.

My thoughts moved on. Were all of these people in the biographical section of my library simply "accidents," volunteer flowers that happened in their time? Or were they prepositioned by God and cultivated by mentors? And are there men and women today, perhaps in our church family, who are like those named on the spines of my books? Men and women waiting to be identified and cultivated? Were any of these people—named in my Bible and found on my bookshelves—like Ben Jacobs when he first came to us?

My eyes grew heavy as the fatigue caused by a sleepless night swept over me. Barely alert, I prayed, "Lord, you know how often Gail and I have asked for clarity on what the next chapter of our lives should be about. We want to stay here in New England if that's possible; we'd like to stay a bit longer in this church family. Frankly, we like doing what we're doing. But I can't talk to this church about rearranging itself, about preparing for a wild future, without recognizing that you may want to first rearrange Gail and me in some way we'd not expected. So, Lord, while I'm in the mood in this early morning hour, I'm asking you: please speak to us in whatever way you choose. We'll listen. And if that means becoming people who major in cultivating deep people, then I'm ready to take my best shot. I ask that you'd also give Gail the same call if that's your best for us. We need to be together on this idea . . ."

I dozed in my chair for the next hour and then awakened to the noises of Gail arranging our breakfast in the kitchen. A new day had begun.

SEPTEMBER 10

Morning, the First Summer

From my pastoral notes

> *Tom/Monica O'Donnell. Serious Christians. Came*
> *to us from Illinois the same year that Gail and I*
> *arrived. Tom is an environmental engineer (grad of U/*
> *Illinois). Monica (Oberlin) is a freelance editor. Mar-*
> *ried nineteen years; three teenaged children. Monica:*
> *great leadership sensitivities. Big-picture person.*
> *Good at making an idea become operational. Obvious*
> *that she could run this church out of back pocket*
> *and make it hum. Says exactly what she thinks. Tom*
> *into details, a doer. Likes being on a team that makes*
> *things happen. Impatience is obvious when things are*
> *stalled. Hobby: antique cars; has a restored 1964 Ford*
> *Thunderbird.*
>
> > *Geoff Handley (wife Sharon): Chair of elders,*
> > *in road construction. Steady, supportive, highly*
> > *respected. Great loyalty to Jesus.*

GEOFF HANDLEY, MONICA O'DONNELL, AND RICH FISHER were already seated at a table in Friendly's Restaurant when I arrived for our breakfast meeting the next Friday morning. As

I approached the three of them, I thought about how fortunate I was to have friends like these three.

After we'd ordered our breakfasts and bantered a bit, I asked Rich if he'd update Geoff and Monica on the events of the past week or so.

Rich started by describing a dream session and then told how he and Carly had decided to make one happen with people in the congregation. Geoff and Monica had both been invited but had declined because of previous commitments. So this breakfast, six days later, was their first chance to get filled in on what had happened.

Rich described how everyone came alive to the idea of raising up a fresh group of leaders. From there he went on to underscore for Geoff and Monica the fact that the discussion centered on cultivating spiritual leaders—or deep people, which he took the time to define—rather than simply resurrecting the old leadership training concept. As it had for me, the high point of Rich's report came when he told about Ben Jacobs and his enthusiasm for the men who had mentored him into Christian growth. Both Geoff and Monica were amazed at Ben's effect on the group.

"Who would have thought?" Monica said. "I remember thinking that Connie Peterson was making a terrible mistake when she said she was going to have Ben in her home. Obviously, I couldn't have been more wrong."

Our conversation was interrupted when our waitress brought our breakfast orders to the table. After thanking her, Monica said a blessing over the food, and we began to eat.

Rich broke the silence with this comment. "Does it make sense if I suggest that maybe God brought Ben Jacobs to us to show us what's possible when a church decides that cultivating deep people is a top priority?"

It was a question that didn't need an answer.

After Rich had said a few more things about the dream session at his house, Monica asked, "Rich, what do you think was the most important thing that came out of the evening? If there was just one takeaway, what was it?"

"Good question; easy answer," Rich responded. "Everyone felt that Pastor Mac would be the right person to put an effort like this together."

"What about Gail?" Monica asked. "Why didn't anyone consider—?"

"Hey, you didn't let me finish," Rich interrupted. "Everyone agreed that if Gail would get into this thing with Gordon, we'd have everything necessary to do this right."

A bit embarrassed, I stayed silent.

A FEW MINUTES LATER, RICH FISHER BEGAN TO TALK ABOUT the conversation he and I had on Tuesday at the high school. Once again he raised the issue of my involvement in the process.

"I told Pastor Mac about the dream session and challenged him to think about the possibility that he's the guy to lead an aggressive effort at grooming a new generation of deep people. I told him that I'd come to the opinion that we needed to redefine the role of pastors."

More than once I'd seen Rich come alive with enthusiasm when he was trying to sell an idea. This was one of those times. Rich Fisher was on a roll.

"You know," he said, "I've been around just long enough to have watched churches turn their pastors into managers. On Sundays they're expected to preach and inspire us. But then, when Monday comes, they're supposed to be at their desks, running an organization. They oversee staff, crunch numbers, start and kill programs. Oh, and if they've got time left over, why shouldn't they be therapists? So when did we stop asking our pastors to give their primary energies to the thing they were called to do: turn people into disciples of Jesus, become spiritual leaders who can help the church do what it's supposed to do?"

Monica broke in. "Well, Rich, you're onto something. And we've got a pastor and his wife who can do what you're saying. They know how to grow people. I've seen them do it."

Again, I was embarrassed. How else could one feel, sitting there at the breakfast table, listening to this conversation, which was going on as if I wasn't there? I'm not even crazy about putting this all into print. But I'm going to do it because I want those who are interested to see what it means to hear God speaking through one's colleagues and friends.

Rich continued. "So Geoff, here's what I'm thinking. The elders have an opportunity to think and pray through a shift in the way we do things at the pastoral level. It's a new view of ministry. And it begins when you people tell the pastor to go out and make disciples . . . and really mean it. If you elders are persuaded, among the very first things you'll do is rewrite the lead pastor's job description. This is not an add-on to his job we're considering. It's a major revision of his responsibilities. And everyone's got to realize that."

All of us waited to see how Geoff Handley would respond. It was the elder chairman's turn to take this idea one step further.

"I've heard everything you've said, Rich," Geoff finally said. "I think I can take this idea to the elders with a strong endorsement that it be considered. As we say in my business, let's run it up the flagpole and see who salutes."

Rich was obviously delighted by the way the breakfast conversation had gone. I was certainly stimulated. An hour later, when we prepared to leave, everyone seemed to have the feeling that something new in the life of our church was in the making.

OUT IN THE PARKING LOT, I CLIMBED INTO MY TUNDRA AND started the engine. Suddenly, there was a rapping on the window.

It was Monica O'Donnell. I turned off the engine and opened the door. Monica immediately began to speak.

"Pastor, I have one more thought, which may not be new, by any means. Let me preface it by saying that Tom and I have watched you and Gail for all the years you've been at our church. We've often said that you are not really Gordon, and Gail is not really Gail. For lots of us, you are Gordon-and-Gail. Your greatest contribution to the people in our church is the way you relate to each other. Many of us have learned how exquisite a marriage can be by watching you two. We know you've had your challenges, just like a lot of us. But you've even taken your challenges and made them something that we could learn from."

"Monica, thanks for that," I said. "I'll tell Gail what you said when I see her."

Monica quickly went on. "The thought I have for you is this. I really believe that what we talked about in there has tremendous potential. But it's only going to work if you do it in partnership with Gail. If you do it alone, you might be successful, but not nearly as successful as you'll be if you do it with her . . . and do it as partners. I want you to hear me on this, now: it would need to be as much *her* thing as it's yours."

"What you're saying is important, Monica. Gail and I have already had a lot of conversation about her place in this, and what you've just said confirms that we're on the right track."

Monica looked away for a moment. I thought I detected tears in her eyes, and I sensed that there was emotion behind what she was wanting to say to me next. It was best to remain silent until she was ready to speak again.

When she had herself under control, she looked me in the eye and said, "I hope this doesn't come across as disrespectful, Pastor, but the women in our church need—they *need*!—to see as many examples as possible of men and women teaming up as partners in leadership. And if you're going to pour yourselves into young, would-be . . . um . . . *deep people*, then do it as partners; show them how two people can make something happen together.

"I know that we're doing a lot better than many churches I've heard about—I'm not forgetting that I'm vice chair of the elders— but we still have miles to go before we sleep. You and Gail need to make this great idea happen as partners! And don't ever forget this: every woman in this church will love you forever. And our dear husbands? They'll learn something valuable."

Monica didn't wait for me to respond. She didn't say good-bye. She simply turned away and headed for her car. She can be very dramatic when she wants to make a point.

SEPTEMBER 10

Evening, the First Summer

From my journal

> Beautiful fall evening last night. Gail and I walked for
> an hour. We talked almost the entire time about the
> great idea. She's obviously on board with this vision,
> and when you have someone who sees it as clearly
> as you think you do—and she does—something good
> has got to happen. I think I'd tell anyone who really
> wants to do the sort of thing we're imagining that
> they should not take a step forward until they have a
> partner to help make it work.

"DO YOU SEE US AS A PARTNERSHIP?" I ASKED GAIL WHEN I
got home that evening.

"I've always thought that. Is there an alternative relationship
I don't know about?"

"Yeah. Our relationship could be an old-fashioned hierarchy.
You know the old way: I make decisions; you make meals. I earn
the living; you keep the house. Come to think of it . . ."

"That sounds like some man's way of looking at things," Gail
said quickly. "I've always liked the partnership model. So forget the
other idea. Tell me, where did that question come from anyway?"

"After breakfast at Friendly's this morning, Monica O'Donnell stopped me out in the parking lot. What she said touched me very deeply."

"And that was?"

"She said that she and Tom and others learn a lot about married life and how to work together from what they see us do. And she used the word *partnership* to describe their view of us. It amazes me that people watch that much."

"How many times have I told you that? Did it take Monica to convince you? People want examples . . . for goodness' sake, most of what you and I know has been learned from the people we watched. It's not what anyone says or writes half as much as how they live it out under every circumstance."

"That scares me."

"It should scare both of us. But do you want it any other way?" Gail said. "So what did you learn from what she said?"

"Well, that's how they see us, anyway: as partners. I looked up the word when I got to the office because I thought there might be a sermon possibility there someday. In the Greek the word is *koinonia* . . . it's a business term that describes the relationship of two people who have a mutual interest in some deal. I checked out *koinonia* in the New Testament and found it in Philippians where Paul says he was thankful for their 'partnership in the gospel.' Sometimes it gets translated *fellowship*."

"*Fellowship* is a beautiful word, if that's what it means. You and I have fellowship, don't we?"

"Yeah, but that's an overused word. *Partnership* speaks to me; it's more action-oriented."

I was quiet for a moment and then went on. "I guess I have always wanted our marriage to be a partnership in every way. I've never liked hierarchical relationships. I saw enough of that when I was young. That's what my parents' generation had. My mother and other women like her just assumed that the men would do the heavy lifting and they'd live with the results.

"I like where we're at, and partnership does describe it," I went on. "Most of the time I see us gliding like Olympic pair skaters. If a decision has to be made, we talk it through, and if there's a need for leadership, the one of us who is most qualified gets to be the leader."

"I love that, and I'm grateful for it. But where is this going?" Gail asked.

"I'm thinking about this idea of cultivating deep people. If this is in the future, I really want it to be in *our* future. You need to own this thing as much as I do. My hunch is that we'll both discover that you have as much to offer, if not more, than I do. You can bring a very important perspective to the table that most leadership training efforts fail to recognize."

"Which perspective is that?" Gail asked.

"That there are important aspects to spiritual and leadership development that only a woman can understand."

"I think you're right," Gail said. "And a lot of women have been praying for men to get that." We both laughed.

"I guess that's what Monica O'Donnell was trying to tell me."

"IN THE MOOD FOR A WALK?" GAIL ASKED AFTER WE'D EATEN dinner. "It's such a beautiful evening, and the leaves are just beginning to turn color."

"Let me get my stick," I said. I've had the same walking stick for twenty-five years now.

Soon we were walking a nearby Class VI road that is almost impassable to anything but walkers.

"So where do you think this great idea thing will end up going?" Gail asked. "Are we talking about something that's really doable in a church?"

"Doable? I don't think the Holy Spirit would make us so sure about a thing if it wasn't doable. I think the ball's in our court: yours and mine. My bet is that the elders will get behind this and my job description will be rewritten and made to emphasize some kind of intensive mentoring. They'll want me to keep preaching and leading the staff for the foreseeable future but give my—our—utmost attention to people who want to deepen their Christian lives and become influencers in and out of the church."

"So if the ball's in our court, what do we do next?"

We walked along in silence for a few minutes, while I sought the best possible answer.

Then I turned to Gail and repeated her question. "What do we do next? I think we start looking around to see how many ways there are for people to be spiritually deepened . . . in the church and in other places. It would be interesting to know what organizations in the larger world do to train people and turn them into influencers. Let's start looking to see if God has anything for us to learn."

Gail agreed to my suggestion.

A bit more walking. A bit more reflective silence.

"You mentioned a women's perspective on spiritual leadership," Gail said, finally breaking the silence.

"Yeah. What are you thinking?"

"Well, I'm just remembering Paul's words to the Galatians when he longed for depth in their spiritual lives. He wrote, 'I feel like I'm in childbirth again until Christ is formed in you.' That's what this idea is all about. Raising up a new generation of Christians who really have the life of Jesus growing in them and flowing out of them. We could help make that happen," Gail said.

A moment more of silence. Then she said, "You know what? I'm in."

"Great, you'll be my partner?"

"That's what I meant. I'm in."

We walked a bit farther and then turned back toward home. The Red Sox were playing an interleague game in St. Louis tonight, and the first pitch was scheduled for 8:30 p.m.

We don't always do church talk, you know.

SEPTEMBER 16

The First Summer

To: Rich Fisher
From: GMAC
Subject: Rabbi?

A couple of weeks ago, when we had lunch together at your
office, you referred to the role of a rabbi several times. At
the time I wondered what you meant by that. Today I think
I figured out the answer. More when we have time to talk.

COMING OUT OF THE NEW HAMPSHIRE DEPARTMENT OF
Motor Vehicles, where I'd gone to renew my driver's license,
I ran into Michael Cohen. Michael is the rabbi at Temple Israel
(Reformed) in our city. We've been friends ever since Gail and I
moved here nine years ago. He was among the very first people to
stop by the church office and welcome me to the city.

A week or two after our first encounter at the office, I had
phoned Michael and invited him to meet me for lunch. Soon a
friendship had begun to grow between us, and it has continued
until this day. I have found Michael to be a devout man, humorous,
intellectually astute, and ready to engage in candid discussions on
topics where Jewish and Christian opinions differ. It also does not
hurt that, like me, Michael Cohen loves the Red Sox.

My friend the rabbi knows far, far more about my Christian point of view than I know about his Jewish one. Through the years he has taught me much about the Older Testament and the Jewish way of dealing with it. He has always been patient when answering my questions about Jewish history, worship, and the meaning of various holiday celebrations. Twice Michael and his wife, Esther, hosted Gail and me in their home for the observance of the seder supper (the Passover meal).

So it shouldn't surprise you that when we saw each other outside the DMV, we embraced and then began catching up on each other's lives.

"So how are you feeling about things these days?" Michael asked me.

"Well, church-wise, I'm pleased. Home-wise, Gail and I are doing great."

When I didn't go into further detail, Michael said, "That's it? That's all you're going to tell me?" Michael Cohen never settles for surface responses to his questions. If you're his friend, he wants to know everything. He's a very caring man.

"Um, well, since you've asked . . . The most important thing on my mind today is a new venture that Gail and I are thinking of launching sometime in the next year. We'd like to take thirteen or fourteen people through a heavy-duty experience of intensive learning with the hope that it will lead to a real deepening of their faith and a discovery of their leadership capabilities. I guess you'd say that we're thinking of 'legacy' and what kind of leadership the church might need in a few years from now. I'm not the youngest guy on the block, Michael. Gotta think of leaving something behind."

"Interesting," Michael said pensively, stroking his beard. "So how are you going to leave this legacy?"

"Right now, it's a work in progress, so I'm short on details.

Basically, we're going to try to create a small group of learners who will become quite committed to each other. If they're going to become part of the next generation of leaders in and out of the church, they have to begin to know and trust one another. The key element in this early stage will be their relationship to Gail and me and what we can teach them not just through books but through watching us and seeing how we try to make life work."

"You sound like you've been studying the ways of the old rabbis," Michael said.

"Rabbis? Where'd that come from?" I asked, thinking he was joking. But something in the back of my mind sensed a link with Rich Fisher's "rabbi" comments of ten days ago.

"Exactly what I said. You sound like you're going to invest yourselves in some young people the way rabbis have done for centuries. Surely, you know that Jesus was a rabbi, and those twelve guys of his were his learning team."

"Of course . . . but I don't know that I've thought much about the implications."

"Gordon, Gordon, Gordon, listen to your Jewish friend here . . . You need to reread your own Scriptures and learn something you may never have thought about before. Your Jesus was first and foremost a rabbi. All his ways were the way of a rabbi. If you don't understand the rabbinical contract, you don't really know as much as you should know about Jesus."

Now I felt a bit sheepish. Once again Rabbi Cohen was informing me—gently, of course—that my Christian knowledge of Jesus might not be all I thought it was.

"Okay, Michael. Tell me what it is that you think I might need to know."

"Hm . . . you know, there's better places to talk about this. Maybe I can offer you a few thoughts that will help you and Gail with this group you want to put together. Tell you what . . . how about tomorrow afternoon for coffee at my office? You haven't been to my place in a long while."

Remembering my comment to Gail that we needed to reach out beyond ourselves and see what others were doing to train people, I quickly accepted Michael's invitation.

Later, as I drove home, I kept wondering at this curious conversation with my rabbi-friend. Usually, I was the guy with all the insights about Jesus, but it was clear that Michael Cohen thought he had a few ideas up his sleeve that would be helpful to me as I continued to wrestle with the question: how are deep people cultivated and readied for leadership? *Tomorrow*, I thought, *might be quite an experience*.

LOCATED IN A QUIETER NEIGHBORHOOD IN OUR CITY, TEMPLE Israel is not a megasynagogue. But it has been a spiritual home for Jewish people for seventy-five years. When I arrived at Rabbi Michael Cohen's office door the next afternoon, I was greeted warmly by Ruth Gold, his assistant.

"Michael has been looking forward to seeing you all day, Rev. MacDonald. I'll tell him you're here."

A minute later, my friend was hugging me and leading me to his office. After we'd looked at some pictures of his family and some souvenirs he'd brought home from a recent visit to Jerusalem, we sat down and launched into conversation about Jesus the rabbi.

"I've thought some about this project you described to me yesterday, and I think it's wonderful that you and Gail are going to do this with those young people," Michael said. "As I said yesterday, it's very rabbinical, this idea of yours. You Christians don't realize just how much you owe the ancient teachers when you talk about wanting to train people . . . at least the way you described.

"This way—dealing with just a small collection of people at a time—may be the only way there is to really change the orientation of someone's life. I've never understood why some of your colleagues love preaching to large audiences and doing TV programs. All of that can make a big splash, I guess, and make some money, of course, but it really doesn't change that many people . . . not deeply anyway."

Whoa. There was that word *deep*. Apparently Michael also found *deep* to be a useful descriptor for significant life change.

"You want to change people. You do what you and Gail are talking about: the work of the rabbi," he said.

"Okay, Michael, you've got my attention. What is it about Jesus and changing people that you think I might not know?"

The rabbi laughed. "Gordon, let me say this with kindness. You Christians sometimes act as if you've copyrighted Jesus and can make him into anything you want. For some of you he's a solid right-wing American. Others? Yourself, maybe? You obviously revere him; you honor him in a most admirable way. But sometimes Christians seem to forget that Jesus was first and foremost a Jew living in the great stream of Jewish tradition. Everything about Jesus was Jewish, including the fact that he was a rabbi."

"So why do you think the rabbi thing is important?" I asked.

"Because rabbis had something of a formulaic way of teaching, and it worked very, very well. If you know a bit about the ways of rabbis, it might affect the way you do this project of yours."

Michael Cohen went on to give me a lesson in rabbinical history. "In the time of Jesus, there was a whole class of righteous men known as rabbis. *Rabbi* means teacher, of course; you know that. Some taught in the temple area of Jerusalem; others were itinerant rabbis. They traveled from place to place, teaching in synagogues and wherever people would listen. If their teaching was appreciated, people would give them gifts . . . donations, if you please."

Rabbi Cohen was on a roll. His hands were in constant

movement as he spoke. He was transformed into the teacher, and I was the learner. I loved it.

"Each rabbi was distinctive. He would have a unique interpretation of the Torah, and this is what he was known for. Some rabbis were militant and encouraged people to insurgency against the Romans. Others were very contemplative and lived in the desert, kind of like John the Baptist in your Bible. Most other rabbis were somewhere between those two extremes."

"So where would you think that Jesus fit?"

"Well, Jesus' message was about love . . . as in 'Love your enemies' or 'Forgive those who persecute you.' Not a message to be welcomed in the larger population, by the way. Now, Jesus wasn't the only one to ever talk about love, but he had a very unique way of talking about it. I think a lot of us Jews could get more interested in Jesus' gospel if there weren't so many complications. Mostly the problem we have with him has less to do with Jesus and more to do with a lot of his followers."

I understood exactly where Michael Cohen was going with that comment. But both he and I knew that this was not the point of our conversation today.

"Let me tell you a few things about the ways of rabbis that might influence the way you deal with these—what did you call them?—growable people. By the way, I like your term *deep people*. I may do a sermon about it in one of our Shabbat services myself."

"Well, Michael, let me know when you preach about it. I'll come and listen," I said.

"Jesus, like other rabbis, was not just a preacher, you know. In fact, that may not have been his most important contribution."

"What do you mean by that?"

"Among the highest priorities for a rabbi were his handpicked students. Rabbis always had students—each called a *talmid*. The group would have been called the *talmidim*. There was usually a close following of these students—disciples, you Christians sometimes call them. They were very dedicated learners.

"It was customary for a young student to approach a rabbi with the question, 'May I follow you?' Sometimes rich Jewish families pushed hard to get the best rabbis to make their sons part of the *talmidim*. A good rabbi, you know, was like a college or university today. You may remember that your Saul of Tarsus liked to tell people that he studied under Rabbi Gamaliel, who was one of the best of the best at that time. When Saul dropped Gamaliel's name, it was like saying today, 'I went to Harvard.'"

I lifted my hand almost like a student might signal that he wanted to ask his teacher a question. "But," I said, "Jesus picked his disciples."

"Sure, you're right about that. But take a look at where Jesus came from. Nazareth! That was a pathetic town. Who in their right mind would follow a rabbi from Nazareth?" Michael Cohen said with exaggerated sarcasm. "Why, if you were anybody, you wanted a respected rabbi from Jerusalem. So I suspect that if Jesus wanted disciples, he had to do a little recruiting. Just my opinion, of course."

Michael went on to talk about a rabbi and his selection process of disciples. "That phrase, 'Follow me,' that I hear Christians use, that's a standard rabbinical response to a young man's request. It meant that he could join the others who were in the rabbi's traveling school. And if the young man did so, he began with the understanding that immediately he was under what I call the rabbinical contract. Not only did he agree to follow, but the closer he got to the rabbi, the better. Remember when the mother of two of Jesus' disciples asked if her sons could sit on either side of him? That's a Jewish mother wanting her boys to get as close to their rabbi as possible."

"So what is this rabbinical contract you mentioned? Was there something signed?"

"No, of course not. It's my way of saying that everyone under-stood that if you were selected to be one of the rabbi's learners, you learned in a certain way."

"Which was?"

"Well, rabbis tended to teach in what I call a *spiral*. First, there would be instruction. And when the rabbi instructed, the disciples were to sit in silence. That's a rabbinical term. They listened and then memorized what the rabbi taught them. What he taught was sometimes called the rabbi's *word*, or *gospel*. He taught them the Torah and offered his version of what the Torah meant. Then when he permitted, the students would ask questions: 'What does this mean?' and 'Why didn't you see it that way?' The students might quote interpretations of other rabbis and ask him to make comparisons.

"Then when the teacher concluded his instruction, he left the students alone to discuss what they'd heard. They would argue and debate until the rabbi's word was fully digested. Now his word was, you could say, in them."

"So," I said, "when Jesus says, 'Heaven and earth will pass away, but my word will not'—"

"—'pass away,'" Michael finished my quote. "I've heard that line a hundred times. It's Jesus' way of saying that what he's taught his disciples isn't going to expire or become null and void. He's saying that they could take his teaching to the bank."

We talked about a rabbi's use of riddles and stories and prov-erbs. Apparently, these ancient teachers didn't feel the need to explain everything they said. They just threw things out there— like a gardener might sow seed—and let it find its own way into the lives of the listeners.

"The second way a rabbi taught," Michael explained, "was through imitation. Now the spiral tightens a bit. Disciples watched their master—another word for teacher—like a hawk because they believed that the Torah came to life in him. His very way of life was an animated version of Torah, and the followers would want to mimic him in every way, to the last detail. When your Jesus said that he was the way—"

"—and the truth and the life," I said, finishing Michael's sentence.

"Yes, the truth and life. When he said that, he was saying, 'I am acting out my own word in living color. Copy me and you bring the Torah to life.'"

"Christians talk a lot about wanting to be like Jesus," I said. "I mean that's at the root of our way of seeing things."

"Of course you'd want to be like Jesus. Any Jewish disciple would have said that about his rabbi. He would try to eat like his rabbi; walk like him, talk like him. Hey, there are writings describing how students—forgive me this indelicacy—studied the way their rabbi went to the toilet because they wanted to be just like him in every way."

"I'll try to forget what you just said, Michael," I said with a grin. "There are limits to this legacy idea."

"Well, just remember that a student's greatest aspiration was to become so much like his rabbi that people wouldn't see a difference between them."

"So that's why Paul said that he wanted to know Jesus and be just like him."

"You've got it," Michael said. "Your Paul talked about being an example. I've read his writings to—what's his name? You know, the young man who wasn't all Jewish . . ."

"Timothy?"

"Yes, sure. Timothy. Paul says to him, 'Be an example in the way you talk and live and love people' . . . and some other things. Paul's talking rabbi-talk, and he's saying, 'You copy me and your people will copy you.'"

We talked about the implications of rabbinical imitation for a while, and then Michael went back to his outline of the rabbi's teaching cycle.

"The third thing a rabbi did could be called *examination*. Now the spiral is really tightening and ready for another circle of teaching. A rabbi constantly tested his students. He gave them little assignments to teach other people, for example, so that he could know if they were learning what they should."

"I never thought about that," I said. "So when it says that Jesus sent his disciples out to preach, it was kind of a quiz. And when they came back, he wanted to know how they'd done, what questions they had."

"Exactly," Michael answered. "Any rabbi would have done that sort of thing. You also have stories where Jesus let learners fall into embarrassing situations. I've read them many times. Rabbis didn't mind allowing their students to fail. That storm story where he said to them, 'Where is your faith?' is an examination moment. When he told them to feed that big crowd of hungry people, he was challenging them to do something special. When he scolded them about the children they'd tried to keep from bothering him, he was rebuking them, correcting them. He was saying, 'I happen to like kids.'

"Hey . . . we Jews may not see Jesus the same way as you Christians believe in him. But we know a good rabbi when we see one, and he was pretty good."

I loved this conversation. So many things I'd known about Jesus over my years as a preaching pastor were coming alive to me in a new way. All these things Jesus had done with his disciples: they were—as Michael was saying—the work of a rabbi. *The rabbinical contract*: why hadn't I heard of this before? It could form the foundation of our great idea.

"We've got one more thing to talk about, and it's this," Michael said. "The relationship of a rabbi to his students always came to an ending point. This relationship was not like a marriage."

"Ending point?"

"Gordon, you need to read your Bible more," Michael said with a good-natured wave of his hand, pretending to be dismissive of my Bible knowledge. "This morning as I thought about your coming this afternoon, I got my copy of the Christian Bible and reread Jesus' conversation with his *talmidim* in the gospel of John.

"What do you think," Michael asked me, "Jesus meant when he said to his students, 'I'm going away . . . It will be good for you . . . You've been my servants, but now I regard you as friends'? What's happening here? I'll tell you what's happening: he's releasing those men from the rabbinical contract. They're free to go. In fact, he expected—he even wanted—them to go and teach others just like he'd taught them."

"The Great Commission," I said.

"The great what?" Michael asked.

"The Great Commission. Christians say that Jesus sent the disciples out to make . . . well, more disciples, and that's why we believe in evangelism and sending out missionaries."

There was a thoughtful silence, and then Michael said quietly, "Yes, I know a lot about that evangelism thing. Let's agree to disagree on what all of that means."

I nodded.

"But," Michael said, "what you call this—this Great Commission, is it?—is, again, what any rabbi would have said to his students. 'Go on out and broadcast what I've taught you. You've been my *talmidim*; now go out and recruit your own.' And that's what they did, except Judas Iscariot, of course.

"Your Christian champion, Saul of Tarsus, was saying the same thing when he wrote to Timothy, 'What you've received—*received*, there's another rabbinical term—from me, teach to others who shall then teach it to still more.' What do you know? Paul's talking like a rabbi and expecting Timothy to act like one too. You've got the Jewish tradition embedded all over your Christian Scriptures, don't you see?"

"Okay, Michael. I get it."

"Now, one more thing. I think you said that you're not going to do this thing with volunteers. You're going to select your candidates carefully."

"You got it."

"Now, where are you going to make this rabbinical thing happen?"

"We're thinking we'll do it each week in our home, a full evening almost every week for a year. I don't want to do it in a church building. I want our connection with these people to stay outside the institution where there's some sense of larger reality."

"A very good idea, my friend. You know what? I think you and Gail are going to be thinking like rabbis soon. You Christians are finally going to learn that the way Jesus did it is the way it should have been done all along. Get your teachable young people and push them hard to learn. You'll produce some . . . *some* . . . of those deep people. I'd love to watch this in action."

"Tell you what. At the right moment, Gail and I will invite you and Esther to join us for an evening. Give us some time."

"We'll be there when you invite us."

Soon after, Michael Cohen and I knew that we'd reached the end of this conversation. But he couldn't seem to avoid one more question. It revealed once again the *teacher* in him.

"What's the most important thing you think we talked about?" he asked.

"I suppose that I learned that our great idea—that's what we've been calling it so far—just might work best if we do it something like the way Jesus did it."

Once again, Michael gave me a hug.

With that I left his office, said good-bye to Ruth Gold, and headed back to church. I couldn't wait to tell Gail, the Fishers, and the pastoral staff how much I'd learned and how excited I felt about the great idea.

OCTOBER 5

Early Evening, the First Fall

To: Elders, Church Council
From: Geoff Handley
Cc: GMAC, Pastoral Staff, Gail MacDonald
Subject: Deep People

Could you all please join me at a special meeting next
Tuesday evening (7:15 p.m.)? We're going to have a dream
session (ask Rich Fisher what that means) on an idea that's
coming from Pastor Mac, Rich, and a few others. Please
come to this meeting having prayed for wisdom. It could be
an important evening.
GH

TWO WEEKS LATER, THE ELDERS, THE COUNCIL, AND MEM-
bers of the pastoral staff gathered in the commons for a special
meeting called by Geoff Handley. Only one person, Gilberto
Silva, was missing. His Brazilian company had called him back
to São Paulo for a long-range planning project. I should add that
Geoff had phoned Gail and asked her to be at the meeting since
the subject matter was as important to her as anyone in the room.

Ken Squires (he and Winn Rilkey were old Discovery
Group people) began the meeting with a brief Bible reading and

comment. "Geoff wrote in his e-mail that the subject tonight is the search for deep people. *Deep people*: what an intriguing term. In view of this, I've decided to read some lines from the letter that Paul wrote to Titus." Saying this, Ken put on his half-glasses and began to read: "'The reason I left you in Crete was that you might straighten out what was left unfinished and appoint elders in every town as I directed you.'

"Not a particularly memorable reading if you stop there," Ken said. "But when I looked at it this morning, I was reminded that people back in New Testament times must have been just as concerned as we are about leadership. I think Paul gave Titus a difficult job. He asked him to appoint leaders in a bunch of churches. So how did Titus do that?

"To assist him Paul gave Titus a list of qualifications he could use in order to spot leadership potential as he went from church to church. Listen to this list: 'blameless' . . . well, that leaves me out . . . 'solid marriage' . . . I think I'm in there . . . 'having children who would not betray their father' . . . 'even-tempered, not a drunkard, not violent, ethical and moral in their work, hospitable, loving the good, self-controlled, holy . . . disciplined . . . solid in an understanding of the faith.' Rather intimidating at first glance, isn't it? I wonder if Titus would seriously consider me for leadership? I mean that's high-bar stuff.

"But the most important question is, where do you find people like this? Do they just come out of the woodwork? This list is all about the character of a person . . . leaders with Christlike qualities . . . deep people.

"Some time back, Pastor Mac gave me a copy of an old book called *Spiritual Leadership* by Oswald Sanders. I've read it so many times that it's beginning to fall apart. Here's one of my favorite quotes when he tries to define spiritual leadership—the stuff Titus was looking for: spiritual leadership 'is the power to change the atmosphere by one's presence, the unconscious influence that makes Christ and spiritual things real to others.' I guess what Paul was saying to Titus was, 'If you find people like that, appoint them to leadership. And if you can't find any, cultivate them.'

"*Cultivate*," Ken repeated. "That's another new word that Pastor Mac's been using over the past few weeks. And I think it fits very well in this reading. And it's what this meeting is about. Let's pray.

"Father, thank you for the worldwide family of people who follow Jesus. We're just a small part of the clan, but we're grateful for our privileges. And here we are in this room, men and women who have been entrusted to lead this church, to serve you and those whom you love in this world. We're humbled.

"Lord, we have big ideas to mess with, and we need a level of wisdom that is beyond most of us. Give Geoff, Monica, Rich, Pastor Mac and Gail, and anyone else on the agenda an exceptional ability to lead us tonight. And when we leave, I pray that we'll all feel that we've participated in something very special, something very pleasing to you. In the name of the Lord Jesus, I pray these things. Amen."

There was some silence in the room after that prayer. We must have all had the same feeling: that we'd just heard the praying of a deep person.

Finally, Geoff spoke up. "Ken, thanks for that." Then looking about the room he said, "We're pleased that the council members and staff are here with us elders. And Gail, thanks for coming. We value your input."

Geoff took a deep breath, looked down at notes on his tablet computer and then back up at us, and said, "For a while now, the pastor has been urging us to make the cultivation of deep people our number one ministry priority. He usually calls it a 'great idea.' I'm behind his great idea 110 percent."

For the next few minutes Geoff reviewed in bulleted form the things he'd been hearing me say:

- We are living in new times that require new kinds of leadership.
- The next generation of leaders will have to be cultivated.
- We are not talking about a new program but a whole new way of doing ministry.
- Such an effort may mean a reshuffle of the responsibilities of the senior pastor and others on the staff.

Geoff then turned in the direction of Rich Fisher and said, "I'm grateful to Rich, who did something a few weeks ago about Pastor's concern. He and his wife gathered a bunch of people together—I wish I could have been there—to kick around this issue for an evening. And after a full evening, they came up with one basic action item to send on to us: that we mandate Pastor Mac—and Gail, if she's willing—to explore this great idea and tell us how they think it could be made to work. Rich, why don't you fill us in on what happened that night?"

"Thanks, Geoff. Carly and I did get a bunch of people together, and some of you were there. Part of what drove us was the observation that too many churches tend to wait until something goes wrong before deciding to do bold things. At the high school, for example, we're imagining what life in our city is going to look like five, seven, even ten years from now. We're laying tracks toward that future. And that includes asking ourselves questions like these: How will our city grow and change in the next few years? What will schools have to do differently to prepare students for life in an adult world? What kind of leadership will we need to make that happen? And what can we do to accelerate the professional development of those leaders?

"A church needs to be asking questions very similar to these," Rich said. "So the issue we dealt with at our house a few weeks ago was this. I've put it in the form of a question."

Rich swiveled around in his chair and turned over a page of a flip chart. We all read: *Is there a way to produce a continuous flow of men and women who are mentored into spiritual depth and trained to lead when God calls them?*

"We had a great conversation that evening. It mainly centered on biblical leaders and what they could teach us about leadership today. When our evening ended, we agreed that we should ping Geoff and the elders on this and express our sense of urgency that some form of cultivating deepening people (as we are now calling them) be pushed up to the highest level of ministry concern."

Geoff invited questions for Rich. And because we're New Englanders, there were more than a few. Like:

- Are you talking about adding more staff?
- Would this great idea affect the budget?
- Is this just about wanting to make the church bigger?
- What kind of leaders are we talking about here? Decision makers? Bible study leaders? Program coordinators?
- Are you saying that our present leadership is inadequate?

Some questions had real merit. Others seemed premature or knee-jerk. Of course, some had no obvious answers. But Geoff Handley handled each with respect.

Then Winn Rilkey said, "Geoff, Gordon and Gail have been

awfully silent through all of this. Are we going to get a chance to hear what they're thinking?"

"Most certainly," Geoff responded. Turning to me, he said, "Gordon, you or Gail want to talk for a few minutes?"

I suggested that it might be time for a break. "Some people would probably love to go down the hall for a moment," I said, "and some others are probably wishing they could read their text messages."

Geoff agreed, and we took a time-out for ten minutes.

When everyone had left the room, I turned to Gail. "What are you hearing?" I asked. Gail's gotten used to that question from me. I trust her ability to smell out attitudes and biases that I would have missed by myself.

"I think everyone's tuned in," she said. "But they've got to be reassured that this is not about doing more busywork in the church. We're all tired of the message that we've got to do more and more and more. We're too busy as it is."

As I turned away, Gail tugged at my arm. "They're getting the message," she said. "There's a spirit of agreement in the room. Just make sure they realize that this great idea implies a whole new approach to pastoral leadership. You—we—can't get serious about this if they expect you to continue doing all the other things you've always been doing. This is something new."

OCTOBER 5

Later Evening, the First Fall

From my journal

> Last night's meeting with the church leadership was
> outstanding. Gail and I felt the support of virtually
> every person in the room. Everyone is beginning to buy
> into the great idea; they actually seem (to borrow Hank
> Soriano's favorite line) to understand what we're saying.
> But getting this far has been the easy part. Now we
> have to start filling in the details, getting practical,
> finding out if we're up to this. Sometimes, after I've
> talked with such enthusiasm about the great idea,
> I feel a follow-up touch of fear. I hear myself
> wondering if we've managed to talk everyone (even
> ourselves) into something that's really not possible.

WHEN GEOFF HANDLEY RECONVENED THE MEETING, HE said, "Gordon, Gail, the floor's yours."

"You can't know," I began, "how much this meeting means to me. I know I've blabbed on and on about this great idea for a long time. But this past summer, the Lord seemed to stoke up the fire even hotter in me. Sometime I'll tell you about the moment at Fenway Park when it all started coming together in my mind."

"Was Boston winning or losing?" Bruce Bartlett quipped.

"Come on, Bruce," I said. "I'm trying to talk like Moses here."

If there was any tension in the air, it was broken instantly by our laughter.

"There are four things that are really important to Gail and me this evening," I said after the laughter had subsided. "I'm going to speak to the first three, and Gail will speak to the fourth.

"The first is personal, about us. Gail and I are moving into our latter years of pastoral life. I'll always be a pastor even after I step down from this responsibility. I may not get paid then, and I may not be in charge of an organization—and that's certainly okay—but I'll always have a pastoral concern for people. It's my call and my gift. And it's Gail's also.

"But here's the point. We think that as a person moves into the latter years of his or her leadership, the priority needle has to point more and more in the direction of investing in younger generations. We love our generation; our closest friends are of similar age. But our passion and my point of call is for those younger than us. We long to pour whatever God has given us into them and then to say the same thing Jesus said to his disciples: 'It's best that I go away.' In effect he handed on his mission to them with the anticipation that they would expand it exponentially. And you know what happened. The disciples accomplished exactly what he prepared them to do.

"I long, and Gail longs, to do that very same thing. Maybe that's part of the reason I've kept referring to this as simply a great idea. We don't have a satisfactory name for it yet. And it's still just an idea. But everything in my heart tells me that it's not a small idea. It's a great idea. Done right, it will accelerate our church into the future."

For a few minutes I told the people around the table of my visit with Rabbi Cohen and how he had given me a fresh perspective on the rabbinical work of Jesus. I spoke of the *talmidim*, the disciples, whom Jesus had selected and molded into people who would learn from him and emulate him.

"Ironically, my friend Rabbi Cohen gave me a look at Jesus and his priorities that I'd not had before. Over the past week I've found myself looking at everything I do through the rabbinical lens. Doesn't always work, but it sure provokes thought.

"This leads me to my second point. You are good leaders. You're our current version of deep people in this church. And you have to take seriously the changes that are going on in our society." I spoke these words slowly so that everyone would realize how deeply I believed in what I was saying.

"Men and women, the church of a few years from now will look nothing like the church of today. The recent economic realities, the problem of epidemic joblessness, the changing sociological patterns in our country, the shift in philosophical thought, the technological revolution . . . even the broad changes in the world of international politics: these are all affecting us dramatically.

"We have to keep asking ourselves what it means to live integrally as Christ-followers so that the people we connect with see something in us that is redemptive and constructive. If we don't know how to do that, then we can anticipate falling into irrelevance.

"So we have to begin to enlarge our core of deep people who can help do this. They will build tomorrow's church when most of us at this table are gone.

"Now, Gail and I have talked about this endlessly. And we are aware that there are a number of unknowns. Nonetheless, let me tell you where we're coming from. As you can easily discern, we're greatly attracted to this challenge. But we're attracted as *partners*. I couldn't do this alone . . . no way. Without Gail—and Monica O'Donnell has already reinforced this for me—I'll be hung out to dry. So although Gail is not salaried and although she is not a part of the official staff, Gail must be a player with me on this if we are to go ahead with it.

"But there's one thing I've got to make clear to you all. Please don't go a step further on this great idea until you have agreed that my ministry priorities are going to change. There will be meetings I'll no longer attend. There will be dinners and parties where we'll not be present and personal invitations we can't accept. Our eyes will be fixed on a smaller group of people who need our attention in order to grow and learn.

"You'll have to protect me when folks in the congregation ask, 'Where's Gordon? Why can't I get to him?' And you'll have to stand behind me when someone is frustrated because I'm not doing what they think the lead pastor should be doing. I don't want to scare anyone, but I see this as a major departure in the way we've done church for many, many years.

"Let me speak briefly about a third point that remains undeveloped in my mind but is nevertheless very important. I think we need to begin to consider our church a teaching church in the same way that some hospitals are called teaching hospitals. Our slogan might be reduced to three words: *training, training, training.*" I thought of Hank Soriano when I said that.

I continued. "For me, a teaching church would mean that I'd give a large part of myself to our great idea of cultivating deepening people and would ask you as church leaders to set an example by allocating 20 percent of all your leadership time to either training or being trained. Everyone—beginning with myself—needs to be defined by the training motif. The questions we'd start living by are: *What are you learning? Who are you teaching? What are the results?*"

Then I turned to Gail and invited her to speak.

"I only have one thing to say, and if Gordon doesn't mind me putting it this way, it's the most important of the four points, the biggest of them all."

That got everyone's intensified attention.

Gail went on. "This great idea is, at its base, a spiritual work. Again, it's not about talents and management. It's about God's deepening work in the lives of people. And when we see it happening, we will all agree that the Holy Spirit of God was in the midst of it. Without that spiritual power, we won't make it to first base.

"As some like to say, prayer is the main event, the key to whatever success we all might enjoy. And you can be sure of this: the spiritual enemy will take notice. If we're making headway, there will be opposition and obstacles of some kind. We all have to come together and tap the resources of heaven on this one."

There was a thoughtful silence when Gail finished. I sensed no obvious resistance to anything that had been said.

Just as Geoff Handley was about to bring the meeting to a conclusion, Ken Squires raised his hand. "Yeah, Ken. You began our evening; you might as well end it."

"Well, I just wanted to say this last thing. I love, I really love, the notion that our pastor and his wife would invest themselves in young leaders. But I want to underscore something Gordon said a few minutes ago: *we present board members also need continuous training.* We need training in spiritual life, in being effective board members, in knowing how to give spiritual ministry to the people of our church. And remember: you heard this from one of the oldest guys in this room. So, Geoff, I plan to push for the development of this great idea."

The evening ended soon after with agreement on a proposal that we would all meet again in a month. At that time Gail and I would talk about what we thought was possible and how we might go about it.

Before we left the room, Gail and I got together with Rich Fisher to see how he felt about the evening.

"I'm overjoyed," Rich said. "I think God is going to do something big in our church. When can we talk again?"

As we drove home that night, Gail and I talked about the evening and both agreed that, so far, everyone was aboard. Still, we could not help but wonder: *What are we getting ourselves into?*

OCTOBER 13

Late Morning, the First Fall

To: Mercedes Perez
From: GMAC
Subject: Meeting

Mercedes,
Would there be any time on your calendar in the next week
or two for a conversation? I would like to visit the hotel's
training center and ask you some questions about your con-
cepts of training. I have some learning to do.
GMAC

To: GMAC
From: Mercedes Perez
Subject: Re: Meeting

GMAC,
I'd be delighted to meet with you. How about Wednesday,
Oct. 13, 11 a.m.?
MP

To: Mercedes Perez
From: GMAC
Subject: Re: Re: Meeting

MP,
Consider me already there.
GMAC

THREE WORDS DESCRIBE MERCEDES PEREZ: *BRILLIANT, GRA-cious,* and *humble.*

Mercedes went to college at Baylor and then headed to Dartmouth, where she got an MBA at the Tuck School of Business.

One of America's largest hotel groups recruited Mercedes out of Tuck. She moved through their training programs at break-neck speed, and eighteen months later was running a hotel for the chain. Mercedes was that good.

Now, six years later, Mercedes directs the Northeast Center for Professional Enhancement, where personnel from scores of East Coast hotels owned by the parent company come to participate in training programs. Sooner or later almost every hotel employee in the chain's eastern section makes his or her way to Manchester to learn from Mercedes and her people.

Everyone loves Mercedes. Check into any hotel owned by Mercedes's company and drop her name (as in, "She's a personal friend") and you'll get VIP treatment.

When Mercedes came to our church, she was an immediate hit with all of us. Even the most taciturn of New Englanders were charmed by the warmth of her Latina spirit and her servantlike ways. Because she never tried to impress us with her professional credentials, it was a while before anyone realized that Mercedes Perez was an outstanding business executive.

But let me put it another way: Mercedes Perez is a deep person.

On Wednesday, I arrived at the Northeast Center fifteen minutes early. The Center is adjacent to one of the hotel chain's New Hampshire properties. The receptionist at the front desk recognized my name immediately and escorted me to a small conference room where Mercedes was finishing up a meeting with what I later learned was a corporate accounts training group.

When the group was gone, Mercedes invited me to take a seat at the conference table.

We chatted for a few minutes about her recent trip to Texas to see her ailing mother, and then I restated my wish to talk with her about the training center and its programs.

Mercedes reached for a file folder off to her right. On its tab, I read, "GMAC, Wed, 11." When she opened it, I saw several pages of handwritten notes. It was evident, as well as predictable, that she'd prepared for this conversation.

The folder contained a brochure that she handed to me. It described the Northeast Center and its purpose. On the back page was a schedule of all the training programs for the year. As I scanned the program offerings, I thought I saw any number of them that would be profitable for church leaders.

"Give me some context for your interest in the Center," Mercedes said when I looked up, "and then I may be able to pick out some things that would be useful for you."

"Well, here's the short story," I said. "The elders, council, the pastoral staff, and I have been talking for the last couple of months about how to enlarge the number of people in our church who could be called spiritual leaders. We've started referring to them as deep people, and our newest buzzword is *cultivation*. It means that we want to identify growable people and pay a lot of attention to them. We sense huge changes coming in how churches will do ministry, and we're concerned that we're simply not finding and preparing future spiritual leaders to deal with those conditions."

"Sounds like you've been hanging around here," Mercedes said. "The hotel industry is knee-deep in massive changes too. And to use that buzzword of yours, we also have to cultivate new leadership as fast as we can. In fact, you'll hear the same concern all over the corporate world."

I told Mercedes about my visit with Rabbi Cohen and how he gave me a tutorial on how students were taught in Jesus' day. I said that I now felt I had all the information I needed about how training or cultivation happened in a traditional religious context, but that I wanted to move outside the so-called religious world and see if there were things to be learned from people in the profit sector. I said to Mercedes, "How do your people do it? What could we learn from you?"

Mercedes responded with questions of her own. "What makes you so sure that you've got to change the way people are trained . . . or cultivated, as you say it?"

"All I know is that the world around us is in flux every day," I said. "Any organization, even a church, that doesn't change at nearly the same speed that institutions around it are changing is headed for serious trouble. We know that technology, social re-arrangements, spiritual orientations, economic realities—to name a few—are going to present the church with challenges no one's ever faced before. We've got to have leadership in the church that understands this.

"Look at yourself, Mercedes. You're a good illustration—a great one, in fact—of change in the larger world," I said. "Who would have predicted twenty-five years ago that a single, professional woman out of Dartmouth would be a top executive in the hotel business today?"

"And don't forget that the woman's name is Perez," Mercedes said with a smile.

"Well, there you are," I said. "Anyway, Gail and I decided that one of the first things we needed to do was to get outside church boundaries and find out how other organizations cultivate leaders. We thought there might be quite a lot to learn. You were the first person I thought of, Mercedes. So, to be honest, that's why I'm here: to learn from you."

"Pastor Mac," Mercedes said with a broad smile, "I should be learning from you."

"Maybe a little bit on Sunday, Mercedes. But from Monday to Friday you're the one who has something to say."

I continued on with my explanation of why I'd asked to visit. "Here are some of my questions. I'd like to know why your company thinks leadership cultivation is so important that it spends big bucks for this training center. Then I'd like to know how you've learned to identify the teachable or growable people who come here. Obviously, I'm curious about the methods you use in training. And, finally, how do you measure the results you're getting?"

"Have you asked," Mercedes said, "what you want your teachable people to be like? For example, is your goal to turn them into pastors like yourself?"

"Oh, no, not at all. We want most of them to be like you, Mercedes: men and women with day jobs who want to make a difference wherever they go . . . in the church or in their work or their neighborhood. We're convinced that if we do this right, God will give us new generations of leaders who understand the times and how a church can thrive in the middle of it all.

"And, by the way, this is not a drive to recruit supervolunteers," I went on. "It's driven by a conviction that a church's first task is to bring out the very best that God has put into people. We're very much aware that this was Jesus' rabbinical strategy."

"Okay, I see this goal you have in mind," Mercedes said. "So where do you want to start?"

"Let's start with the hotel's philosophy of training. Maybe this is a kindergarten-level question, but why does the hotel company create a training center like this and put one of its very best people in charge?"

Mercedes's assistant entered the room at that moment and handed her a note. She read it and simply said, "Please tell Josh that I'd appreciate him being here in about forty-five minutes." The assistant nodded and left the room.

Mercedes returned to the conversation and rephrased my question, probably to divert attention from herself. "You're interested in our training philosophy. You're assuming, of course, that we have this all figured out, Pastor Mac. But anyway, I'll take my best shot at your question."

Mercedes looked at her notes and said, "Let me simply throw out a bunch of training insights that are important to us. If any of them arouse your curiosity, we can discuss them."

I took out a pen and an index card from my shirt pocket.

"First," Mercedes said, "we believe that a business can be only as good as its training. Our very best people are expected to allocate a significant portion of their time to training. You couldn't last long around here if you didn't do that. We train constantly. We teach people to grow by growing ourselves. It's sort of like painting a huge bridge. The minute the painter finishes at one end, he goes back to the beginning and starts again.

"Trust me on this," Mercedes continued. "If you skimp on training, you spend more and more of your time problem solving. Bottom line? We make big investments in training because training is less expensive than problem solving."

I proceeded to write down on my card: *Training—constant, never stops, painting bridge, money: don't skimp.*

Mercedes went on. "Every training module, every training meeting begins with a reaffirmation of our core business. On the surface we may appear to be selling a night's sleep, selling meals in our restaurant, and selling space to hold conventions and weddings and a score of other things. But our core business, the thing that defines all these functions, is hospitality. We're in the hospitality business. That means we want our customer to feel as comfortable here as if he or she were at home. The feeling of *home* is our standard of performance for hospitality. Of course, we're assuming that the customer likes his or her home."

We talked for a little while about how hospitality works in a hotel. The importance of the congeniality of staff, the choices made in décor, the style of music played in the restaurant and in the elevators, the freshly baked chocolate chip cookies at the front desk, concierges with reassuring answers for every question, databases that record the tastes of frequent guests, quick response times to complaints, reliable transport to and from the airport. It made me wonder what the equivalent of hospitality is in a church like ours.

I wrote down on my card, *Define core business, constantly reaffirm it, what is our standard of performance? What does hospitality look like in a church?*

Mercedes said, "There's more. Let me jump ahead.

"Here at the Center, as I said before, we talk about continuous personal growth. We want every employee to take advantage of the opportunities we offer for personal and professional development. And I'm talking about everyone here: those you might think as holding down the most menial jobs and those who work at the highest management levels. Some of the very best people in this company started at the bottom—driving the shuttle to the airport or working on the night shift cleaning staff, for example—and because of our training program, they have gone on to flourish in management careers.

"If we spot a person with unusual talent and personality, we have a training track that offers an overview of the entire industry. We've seen all kinds of people go through it: room service personnel, a concierge, a maintenance supervisor, and one of the airport shuttle drivers. Some of them have gone on to very responsible jobs as a result.

"We want our people to think boldly about the possibilities of professional advancement if they're motivated. Not everybody's a dreamer, of course, but when we meet one, we do what we can to help make their dreams come true. Frankly, if you wanted a better learning experience in the hotel world, you'd have to go for a degree in hotel and restaurant management in a major university. And even then, you'd want to come here after you had your degree and go through our job-based training program."

I wrote down, *Create a desire for continuous growth, big-picture thinking, watch for dreamers, job-based training.*

"We are very careful to match right people with right training," Mercedes said. "Our HR department regularly confers with our department managers so that all training modules reflect exactly what the managers think their people need."

I wrote, *Identify needs; match with critical topics.*

Mercedes continued. "Let me throw out one or two other things that might be important to you, Pastor Mac. Here at the hotel we train our people in groups, and we try to create experiences where people learn from peers, not just the executives and managers. That means cross-training where people teach each other their jobs. And it means teaching everyone to think like team members. We love to form learning groups that stick together for a while. Sometimes they don't realize it, but they egg each other on to enjoy their jobs more and to take pride in what they're doing."

Now I wrote, *group learning—teaching each other—importance of longevity.*

Recalling Michael Cohen's *talmidim*, those rabbinical disciples who formed a culture of learning around their rabbi, I jotted down, *Learning groups . . . like disciples.*

When I looked back up, Mercedes was saying, "We know that the success in training people in our business requires that you set a very high bar."

"A high bar . . . ?"

"High bar. That means that you stretch your people. You push them to go far beyond where they might have gone on their own. Even the little things are important. For example, we tell people right up front that attendance at every session is mandatory. No one misses. You don't come and go as you please in our program.

"We create disciplines that build a kind of pride of achievement and belonging into our people. A little bit like the marines, you know. Everyone learns to arrive at scheduled meetings five minutes before starting time. No one sits outside the circle when we're dialoguing. We all stay through the duration of a meeting. Everyone participates; there are no silent members in the conversation. And normally there are no visitors allowed during a session.

"We make all of this very plain to each person long before they enter the process, and we tell them that if they're not prepared to commit to these disciplines, then we don't want them to sign up for the program. Which is really a way of informing them that they probably do not have a long future with our company."

Mercedes got very serious all of a sudden. She leaned toward me and said quietly, "This is one of the things that has always bothered me about how some people treat the church, Pastor Mac. Because we don't want to offend anyone in the church, we do not ask much," she said. "People in the church come and go as they please; they arrive late, leave early, maybe not show up at all. They are asked to prepare things, and often they do not. They are challenged to get into the action, but they sit back and let someone else do the work. No one can respect an organization like that.

"If people here acted like a lot of people do at church . . . Let me be honest with you; I'd have to fire them or be fired myself. Yet everyone at church says that what we do there is the most important thing. We talk about life and death, God and heaven, eternity . . . abundant living. Forgive me, Pastor Mac, but it sometimes seems to me that people are lying to one another . . . just saying meaningless words. What gets your top loyalty shows what you really believe."

I could only respond, "I fear that you're right, Mercedes."

On my card I wrote, *high bar, no compromises, don't admit those who resist disciplines.*

Mercifully, Mercedes changed the subject. "Sorry . . . Let's see if I left anything out on my list." She referred back to her notes.

"Ah, I overlooked two things. When we invite people to enter a training track, we always tell them why we have selected or approved them. It's very, very important for everyone to know that they've been observed and what we've seen and appreciated in them. So many of our people come out of families and homes where no one ever tells them that they are valuable for anything except earning money. So if this hotel can be the one place where they learn that they are competent and valued, we want that to happen."

I wrote, *Inform people: why they've been chosen.*

Mercedes and I talked for a while longer about parallels or nonparallels between church and hotel, until there was a knock on the door. When Mercedes opened the door, I saw a young man standing there.

"You asked to see me, Ms. Perez?"

Mercedes said, "Yes, Joshua, I did. Come in; I'd like you to meet a colleague of mine."

OCTOBER 13

Almost Noon, the First Fall

To: Bruce Bartlett, Rich Fisher
From: GMAC

I'm with Mercedes Perez at the Northeast Center. You won't
believe what there is to learn here. Feel like I'm drinking out
of a fire hydrant.

"THIS IS JOSHUA KIM FROM OUR CONVENTION SERVICES
office," Mercedes said to me as she pulled a chair away from the
table for Joshua to use.

When the young man was seated, Mercedes said, "Joshua,
this is Mr. MacDonald, and he and I have been discussing the center's training program."

After Joshua and I shook hands, Mercedes said, "Joshua, I'd
appreciate it if you could describe for Mr. MacDonald your experience in the recent convention development sessions you went
through. Don't worry about details . . . just some impressions."

Then Mercedes stood up and said she had to check on something and left the room. Later it dawned on me that she had
staged this brief exit so that Joshua would not be intimidated by
her presence and say only things he thought she'd want to hear.
Would an ancient rabbi have done something like this to test his
students?

110

"Impressions?" Joshua said after Mercedes was gone. "How many hours do you have? I have a hundred of them."

It didn't take long for Joshua Kim to get started, offering a confident response to Mercedes's request. "The training program here makes you feel that the hotel believes in you and cares about your future. From Ms. Perez on down the org chart, people make you feel that you belong here. Everyone makes it very clear: they want you to learn all you can about your job and then about the jobs that others do. It's obvious that they're watching to see if you have the hotel business in your blood. And if you do, you get the message that there's a future somewhere in the company just for you.

"The training sessions are never a waste of time," Joshua went on. "You're expected to do your homework and come prepared for every meeting. If you're unprepared, it will show really quick. So some people learn the hard way that the training here is not to be blown off."

Joshua continued. "I've appreciated the fact that one or two of the top people in the company are always in the room, right at the table, with us. They listen to each other's presentations; they listen to us; they ask questions about what we've said, and they tell us stories out of their own experiences. Again, their being there sends a strong signal: what you're learning is important, and you yourself are important.

"Oh, and, this too . . . I think the program challenges me to see that I'm responsible for my own development down the line. The company isn't going to do everything for me. I've got to take responsibility for my own growing. There may be times when the hotel's business reputation will be in my hands, and I've got to be able to represent it with dignity and professionalism."

About the time Joshua finished, Mercedes reentered the room.

As she took her seat, I asked Joshua, "So if I asked you to tell me the company's elevator story, how would you answer?"

I could sense Mercedes suddenly become very attentive.

Joshua hardly paused before answering. "Oh, that's easy," he said. "We're in the hospitality business. We make people feel served, safe, and satisfied. And my particular contribution is to help corporate clients come to our properties and experience conferences and conventions that meet all their objectives and that are free of any problems or distractions."

A moment or two later, Joshua was gone.

"Served, safe, and satisfied," Mercedes repeated Joshua Kim's words. "Where did that line come from?"

"Must have grown up in a preacher's home," I answered. "Three points, all beginning with the same letter."

Mercedes nodded. "Any more questions?" she asked me.

"I don't want to overstay my welcome, Mercedes. I need to go back to the office and process what I've heard. Besides: you've got a training center to run."

"The center can wait a bit longer. Seems to me that Joshua's ready to handle everything around here," Mercedes said. "Why don't you join me and my teaching team in the dining room for lunch? You'll enjoy them. They'll make sure you feel served, safe, and satisfied."

And then Mercedes Perez said one more thing as we left the room. "Remember that young man. Someday he'll be doing my job."

She's like a rabbi, I thought.

OCTOBER 13

Early Afternoon, the First Fall

To: GMAC
From: Bruce Bartlett
Do you have a free hour tomorrow or Friday? Claire, Jason, and I want to get with you and assess progress on the great idea. We'd also love to hear about your time today with Mercedes Perez. If you've got a free hour we'll adjust our schedules accordingly.

AFTER LUNCH WITH MERCEDES PEREZ AND HER TEAM IN the training center's dining room, I toured the rest of the facilities. The seminar rooms were equipped with everything (furniture, technology, resource materials) that could maximize a learning experience. The small group of people who coordinated the center's activities were quick (and enthusiastic) to answer any questions I had, and by the time I left, I had more than enough material to read through over the next several days. Being a friend of Mercedes Perez had opened lots of doors that day.

As I left the building to drive back to our church, I found myself captured by a disturbing thought. The quality of space, the equipment, the staff, the information, and the program to which I'd just been exposed all conveyed a clear message: this national chain of hotels believed (really believed!) that identifying and training highly motivated people to pursue the mission was a top priority. Everything I saw and heard that day underscored this commitment.

Then, I asked myself, if a visitor came to our church and assessed the space, the equipment, the staff, and the process we used to train people, what would that message be?

I didn't like the answer to my own question.

Mercedes's Northeast Center for Professional Enhancement was tiny in comparison to some of the great training institutions in our country: West Point, Harvard Business School, Juilliard, Johns Hopkins. But large or small, the people behind each of these institutions all had their versions of the great idea. *They believed that an organization is only as good as its commitment to training leaders for the future.*

Is it necessary to keep repeating that Jesus believed this also? And that he demonstrated it in the amount of time he spent with a relatively small cluster of people?

As I reached my car, my cell phone began blinking with a text message from Bruce Bartlett. The staff wanted to know if we could get together in the next day or two. I called Kelly Martin and asked her to arrange a Thursday morning meeting at a time that was convenient for everyone.

OCTOBER 14

Morning, the First Fall

From my journal

> *It occurs to me that I have seen a fascinating*
> *similarity between what Mercedes Perez told me*
> *yesterday and what I heard from Michael Cohen.*
> *There are two thousand years between these two*
> *traditions of training. But when you get right down*
> *to it, they're very similar. Imitation, instruction,*
> *examination . . . then send them out.*

"WE'RE EAGER TO KNOW YOUR THOUGHTS AFTER THE LAST few days," Bruce Bartlett said when the pastoral staff (Bruce, Claire Dustin, Jason Calder, and I) gathered the next morning in our conference room.

It took me about twenty minutes to review my positive reactions to the elders/council meeting. Then I went into some detail to describe my conversations with Michael Cohen and Mercedes Perez.

My staff colleagues listened intently, and when I finished, I reversed the question. "Now, tell me what you're thinking," I said.

I didn't have to wait long for a response.

Claire was first to speak. "Let me give you two impressions

115

I'm getting. First, it sounds like your time with Michael Cohen and then with Mercedes and her people reinforce our conviction that training is top priority, non-negotiable, if a church desires a future. And we're saying we want a future.

"My second thought is Rabbi Cohen's description of how rabbis cultivated disciples and Mercedes's description of the hotel's commitment to developing its people both say a similar thing: that you go for depth of character first and then follow on with the practical stuff of technique and method. And I think this is an important distinction about our great idea: depth comes before competency."

For a millisecond it hit me: Claire had said "*our* great idea." It signaled to me that more and more people beyond Gail and me now felt that they owned the vision of developing a new cadre of deep people. I loved that.

Jason Calder took our conversation in another direction. "One thing that bothers me," he said, "is that most leadership training activity I've heard about is open to anyone who *thinks* he's a leader. So what you too often get are wannabes, people who show up for the wrong reasons. The other night the worship team read that story in Luke where Jesus turned away three volunteer disciples. And it occurred to us that you never hear of Jesus opening up places for volunteers among his disciples. He selected his people; they didn't select him. And Mercedes seems to get this idea too. Apparently, she and her staff are not going to monkey around with people who aren't fully invested in the possibilities of growth."

"You're right, Jason," Bruce said. "It seems to me that when you open leadership development to everyone—you know, kind of just one more public meeting—the effort gets degraded. People looking for something really serious think it must not be worth it, and the volunteers you talked about often show up there because they're hungry for recognition or the perceived power that they think leaders enjoy."

"Or they just want to get close to the pastor and others they think are important in the church's life," Claire said.

"I'm listening carefully to you guys," I said, "because you're verbalizing things I've struggled with. Remember what you've said, because these observations will become an important part of the process when the elders get together again."

Our conversation went on for a while longer, and then I asked the staff if they could help me with something. "It may be time to start breaking down the great idea into four or five operating principles . . . you know, talking points that anyone can grasp. I want to be able to say, 'This is the way we want to cultivate deepening people in our church.' Any thoughts?"

Everyone became quiet. Someone suggested that we refill our coffee cups, which we—well, three of us, anyway (Jason wasn't into coffee)—did. Then we returned to our seats.

Bruce was first to speak. "I think the first talking point might reflect what Jason said a few minutes ago: that you can't—in fact you mustn't—try to involve everyone in the great idea . . . not all at once, anyway. If we're not looking for volunteers, as he puts it, we will have to begin with the principle of selection. Who's ready to be a part of such an initiative?"

"Gail and I have felt that way from the beginning," I said. "So I agree with Jason, and I hear you now, Bruce. Here's my thought . . . I think we should try to emulate the way Jesus worked with his disciples as closely as possible.

"Gail continuously reminds me that Jesus did nothing in the way of disciple-selection until he'd prayed and prayed hard. I think he was telling us something—that this most critical event— selecting growable people—has to start on your knees.

"Then he began identifying people who he sensed had a potential for depth and service and invited them to learn with him. You have to believe that not everyone said yes to Jesus' invitation, but that's the way he kicked off his public life as a rabbi, and that's the way I'd like to start."

Claire spoke next. "If those are the beginning steps, I'd say there has to be some very careful thought given to the qualities you're looking for when the selection process takes place. You can't compromise on this. If you do, you're in trouble from the beginning."

"I think I have an answer for that," I said. "We've been kicking around words like *growable* and *cultivating*. So who are the growable men and women in our congregation? People, younger and older, who have reached a moment in their spiritual journeys where they want someone to push and poke at them and challenge them to enter into a process of spiritual cultivation so that they can become all God has made them to be."

"Okay. You're talking about growing in one's effort to be a follower of Jesus," Bruce said. "A word I'm using more and more is *loyalty*. Aren't we talking about people who want to live loyally for Jesus?"

Claire reached into a bag beside her seat, took out her iPad, and began to type with her fingertips on the screen. The guys forgot what we were saying as we watched her tap away. Then Claire looked up.

"What?" she said, as if shocked that everyone was looking at her.

"We're wondering what you're doing," Jason said.

"Well, I'm trying to record what you're saying and help describe this set of great-idea principles."

"Great. What have you got so far?" I asked.

"Well, you really haven't said that much, but here it is so far. I'm trying to use words you all are kicking around. 'The first objective of the great idea is to identify growable people who hunger to be loyal'—your word, Bruce—'to Jesus.'"

"*Hunger* is kind of dorky," Jason said. "Why don't you just say *expand* . . . to expand their loyalty to Jesus?"

Claire deleted and typed in a few words. Then she looked at us and said, "Needs something more. How about, 'to identify and challenge growable people to deepen their loyalty to Jesus and his purposes.'"

We nodded in agreement, and Claire edited the line on her iPad.

"What's next?" Bruce asked.

Jason spoke up again. "I know I'm the new kid on the block here, but I'm going to throw this out for what it's worth. Just before I went off to college, Pastor Mac and Gail started meeting with the Discovery Group. One night they invited the youth worship team to meet with the group. It was an incredible experience because most of us had never sat with people forty years older than us and had a conversation like the one that happened that night."

"I'll never forget it, Jason," I said. "I remember that evening as one of the great moments in my pastoral life. Watching the walls between two generations come down was amazing. You had a lot to do with what happened. You were a leader that night. The life of the Lord was really in you."

Jason seemed a bit embarrassed at my comment but finally continued. "Well, I was going to say that on the occasions when the worship team and I met with the Discovery Group, we saw what was possible when people work at connecting with one another . . . when they really try to love each other and attempt to help each other grow and accomplish things no one thought possible . . . You know, like Mr. Yost and the others who came to love Ben Jacobs and draw him into our church family."

"Did I hear someone saying my name?" The voice came from the open doorway. There stood a smiling Ben Jacobs. I got up and pulled him into the room with my handshake.

"Hey, Ben, what are you doing here?" I asked.

"Well, today's my day off from the store [Ben works at the Home Depot], and Catherine asked if I'd come down to church and pick up a book someone left for her. I was passing the door when I heard my name."

"I think Jason was about to say something nice about you, Ben, but you interrupted him," Claire said.

"Why don't you come in and join us for a few minutes and hear what Jason's going to say about you?" I said. "We're discussing leadership development . . . you know, the great-idea thing."

"Yeah," Jason said, "and I was talking about the old Discovery Group and what happened to those people when they got so connected with one another."

"Gosh, I'll never forget what I owe those guys. They showed me what community looks like," Ben said. "Catherine is convinced that none of us can ever be strong in the Christian life without intentional participation in a smaller group of people."

"What do you mean, *intentional*? Claire asked.

"It's Catherine's new favorite word. She got it from listening to Pastor Mac too much . . . I guess it's one of his favorite words too." Everyone laughed.

Ben continued. "Most people join a group because they simply like everyone there or because they have something in common. And that is a community of sorts. But add *intentionality*, and it means that somebody seriously commits to a group of people and sticks with them even when there is tension and misunderstanding.

"In intentional community no one walks away when somebody shows their dark side or fails. Everyone hangs in there. It's like in a good marriage: you're intentional about it . . . you accept; you commit yourself to people just like I learned to accept and commit myself to Jesus. And that's one of the things that grabbed me when I first came here. I met people who had learned to like or love each other and to make some allowances for their differences, yet, at the same time, walk in the same direction toward Jesus."

"So, Ben," Claire asked, "we're talking here about leadership development . . . cultivating deep people. How does community relate to that?"

"Well, I'd say that the kind of leaders you want have got to be the first players when it comes to intentional community, and they should know—because they've done it themselves—how to bring other people together and create still more communities. You can't tell other people to do what you haven't done yourself.

"I guess if I were training people to be leaders, that's among the very first things I'd do. I'd make sure they knew how community is built, how it works . . . because they'd done it."

Ben looked in my direction and went on. "Pastor Mac, I don't want to embarrass you, but you and Gail model a kind of intentional community every time you sit together in the front of the worship center on Sunday morning. Your marriage is a community. A lot of us who didn't grow up in homes where there was community watch people like you two . . . and, I might add, the rest of you. We need to see what intentional community and relationships look like."

"Gordon, Ben's saying something we really need to consider," Claire said. "This is more than your generic small group. It's several notches up the line in significance, maybe the way the church will reorganize itself in years to come."

"You better believe Ben's onto something. He's referring to the very same thing I was starting to say when he came through the door," Jason added, becoming more passionate with each word. "My generation isn't going near any church if there isn't a real sense of community . . . I mean real, authentic belonging. So many younger people come out of dysfunctional homes and they're looking for some kind of family experience. Leaders had better know what community means, how it works, and be a part of it themselves."

"So what kind of intentional community are you talking about?" I asked. "What do you younger folks see the people in such a community doing?"

"Jason, could I take a shot at this?" Claire asked. When he nodded, she said, "In the case of the great-idea, we're talking about communities built around serious learning and deepening. And as they learn, their commitment to one another grows. Think about this: is there any significance to the fact that Jesus doesn't talk about the disciples loving one another *until* they'd learned together?"

"So the intentional community that Ben talks about is the *community of learners* that you're talking about," I said to Claire. "Try putting that into words."

Again, Claire began tapping on her iPad screen, and we waited to see what she'd come up with. Finally she spoke. "Well, I'm not happy with this, but here it goes: 'The second objective of the great idea is to form intentional communities of learners where Christlike character is . . . is . . .'"

"Explored?" Bruce said. "Try that."

"What have you got, Claire?" I asked.

She looked at her screen and began typing again. "Good. We're getting closer."

A moment later she said, "Okay . . . this is what I heard you all saying. The second objective is 'to form intentional communities where people work together to understand the nature of Christlike character.'"

Bruce said, "All in favor, say aye." We all said aye, even Ben Jacobs, who apparently assumed he was now part of our discussion.

"Yesterday," Bruce said, "Jason, Claire, and I tried naming folks in the church who impress us as being *deep* in their Christian way of life. And we noted that they had these things in common. I wrote them down . . ." Bruce pulled an index card from his shirt pocket.

"Here's what we said. They have a sense of worshipful reverence for Jesus. Also, you could tell that they really care for others . . . in and out of the church. They have a calmness and a certainty within them when they face difficult experiences. They are unashamed to talk about God's grace and blessing in their lives. They maintain a vigorous devotional life. They have great faith and optimism in God's power. And in one way or another, they influence others. People look to them for inspiration, guidance, and assurance."

"Bruce," I said, "the term Gail and I kicked around this morning that sums up what you've got there is *influence*, a holy influence. It pertains to men and women who renounce mediocrity and embrace the possibility that God can use them in extraordinary ways to serve others."

Ben Jacobs said, "Well, that's what I saw in you guys when I got here. You all welcomed a real jerk who was really broken in a lot of pieces. Guys like Ernie Yost loved me and told me their stories. They listened to me and answered my questions. And when I disappointed them, they didn't turn their backs on me. They simply kept loving me. And each of them did it in a different way. *Holy influence*: I like that, Pastor Mac. That's what I experienced. And look! Here I am. Sitting at this table with folks like you. You have no idea how different it could have been for me. I was walking straight into disaster city until I got here."

I thought, *Every church needs a Ben Jacobs hanging around the office who can remind us each day of the "business" we're in.* The truth is that we're supposed to be engaging with people—using Ben's words—who are walking straight toward disaster city.

Claire went back to her iPad again. "Okay, Ben . . . you guys . . . listen to this," she said. "'Third objective: to help people

123

discover and refine their own ways of influencing others in the name of Jesus.'"

"It's a start in the right direction," Bruce said, grinning. "Can you live with it for now, Gordon?"

"Yeah," I responded. "It is a good start. I'll want to hear Gail's perspective tonight. So, we're up to three objectives . . . but something's still missing. Anything else occur to any of you? Ben, could you hang on with us for a few more minutes? We might have something here you could help us with."

Ben said he would.

"Well," Bruce said, "you may be looking for an exit or a transition strategy to the great-idea initiative. As people finish the process, what happens to them? Do we just drop them, let them figure out on their own what they do next? Sounds like we don't care what they do. That would be absurd."

"I agree," Jason said.

"So what are we saying?" I asked. "That the great idea is not complete until we help people figure out what they are supposed to do with what they've experienced?"

"Wouldn't Mercedes Perez say they do that at the hotel center?" Claire asked.

"Sure, of course she would," I said. "She'd say that training opens the door to all sorts of opportunities but that the effort would be a failure if each person doesn't discover a way to put what they learned into action and where they can best fit into the community.

"Can I suggest that we remember that we're not just wanting to cultivate deep people to do things in the church? If this great idea is as successful as I think it could be, there will come a time when we'll have more deep people than the church can accommodate. We have to be willing to see them exercise their extraordinary influence in other places . . . other Christian ministries or in the service organizations of the city."

Ben said, "That would be an incredible thing to see."

"Well, do your thing, Claire," Bruce said. "Say that. Write something brilliant. It will be the last of Gordon's talking points."

And she did. A couple of minutes later Claire read, "'Fourth objective: to point people toward opportunities in the church and in the larger world.'"

"I could salute that. What do the rest of you think?" Bruce asked us.

Everyone nodded in agreement.

"Claire, could you e-mail those four objectives to me as soon as it's convenient?" I asked.

"Convenient?" Claire said. She tapped a few times on her iPad screen and said, "It's in your in-box now. Oh, and I sent a copy to Gail too."

"Okay, guys," I said. "I suspect there's more to say here, but we've made some good progress. There's one other thing you might be thinking about."

"What's that?" Jason asked.

"I need to find an appropriate name that identifies this effort. No one's going to be impressed if all we keep saying is that we're working on a great idea. So the next step is to figure out what we're going to call this thing that we think is so exciting."

For a few minutes Bruce, Claire, Jason, Ben Jacobs, and I kicked around some ideas, but I became a bit of a footdragger. Everything they came up with seemed too slick or too vague. Then again, it might simply have been that I was tired of making decisions.

OCTOBER 14

Late Morning, the First Fall

On my voice mail

"Pastor MacDonald, this is Annie Huntoon calling. My father was taken to the hospital yesterday. They're worried that he may have had another heart attack. It would mean a lot if one of the pastors could drop by and pray for him."

AFTER THE STAFF MEETING (PLUS BEN JACOBS) ENDED, I left the church office and drove to the hospital to see George Huntoon, who had been chair of the elders when I first came to the church. This was his second time in the hospital this year.

My suspicion was that we would not have this godly man—this deep person—with us much longer. In the past months, I'd tried to see George whenever I could so I could be sure he knew how much he was loved and appreciated by our congregation.

When I entered his hospital room, George seemed very alert and glad to see me. Typical of this grand old New England man, he didn't want to talk about himself. He wanted to know about everything that was going on at church.

Soon I was telling him about our progress in the development of the great idea, and he was delighted. When I said that it appeared that Gail and I would spearhead the cultivation process of young leaders, he said, "Good! It will take twenty years off you. Those kids will keep you going and going and going." He paused while he coughed. "So what is this great idea going to be called? If I'm going to pray about it, I'll have to have a name."

"I don't really know, George. That hasn't been the most important thing in the discussions so far. When someone like you wants to know what's going on, we use words like *cultivation, discerning, deep people, leadership development, growable, discipleship.* We know we want this effort to be a mix of leadership issues and discipleship issues. But that's as far as we've gotten.

"Underneath it all," I continued, "we know that we're on the search for potentially deep people: deep in the love of the Lord, deep in their desire to follow Christ, deep in their willingness to serve in the church or the larger world—"

"Don't waste time finding some big, fancy name," George interrupted. "If God's in it, it won't need a big name . . . just some handle that people like me can use to refer to it. I do like that word *cultivation,* probably because my father and his father were farmers. Oh, and I love that term *deep people.* That reminds me of our old farm well. You see? Words like *deep* and *cultivate* send a message that even an old duffer like me can understand."

Just then a nurse came into the room to read George's chart and check his heart monitor. I stood off to the side and waited until she was done.

When she left the room, George picked up right where we'd left off. "I still like that word *cultivation,*" he said again. "Tell you what: just try calling this great idea of yours *CDP . . . Cultivating Deep People.* See if it fits what you're trying to say."

A short while later I left the hospital with three thoughts, each in its turn, swirling in my mind. The first was George Huntoon's suggestion for a name. *CDP, CDP, CDP . . .* I kept saying to myself. I could go with that.

And my second thought was, *Won't it be fun to be able to tell everyone that George, one of the deepest people our church has ever known, was the guy who gave the great idea its name?*

Then a third thought: *If Gail and I do this CDP thing—which appears likely—I won't be making as many calls in the hospital much longer. Other people will be visiting the George Huntoons of our congregation.* And that was not a happy thought. I love that man.

OCTOBER 14

Dinnertime, the First Fall

To: Geoff Handley, Monica O'Donnell, Rich Fisher
From: GMAC
Subject: Name

Wanted you to know that I've had some great conversations with staff, Gail, and George Huntoon. George wants us to call our great idea CDP—Cultivating Deep People. Frankly, I don't want to waste a lot of time finding and debating the perfect name for the great idea. And besides, I think George's name is pretty good. I'd like to run the name past Gail, but my own feeling is pretty positive.

IT WAS 4 P.M. THE AUTUMNAL NEW ENGLAND SUN RESTED low in the western sky, making driving in that direction a bit difficult.

After a day of nonstop talking—a breakfast with some young adults in the church, the staff gathering, the George Huntoon visit, and two pastoral counseling conversations—I was headed home tired but very eager to see Gail.

My partner in life had been gone for two days—an annual getaway with a close friend—so we hadn't had much of a chance to talk about my hotel experience, the staff meeting, or the latest surprise of the day—George Huntoon's suggested name.

Soon after I was in the house, we were deep into conversation.

"Cultivating Deep People . . . CDP." Gail repeated the words after I told her about George's idea. "Sounds like what you do when someone's had a heart attack."

"No, babe; that's CPR. This is CDP: Cultivating Deep People."

"And you're happy with that?"

"I got used to it pretty quickly. It does describe exactly what we say we want to do."

"Well, you're probably right. But maybe someone will come up with something better. On the other hand, it's kind of special that the name would come from a veteran leader in the church."

As we ate dinner together, I described to Gail all the other experiences I'd had while she was gone, and after we'd cleared the table and loaded the dishwasher, we spread out the training literature that Mercedes had given me. Since this was my first time to study what I'd been given, I'd be less than truthful if I didn't admit I was overwhelmed.

"Mercedes's company is obviously far more committed and more thoughtful about training its people than our church has ever been," Gail said. "And, really, when you get right down to it, they're doing it to make money. On the other hand, we keep saying that we want to bring people to Jesus and change the world. But anyone can see that in terms of sheer effort and excellence, Mercedes's company has a passion that seems far greater than ours."

"Well, to be frank," I said, "that's the same feeling I had when she introduced me to a young man from one of their departments and asked him to describe what the hotel's training meant to him. I'm going to tell you: that kid was really impressive. I kept saying to myself while he talked, 'Do we have *anyone—anyone!—* in our congregation who'd sound like this if they were asked how the church was helping them grow into everything God called them to be?'"

"So, did you have an answer?" Gail asked as she poured us some fresh coffee.

"Not exactly . . . So maybe this is another one of those ways that God speaks into our hearts and says, *Get busy.* I mean, look at this stuff . . . Mercedes and her people really know what they're doing."

"So tell me, what were the most important takeaways from your time at the hotel?"

I got my laptop and found the "Reflections" file, where, the night before, I'd refined my notes from the hotel visit. "Let's see . . . First, all training at the hotel is done in a group context. Second, selection of participants is everything. Third, people are pushed hard to learn. Fourth, there are expectations about preparation and participation, and no one is an exception. Start slacking, and you're out of there. There are several more ideas, but these are the most important. I heard pretty much the same ideas in the staff discussion this morning, except for the prayer element, of course. But you can be sure that Mercedes prays about these things even as Rich Fisher prays for things at the school."

Gail seemed thoughtful. "Can our church match the quality that Mercedes has accomplished at the hotel?"

"Well, why not? When the staff took a cut at operating principles we might embrace, it was clear that they were aboard and highly motivated. And the leadership? You've heard what they're saying."

"But are you confident that we can push people in a church as hard as they do at the hotel?" Gail asked.

"Jury's out on that one. But why not have just one activity in the church where you refuse to allow mediocrity, laziness, or spotty participation to be the standard?"

I could feel myself getting worked up about what I was saying.

Perhaps my feelings were connected to a pastoral lifetime of frustration when I have felt that too many people—and we pastors are no exception—are long on words but short on action.

"At this point in my life," I said, "I'm not going to give myself to one more church function that starts off hot and runs out of gas eight weeks down the road. It would be better to invest our energies in six growable people who are willing to pay the price to mature in their faith than to waste time with one hundred people who want to play religious games but won't be any different at the end than when they started. I'm just not going there again. I'm eager to see the ministry to be about growing deeper people."

Tough words—probably better left unsaid. But I felt much better having gotten them off my chest.

Later, after the evening news, Gail and I retreated to the porch and picked up the earlier conversation. She wanted to hear more about the staff conversation that morning.

I told her about the four talking points we'd put together.

"What did you come up with?"

"Wait a minute . . . Claire e-mailed the points to me from her iPad." I got up and found my BlackBerry. As Claire had promised, the information was there.

When I sat back down, I said, "Now these words are pretty raw . . . totally unedited. Nothing's in concrete. We probably have a long way to go before we can dance with this stuff. Anyway . . . I'll read them straight through."

After I'd read them and we'd had a chance to talk about their implications, Gail said, "Those are really quite good . . . quite good," Gail said. "There's a lot of possibility inside those points. I could get very excited about helping to make those things happen."

Not long after, we both admitted how tired we were and headed off to bed.

OCTOBER 14

Midnight, the First Fall

To Do

☐ *Edit list of CDP selection criteria.*
☐ *Copies to Handley, Fisher, O'Donnell, staff*

WE MAY HAVE GONE TO BED, BUT NEITHER GAIL NOR I COULD get to sleep. An hour passed, then another. We tossed and turned, reshaped pillows, rearranged the blankets—nothing worked.

"My mind simply won't turn off," I finally said to Gail.

"Mine won't either," she said.

"Want to get up for a few minutes?"

"Sure, why not?"

We put on our robes and went out onto the porch. An October moon was nearing its full stage, and it seemed as if the backyard was fully illuminated. Gail thought she saw a deer at the edge of the woods. But if it had been there, it was gone quickly.

"I don't know what you've had on your mind," Gail said, "but I've been thinking about the kind of people we want to get into this CPR—"

"It's CDP, sweetheart. Cultivating deep people."

"Okay. CDP. Anyway, I've been thinking about how we go about inviting people to become a part of it."

"And . . ."

133

"Well, everyone seems to be in agreement that we won't take volunteers. We are agreed, aren't we?"

I said we were agreed.

"So that means that CDP isn't the sort of thing you announce on Sunday morning and invite people to sign up in the commons."

"Hadn't really thought about it that way, but you're right. I will have to preach about it somewhere down the line. If it's going to be a high priority in our ministry, the people will have to know why and how it works. So where are you going with this?"

"Well, let's take ninety days to formulate a list of about thirty people. We could encourage the staff and the elders to quietly make recommendations of men and women they think fit the criteria for the CDP venture."

"Do we know what the criteria are?"

"I've got some ideas, but you probably do too," Gail answered. "But, again, the most important thing is to start with prayer. We ask the Lord, and we believe that he'll bring people's names to our hearts. Then we watch them for a few weeks . . . talk to them . . . observe them with people . . . see if we think they'd fit. Let me work this selection thing through. In the end we'll narrow the list to the twenty most qualified."

"Sounds like General Marshall's black book," I said.

"Uh . . . yeah . . . General Marshall with the black book. Something like that."

"So what would be the criteria?" I asked Gail.

"Well, we've been using the word *teachable* a lot, and it stands out in my mind as the first thing. Of course, I'm assuming that there's already a clear devotion to Jesus. But after that, any lack of teachability is the first deal-breaker. You don't want someone in this learning community who isn't curious and doesn't want to learn. You want men and women who are determined to grow and to be taught."

"So what's the opposite of teachability?"

"Proud . . . smug . . . know-it-all . . . shallow . . . stubborn . . . arrogant . . . that enough?"

"Helps to know who you don't want to consider. So then, what are words that define teachability?

"Well, what I just said: *curious, inquisitive, hungry to learn, humble, disciplined* . . . that enough?"

"Yeah. Here's a second thing to look for. I think you want to look for a pattern of faithfulness and dependability."

"Reason?" Gail prompted.

"Simply because the effectiveness of the experience breaks down if you bring people in who make commitments and promises and then don't honor them. My suspicion is that we're going to ask a lot from these people. You get one or two of them who aren't reliable and the cohesiveness of the whole group breaks down."

"Okay, makes sense. Faithful and . . ."

"Dependable," I said.

"Dependable . . . right."

I was on a roll now. "Can I suggest that we put *social skills* on the list of things we're looking for? We want to work with people who know how to listen and respect others. And we want them to be reasonably comfortable about expressing themselves."

"Okay . . . social skills . . . How about *social maturity*?" Gail said. "That's what I think you're talking about."

"Sounds good."

"Let's also agree," Gail said, "that we're not going to choose people who are struggling with significant personal problems. We're not starting a support group or a therapy group. It occurs to me that we've got to be firm about this because we'll probably get pressure to invite some people who need lots of help. And we've got other groups in the church for that purpose."

"Good point . . . what else?"

"*Participators* . . . I can't think of a better word, but we want people who are willing to dive in and participate. We can't have people who sit silently time after time and let others carry the burden of conversation."

"Good . . . I agree . . . that's important," I responded.

"I think we also want to discern whether or not a person has shown any potential for leadership of some kind," I said. "Have there been those who have followed this person for any reason? Is he or she respected?"

"Okay, so we look for *respected*. Anything else?" Gail asked.

"Well, it may be a bit vague . . . maybe not . . ."

"What?"

"I think," I said, "that we need to ask ourselves, 'Is this person ready to learn how to think like a servant?' How do you put that into words? But it's really important."

We were silent for a moment, trying to think of anything else to add to this list of selection criteria.

Then Gail broke the silence. "This servant thing you just mentioned. It's most likely to come about if they see you and me as servants . . . serving them, serving each other, serving others. They'll become servants if they see us as servants."

"Are we demanding too much with this list?" I asked. "I mean, when I think of the things we've just put on this list, I don't think any of Jesus' disciples would have qualified at the beginning."

"Well, you're right. If anyone had all these qualities, they wouldn't need us. But let's agree that we're looking for people who are growable in these directions."

That seemed to satisfy us both.

It was now 1:45 a.m. Gail stood and stretched. "If I don't get some sleep, I'm going to need CPR." Maybe it was a silliness that arises out of fatigue, but the two of us broke into laughter.

"Hey," Gail said as she looked out the window again. "The deer's back. Look!" Courtesy of the full moon's light, we watched the deer calmly poke its way around the flowers in search of something.

"You won't see that deer again in a few weeks," I said.

"Why not?" Gail asked.

"It'll soon be hunting season. That deer will be deep in the woods in a hiding place that almost no one can find."

We headed back to the bedroom.

When we'd both gotten into our favorite sleeping positions, Gail said, "You've not forgotten, have you, that the night before Jesus called his disciples, he prayed?"

No, I'd not forgotten. So I put my arms around her, and we prayed for this CDP initiative that had no precedent, at least in our church. We asked for discernment in picking the first group. And we thanked the Lord for the elders and the rest of the leadership who appeared ready to support this effort.

I realized as I prayed that for Gail and me, CDP was already a done deal. We were more than committed.

Only then did we drift off into sleep. A day's work—a long day's work—finally finished.

NOVEMBER 4

Evening, the First Fall

Letter to Melanie Capon

> Dear Melanie,
>
> We'd like to invite you to our home on Thursday evening (7:30 p.m.), November 4, for what we're calling a conversation party. After some dessert, we'd like to ask each guest to describe one memorable way some teacher, coach, pastor, or maybe even a parent taught them something very important. How did they do it? Please get back to us with an RSVP as soon as possible.
>
> Pastor and Mrs. MacDonald

AT BREAKFAST ON THE MORNING AFTER OUR MIDNIGHT CON-versation, Gail presented me with an idea.

"Why don't we get a bunch of people to come over some evening and talk about their most memorable learning experiences? We just might get some insights about how people learn and grow that we wouldn't have thought about ourselves."

Gail became so excited about her own idea that it would have been folly to throw cold water on it. Very quickly she compiled a list of invitees: twelve people. She anticipated that one or two might decline and that one or two more would probably cancel at the last minute.

ALL TWELVE ACCEPTED AND, ON THURSDAY NIGHT, November 4, all showed up. Many arrived a few minutes early, and most—the women, anyway—brought hostess gifts: flowers, a plant, some exotic teas, and two kitchen towels. Fortunately we have a basement room in our condo that is quite sizable, and when you set up fourteen metal folding chairs (metal folding chairs will not be part of heaven's furniture), you don't feel crowded at all.

We name-tagged our guests as they came through the front door, since there were those who'd never met before. Most were from the church; a few came from our neighborhood.

When we knew that everyone had arrived, we set out dessert— cake from Bread and Chocolate, Boston Bean coffee, and nuts—lots of nuts.

A day or two earlier, I had suggested to Gail that it would be best if we presented the great idea in the form of a dialogue between the two of us, instead of just one of us making a presentation. "Let's let them see us working together instead of one of us doing all the talking and the other just sitting."

So our introduction to the conversational part of the evening sounded like this:

GAIL: Gordon and I are very thankful to each of you for coming to our home tonight. We've asked you here because we think you can help us. We're thinking very seriously about spending a lot of time with a small group of men and women we believe have potential to be effective leaders in our church and, perhaps, even in the community. If we can do this successfully once or twice, then we'd like to see the concept expanded so that, each year, a larger and larger number of potential leaders of varying kinds appear on the scene. Right now the process we're thinking about is being called CDP... Cultivating Deep People. If you want to know more about what that means or why we chose that name, talk to Gordon or me later.

GORDON: We're not going into detail about techniques and such because we're still forming the process in our minds. But we're at a point where we'd like to consult with some people like you. We invited you because we believe you might have something to teach us. And the subject is just that: how people learn. We've talked with professionals in the world of training, but we think there might be something valuable in the stories of people like you.

GAIL: Here's what we're hoping might happen tonight. We'd like to ask each of you to think back across your life and remember one profound experience in learning. How did it happen? Or who made it happen and what did that person do? Maybe it's what the experience did to you and how you've never been the same since. Some of us may have similar stories, and that's okay. Now, there's fourteen of us in the room, so each of us will have about three or four minutes to talk.

GORDON: Before we begin, I'd like us to go around the room and simply state our names. A lot of us know each other, but we don't want to assume that everyone knows everyone. So Carl, can we begin with you? Oh, it's not fair for any married person to speak for both. We want to hear from everyone.

140

CARL: I'm Carl Klaussen, and this is my wife . . . Oh, sorry . . .

CARY: I'm Cary Klaussen, Carl's wife.

HANA: Name is Hana Tchung. I from Korea . . . not speak English very well.

MELANIE: Melanie Capon. Thanks, Pastor and Mrs. Mac, for having me. [Melanie was a single woman who was a lawyer. She was already on our list for possible CDP involvement.]

The next couple were our neighbors Hank and Cynthia Soriano. They'd accepted our invitation to be part of this event even though they'd never been to any church-related function before. It had been almost five months since the memorable elevator-story night at Fenway Park.

"I'm Cynthia Soriano," Cynthia said.

"And I'm Hank . . . really glad to be invited."

Following the Sorianos was Tyler Ford (also on our original CDP list), Ginny and Vince Kellogg, and Connie Peterson, Ben Jacob's aunt. I'll not keep on with the rest of the names.

When we'd gone around the circle, I said, "Now we're looking for stories, and the best way I know to get this started is to kick things off myself. When I was nineteen years old and in college, I met an older couple—older than me, anyway—who lived down the street from me. He was a Presbyterian pastor, and she was a stay-at-home mom who did a lot of volunteer work in the community. One day I passed their home while they were out in the front yard, and I stopped to say hello. One thing led to another, and I was invited for dinner that evening.

"I had a great time, and they must have also because they asked me to come back a few nights later. As we got to know each other, they poked me with lots of questions and kind of wormed their way into my life. All the time I was watching them closely. I'd come out of an unhappy home life and longed to see a husband and wife who really loved each other. And as far as I could see, they were it.

"I was impressed with the way he treated his wife, his ways of appreciating her, respecting her, and listening to her when she talked. And I couldn't get over the ways she found to make her husband feel loved. She clearly enjoyed him and did everything she could to make him feel respected.

"As the months passed that year, I ended up going there for dinner again and again. They became like surrogate parents to me. But the thing I remember, whenever I look back, was the model of deep, abiding love that they represented. By having me in their home night after night, they taught me what a good marriage looked like. She became the woman that I used to measure against all other women who came into my life. And when I met Gail, I determined to have a marriage with her that emulated all I'd learned from that couple. So for me, that's learning by observing and imitating."

There was a minute or two of awkward silence, and I hoped that I'd not spoken so fluently—it is part of my job—that others felt reluctant to follow. Then Hank Soriano broke the silence. My neighbor! I hadn't expected that he'd speak out so quickly in a group where most people were strangers.

HANK: The most important things I ever learned came when I was on teams: football in high school . . . a team of lifeguards at summer camp . . . a team I worked on when I was in the navy, and a tiger team in the place where I work now.
TYLER FORD: A tiger team? What's that?
HANK: Oh, sorry. It's a group of people that are put

together to solve a problem that no particular unit in the company is responsible for. So the boss picks a number of people, throws the problem their way, and says, "Don't bother me again until you have a solution." That's a tiger team. Get what I'm saying?

TYLER: Got it.

HANK: I'm a team kind of guy. I love seeing how a team brings out the best in everyone. Something in me just becomes electrified when I get with a group that has a mission to win a championship or launch a new product. You have this sense of minds and hearts networking and becoming one big machine. And you find that you can do things, achieve things together that none of you could have done by yourself.

Soon after I started with the company I've been with for twenty-two years, I was put on one of those tiger teams. The VP thought I might have fresh eyes. We had two old guys and three or four of us young ones. Those old guys knew all the shortcuts and the land mines. They taught us kids everything from A to Z. And I think we energized them with our fresh enthusiasm for the work and our willingness to put in long hours. We called ourselves the Boiler Room Gang, and the VP of our division loved us. He threw one project after another at us because we got things done. The team finally broke up when the older guys retired. But I learned then that if you want to grow your career, do it with a team.

MELANIE CAPON: Pastor, Gail . . . can I go next? If I wait too long, I'll be too nervous to talk.

GAIL: The floor's yours, Melanie.

MELANIE: Gail, one of the greatest times of learning

for me was when you gave a bunch of us women the
Briggs-Myers . . . uh . . . uh . . .

GAIL: It's Myers-Briggs . . . the MBTI, Myers-Briggs
Temperament Indicator.

MELANIE: That's it: MBTI . . . I never get that right.
Anyway, learning about my temperament was a life-
changer for me. Gail said we are all wired uniquely,
and the MBTI helped me to understand my own wiring and the wiring of others.

Gail, you helped me learn that I was an introvert
and that I shouldn't be ashamed of it. And I learned
that I was a sensate who has a nose for details. I guess
that's why I'm pretty good at contract law, because
there aren't too many nits that get by me. And then
you helped me discover that I was a perceiver—which
helped me see why I worry over decisions so much.

If you're going to try to help people to be leaders,
Gail . . . and Pastor, I'd urge you to think about teaching
the MBTI to each person. And do it at the very beginning. That way all the people you're working with will
know how to respond to each other. That really helped
all of us women bond. We talk about our temperaments
all the time, and, believe me, there's a lot to talk about.

GAIL: Melanie, that's a wonderful idea. I don't think
we've talked about that yet. But you can be sure we
will now.

To my surprise Hana Tchung, our Korean friend, leaned forward and raised her hand. Carl Klaussen was about to speak, but
I decided to recognize Hana since I knew she would be reluctant
to assert herself.

"Hana, do you want to be next?"

HANA: I want say about prayer. Forgive me. My English not so good. [Hana was constantly apologizing for her English and it was hard to persuade her that this was unnecessary.]

GAIL: Your English is fine, Hana.

HANA: When I was girl in Korea, my grandmother say prayer is most important thing. She say that you can tell how close someone is to God when pray . . . they pray. She get together with other women and pray every week. Five o'clock in morning. When I become woman, I remember her pray and say myself that I would be woman of prayer too.

It great honor to pray for church. Pray for you, Pastor MacDonald. Pray for my friends. And I love hear you pray on Sunday on worship. More important than sermon.

There was lots of laughter at this comment. And Hana was surprised, perhaps embarrassed. She looked at me and said, "I sorry, Pastor Mac. I hope I . . ."

"Hana, you couldn't have said a nicer thing to me. I'd much rather be appreciated for my praying than my preaching."

HANA: Thank you, Pastor MacDonald. This what I want say. Find way to teach people how to pray to God. Pray for each other. Pray for world. Pray for church. This what my grandmother say.

GAIL: Hana, you said it beautifully. Thank you. We heard you.

There were others who spoke up, and we had no trouble getting people to contribute. The stories were riveting, and everyone forgot the time and listened intensely. There were a few comments that stood out and either gave us a fresh insight or reaffirmed what we already thought might be important when you're teaching "growable" people.

For example, there was this from Carl Klaussen:

CARL: My greatest learning experience was near the end of my college days when someone taught me to read. I'm talking about the kind of reading where you get into intimate touch with the author. The key question I learned to ask myself when I read was, "What is the author trying to say?" I'm embarrassed that I often brought biases to my reading and study. I formed opinions about the reading before I was even sure I'd discerned the author's intention. Then I had an instructor who was merciless with me until I learned to read a page with an open, hungry mind. Only when I could tell this teacher *what* the author said, would he let me tell him what *I thought about* what the author had said.

Leaders need to know how to read and read analytically. A lot of Christians don't know how to do that. You'd give your protégés a great gift if you can do that.

BRENT STERNS: I've been a surgeon for thirty years now. My greatest learning experience came at the hands of the man who headed my first surgical team. He said to me the first day, "I want you to watch everything I do. Everything . . . I . . . do. And when you think you're ready to do any of these procedures the way you've seen me do them, tell me, and I'll give you a shot at doing it. But I'll be watching to be sure you do it exactly as you saw me do it." And that's how I got started. One day I told him I was ready to do a simple procedure, and he let me do it.

VINCE KELLOGG: Carl, if I could add to something you said—I think you touched on something really big. The reading is even better if two other things happen. First, learn to read in a group. Let each person in a group read two or three paragraphs, and then let the next person read. Every once in a while someone will say that they'd rather not read out loud, and that's okay. Just tell them to say, "Pass," and then go on to the next person.

When the written text is read out loud, it comes alive. It's never wasted time to read like that. And the second thing is teach them to dialogue with each other about what the author has said. Carl's right about zeroing in on what the author has said. And that's best found out in a group dialogue. You will be astonished what a group can wring out of a reading when they're encouraged to do it.

CONNIE PETERSON: I want to throw in my two cents as the oldest person in the room. I'm a New Englander from the start. And we're not supposed to be people who show much of our hearts. But I've come to know better.

One of the most important things we did in the Discovery Group that Pastor Mac and Gail started several years ago was to learn each other's story. We came to know about each other's lives, and it made all the difference. We came together for a number of weeks, and each of us in turn took an hour and read our stories to the group. Oh my . . . the conversations that happened because of that. And then—Hana, you'll like this—we all gathered around the storyteller, laid our hands on them, and prayed. Sometimes we were at prayer for thirty minutes or so.

Connie is a New Englander: every inch of her. I've never seen her cry. But she began to fight back tears as she described her memories of the Discovery Group and their intimacy in praying for each other. Every one of our guests was riveted on what she said. And some of them were on the edge of tears as they watched her show emotion.

I glanced over at Hank and Cynthia Soriano to see how they were responding, and the look on their faces suggested that they'd never seen anything like this moment before. They seemed transfixed by what Connie was saying and how she was saying it.

"They say that old women my age don't change much," Connie went on. "But I changed . . . a whole lot, and I'd make these people you want to train write their stories and read them to the group. Some of them will fight it . . . I did. But it's one of the best things they'll ever do. And then when they hear themselves being prayed for . . . well, it doesn't get any better than that."

Tyler Ford talked about the man who had mentored him when he was in InterVarsity Christian Fellowship (a parachurch ministry) at college. He told several stories about the man's imprint upon his spiritual journey. And then he said, "I think you should consider making it mandatory for every person you train to have a mentor or mentoring couple that they can go to and reflect on what they're learning. That way they learn from you guys, and then they get a second perspective from their mentor."

Tyler's comment drew a positive response from the group. Someone said, "Why not recruit at least two older Christians to be permanent mentors for every person in the program? You'll probably have to train them too. But it's worth it. Now you double the program's impact."

Ginny Kellogg suggested that we find a way to let each person "shadow" one of us for a day. "Let them follow one of the two of you around, listen in on conversations, see the kinds of pressures that come with leadership. Let them observe you doing your private devotions, even."

That brought a reaction from several people who couldn't imagine the idea.

"I'm not fooling," Ginny said. "Didn't Jesus let the disciples see him pray? I think it would be quite a learning experience for someone to observe an older Christian do private devotions."

Cary Klaussen is much the same kind of reader that her husband Carl is, and she wanted to talk about reading biography. "I'd say that every third or fourth book I read is a biography. I've learned an incredible amount from reading the lives of great people down through history. And I can't imagine training people to be leaders if they do not have an interest in great men and women from the past."

Cary suggested that every person in a training group be assigned a notable leader from the past and become responsible to make a report on what they'd learned about that person's character and way of leading.

After Cary finished, it was Gail's turn.

GAIL: One night, when our daughter was five or six years old, I was brushing her long, blonde hair. She loved for me to do this. Suddenly she said, "You know, sin is like the snarls in my hair." My ears perked up. I wondered what was coming next. She went on to say, "If you don't get the snarls out as quickly as possible, they get worse and worse and then, maybe, you'll never get them out."

"It was a special insight coming from a child," Gail said. "And I thought, what if I'd not been there that evening to hear what she said? And it made me realize the importance of being as present as possible to those you're teaching. You want to be sure you're in a position to hear everything. In our busyness I fear that we miss too much. There were always people present to hear my comments and questions. Now I want to be present to hear the same from others."

NINETY MINUTES AFTER WE'D BEGUN, I REALIZED THAT everyone had spoken except Wilford Jean-Baptiste. I've learned that Wilford, who is from Haiti, is rather quiet when he's in a large group of people. But get him one-on-one, and he's as warm and expressive as any man can be. He just drips with a genuine joy. He and his wife, Martine, are easy to love.

Even though we knew that Martine was to leave (that very same day, actually) to go to Haiti to visit family, we insisted that Wilford join us. He accepted our invitation. But it was clear from the moment of his arrival that he was preoccupied with Martine's traveling. He knew that he'd not get a call from her saying she'd arrived safely at her parents' home until very late in the evening. Now the time for that call was drawing near.

"Wilford, you've been too quiet all evening," I said. "We know your mind is on Martine, and when we say a good-night prayer, we'll remember her. But I'm wondering if there's anything you have to say after listening to everyone speak tonight. What's your greatest learning experience?"

"Ah, Pastor Mac," Wilford said, "I am so *happy* to be here in your home with *you* and Miss Gail. And I have enjoyed *so much*"—Wilford liked to emphasize certain words—"what everybody say this night. It be very hard for me to say *anything better* than what everyone say."

150

Wilford paused. For a moment he covered his face with his hands as if he needed to withdraw from us and think. Then he opened his hands, as if they were doors, and said quietly, "My most important *teacher* was Mr. Experience. No people train me. There were no older *Christians* where I came from. And my father . . . he was *tough, tough* man. He never talk about himself; he never teach me. He just tell *me* what to do, and I must *figure it out* for myself.

"So I learn from Mr. Experience . . . I must figure it out for *myself* . . . and that not really all *bad*. Young people today get too much too easy. There are things that you learn *best* the hard way. You fail. And you fail again. And then, three, four, six failure times later, you figure out how to do something. And you *never* forget it.

"So, I think that you *must*—how do you say it in America?— sometimes *push* people into water and make them learn to swim. In your teaching of leaders, give them some jobs to do, big jobs, maybe, where they might fail the first time. Let them learn from *Mr. Experience*. That's what Jesus did with the disciples. He *introduce* them to Mr. Experience. And they learn very quickly. They learn to be people of the *heart* . . . and people who know what to do."

Mr. Experience! What a way to end this meeting, I thought. Our Haitian friend had capped off the evening with a remarkable story.

Gail said, "Wilford, thanks so much for that. You have ended our evening well." Then, looking about the room, she said, "You have more than confirmed our brainstorm to invite you tonight. Gordon and I have been taking notes furiously, and there are lots of things that have been said that Gordon and I might never have thought of ourselves. So if you hear someday that we're doing some of the things you've suggested, please know that we know that it came from you. Gordon mentioned prayer before. Honey, are you going to pray for all of us?"

"I think I could come up with a prayer," I answered.

Everyone lowered their heads.

"Our Lord and our God, Gail and I want to thank you for these special friends. Some are part of our church; others are our neighbors. We value every one of them. And it's been special to hear them reminisce tonight about times when they learned and grew and became the kind of people they are today.

"We pray for Wilford's wife, Martine, and ask that these last miles of travel to her family's home in Haiti will go well for her. And we ask that Wilford will have calmness of heart, the assurance that his dear wife is under your protection.

"I ask that you will give Gail and me the wisdom to know how to implement what we have heard tonight. It's all been very valuable. Amen."

Soon the group dissolved into several different conversations. The first people to approach me were Hank and Cynthia Soriano. They wanted me to know how much they'd enjoyed the evening and how impressed they were with the people who went to our church.

"We've got to come over to that church of yours someday . . . It's been a long time since we've been a part of a conversation like tonight. And I want to tell you, I'm going to be real interested in how this group thing turns out. Will you keep me in the loop?"

I promised Hank I would.

Then, just as he and Cynthia headed for upstairs, Wilford Jean-Baptiste's cell phone rang, and the room became silent. Wilford answered, heard his wife's voice, and broke out in a huge smile.

"Hallelujah, hallelujah!" he shouted. "She has arrived," he said to all of us. The last thing we heard as he rushed upstairs where he could talk with her more privately was, "I love you, I love you, I love you."

Hank turned to me and said, "Wow. That guy really loves his wife. Everybody in your store like him?"

Thirty minutes later, everyone was gone and our home was quiet. Some had stayed long enough to help us clean up and load the dishwasher. And when they left, Gail and I sat and talked about what had happened tonight. We were filled with excitement. We not only had a slew of ideas to think about, but we were almost disbelieving that Hank and Cynthia Soriano had responded to the spirit of the evening and actually told us that they'd like to visit our church sometime.

I told Gail that what Hank had experienced that evening was probably the best elevator story I could have ever told him. And it came not in words but in people.

NOVEMBER 5–18

The First Fall

Dear Pastor Mac and Gail,

    It mean so much to me to be asked to your home.
Thank you. I pray for you every day and this great idea.

                             Hana Tchung

Gordon and Gail,

    We met some wonderful people at your home. Thank you
for including us. If you do something like this again, we'd
love to be re-invited.

                    Ginny and Vince Kellogg

To: GMAC, Gail MacDonald
From: Connie Peterson
Subject: Thank you

Thanks for inviting me last night. Next time, please warn
me about how good a time we're going to have at your house
so I can prepare myself better not to cry.

GEOFF HANDLEY AND RICH FISHER SCHEDULED ANOTHER
combined elders/church council leadership meeting for Thursday,
November 18. In the days before that evening, Gail and I spent

154

some hours exploring what other churches and pastors might be doing to—using our words—cultivate deep people.

Gail studied the websites of at least twenty North American churches to see if there was any reference to growing leaders.

I took to the phone, calling pastors of churches our size whom I'd met in various leadership conferences in the past few years. Here and there we picked up useful insights (many on how not to do things), but I can't honestly say that we were overwhelmed by what we learned. I found myself wanting to say to more than a few people, "You need to have a talk with Mercedes Perez and Rabbi Cohen."

Some pastors admitted to little effort because their schedules were already clogged with other institutional responsibilities. Others claimed they had good intentions, but there were no materials or curriculum that might help get them started. Where there was an effort to cultivate deep people, it seemed as if it mostly amounted to reading a book or two and getting together periodically to discuss what had been read.

I wrote in my journal one morning:

> It's clear to me that most pastors (including myself in the past) remain convinced that they can preach their church into the future. They pay lip service to the importance of training a younger generation but end up complaining that there are too many other things to do.
>
> A church without a commitment to train future generations of deep people may be like a professional baseball club without a minor-league team where young players are being groomed for the majors.

MERCEDES PEREZ CALLED ME ONE MORNING TO ASK HOW the great idea was progressing.

"The great idea is now being called CDP," I told her. "The letters stand for Cultivating Deep People. The name came from one of our oldest church members, George Huntoon, whom you've probably never met but who, at one time, made a great impact upon this church."

"Cultivating Deep People . . . the name is a good one," Mercedes said. "It speaks of a sound and achievable promise."

I told you. Mercedes is a wise woman.

A FEW DAYS BEFORE THE LEADERSHIP MEETING, GAIL AND I had dinner at Rich and Carly Fisher's home to review what we were learning. They listened and asked what seemed like a thousand questions. When Gail and I left them at the end of the evening, I carried away two distinct impressions: how much they believed in the CDP initiative and how much they wanted to be a part of it.

THE DAY BEFORE THE LEADERSHIP MEETING, THE PASTORAL staff and I spent the day at a retreat center in the White Mountains. I suggested that we spend the morning in a Scripture-based conversation on cultivating deep people.

Bruce Bartlett agreed and proposed that we read through Paul's letter to the Colossians. "I think," he said, "that Colossians is the charter letter on discipleship."

"Reason?" I asked.

"Simple," Bruce said. "Paul was writing to a group of new Christ-followers whom he'd never met. He wanted to see them maintain the momentum of their conversion. We could profit from reminding ourselves of what he said to them."

Early on the morning of the off-site, I spent some of my devotional time rereading Colossians, and I saw exactly what Bruce was saying. When I came to Colossians 2:6–7, I thought, *This is exactly what we need as a theme verse for CDP.* The process we called *cultivation* was right there. "Just as you received Christ, continue to live in him, rooted and built up in him, strengthened in the faith as you were taught, and overflowing with thankfulness."

It was a simple but significant description of deepening people: *rooted, built up, strengthened, overflowing with thankfulness.* That described exactly what we said we wanted to see in the lives of "growable" people.

When the staff got together, we read Colossians aloud from beginning to end. Each of us commented on what we thought we were hearing Paul say, and I sensed a fresh growth in our excitement. The Scripture spoke out to us, and it seemed to be saying, *Cultivate deep people in every possible way.*

Paul began the letter by noting the quality of the Colossian community: "We have heard of your faith in Christ and of the love you have for all God's people—the faith and love that spring from the hope stored up for you in heaven."

"What a wonderful reputation for a gathering of Christ-followers to have," said Bruce. "Almost sounds like an elevator story."

Then we became fixed on the content of Paul's prayer for the people in the first chapter: "We have not stopped praying for you."

The prayer offered insight into Paul's dreams for the development and spiritual maturity of the Colossian people: a knowledge of God's will, filled with wisdom, bearing fruit in every good work, growing in endurance and patience, giving thanks, living like redeemed people.

Jason wanted to linger on these terms. "Let's tell it like it is. Are we seeing many people becoming like this?" he asked. "I can tell you that my friends are looking for Christians who fit this description, and if they don't find some of them soon, they'll be pretty discouraged."

Next, we considered this statement: "In everything [Christ] might have the supremacy."

"What a high view Paul had of Jesus," Claire said. "You know, if you take your eye off Jesus, everything falls apart. This is such a remarkable declaration. Paul's saying to the Colossians that Jesus was Lord . . . that Jesus is Lord . . . and that Jesus will always be Lord of everything."

This led us to conversation about how to make sure Jesus was central to every aspect of the CDP initiative. "We're not out just to cultivate nice, attentive people," I said. "We want Jesus to inform every aspect of their lives."

A little later we came to Paul's statement about his purpose being to present everyone perfect in Christ: "He is the one we proclaim, admonishing and teaching everyone with all wisdom, so that we may present everyone fully mature in Christ."

"Well, there you go," Bruce said. "Here's Paul saying that his business is more about cultivating depth or maturity . . . in Christ than anything else. And that's really supposed to be the business of the entire church. And it's obviously the business of this CDP venture. Perhaps we need to see the CDP idea as something that will ultimately pervade every level of life in the church."

Then we got to my favorite lines: "So then, just as you received Christ Jesus as Lord, continue to live your lives in him, rooted and built up in him, strengthened in the faith as you were taught, and overflowing with thankfulness."

I shared with the group my experience with those words earlier in the morning: *rooted, built up, strengthened,* and *overflowing with thankfulness.* I told them that if and when CDP actually launched, I wanted these words to be the theme verse of the entire venture. "Paul's thinking strength and durability for the Colossians," I said. "He's passionate about them becoming deep people."

We slogged through the passages about heretical teaching and then got to the two contrasting paragraphs that described what the Colossians once were like (violent, immoral, slanderous, liars) and then what Paul wanted them to be like: "Clothe yourselves with compassion, kindness, humility, gentleness and patience . . . forgive one another. . . . teach and admonish one another . . . do it all in the name of the Lord Jesus."

"It's an incredible menu of qualities for building strong community," Bruce commented. "And it's in great contrast to what you see in large parts of the world. If we could cultivate this kind of character in people . . . I'm just excited all over again about the possibilities."

At the end of our time in the Scriptures, the staff prayed earnestly for Gail and me. They asked God to give us the ability to put the whole CDP package together in a way that the elders would support it 100 percent. As I listened to their prayers, I kept thinking to myself, *A few months ago you wondered what the future would look like. And now a whole new opportunity sits waiting out there. This is the perfect effort for an old guy like you. This is your new call.*

NOVEMBER 18

Early Evening, the First Fall

From my journal

> *The staff off-site was a ten out of ten. We had a*
> *great time in the Scripture and agreed on a biblical*
> *foundation for the CDP effort. The men and women I*
> *work with, they are such a cheer to my soul. Now on*
> *to the elders' meeting. A decisive moment.*

ALMOST SIX WEEKS AFTER THE ELDERS AND CHURCH COUN-
cil had gathered for the first time to discuss the great idea, they
met again. This time the expectation was that Gail and I would
offer a more succinct picture of what the cultivation of deepened
people might look like.

Gail and I had spent the previous day preparing. Rich Fisher
and the pastoral staff had provided feedback to us as we finalized
our presentation. Finally, we were ready to go.

Our concern was to offer a vision of the CDP initiative that
would be clear and compelling. We would not be successful, we
told ourselves, if, at the end of the evening, the leadership saw
CDP as just one more program. We wanted them to visualize the
beginning of a process that would eventually lead to the reinven-
tion of how we did church. And we wanted them to own that

process. They had to feel that God was moving us all, not just Gail and me, in a new direction.

When we finished our preparation work, we felt confident that we could justify the allocation of energies and effort to the CDP initiative. We thought the opening statement of the evening might be: *Let's begin by dreaming of the possibility that in five years, our church could be populated by two hundred deep and deepening people, some involved in the ministries of our church and others involved in various initiatives in the world beyond. How can we all make that happen?*

When Geoff Handley called the meeting to order, every elder and church council member was there. Among the invited guests were the pastoral staff and Gail.

Geoff handled the Bible reading himself, reading from 2 Timothy 3: "You, however, know all about my teaching, my way of life, my purpose, faith, patience, love, endurance, persecutions, sufferings . . ." Finishing the paragraph, he simply said, "We're here tonight to consider how that kind of leadership cultivation might happen more effectively in our church. Let's pray that, when we leave here, we will all feel that we have participated in doing something very special, even historic, for our church."

With that, Geoff prayed and asked God to weld us together as church leaders as we contemplated the new generations of men and women who would follow in our steps. When he finished, he turned the meeting over to me.

"Good evening, everyone," I said. "Gail and I have anticipated this moment for some days now. You all know the subject that has been known to many of us as *the great idea*. Now in more recent days, we've given it a more specific name, which I'll tell you about in just a minute.

"Many of you are familiar with the name John Stott. A lot of people would say that he was among the greatest theologians and preachers of the twentieth century. And a lot of people would say that he was the finest Christian they ever met. I would be among them. Dr. Stott was asked one day how he felt about the stupendous growth of the Christian movement in the world. His answer was a qualified one. He was clearly delighted in growth, he said. And then he added, 'None of us wants to dispute the extraordinary growth of the church. But it has been largely numerical and statistical growth. *And there has not been sufficient growth in discipleship that is comparable to the growth in numbers.*' Could I ask you to keep that comment in mind as we talk together this evening?"

Using PowerPoint, I took my best shot at describing to the elders what we thought the CDP initiative might look like. My presentation took about twenty-five minutes.

I started by reminding everyone of the biblical tradition where the older, more experienced person prepared the young for future responsibilities in leadership. From there I talked about my concern that we could no longer assume that spiritual leaders would simply "show up" when they were needed. We would have to develop them.

It was then that I reintroduced the term *Cultivating Deep People*, and I added this tagline: "to identify and prepare people whom God has called and gifted with the potential of extraordinary influence."

From there I traced the latest iteration of our four objectives:

- Identifying growable people
- Folding them into learning communities
  focused on spiritual maturity
- Helping each person discover his or
  her giftedness and calling
- Pointing them toward leadership opportunities
  in the church or in the larger world

"Until recently we've called this initiative *the great idea*," I said. "Last month I visited George Huntoon in the hospital and shared with him what we were dreaming about. When he asked me what we were calling it, I told him that we didn't have a name.

"He simply said, 'Call it CDP . . . Cultivating Deep People.'"

I flashed the words on the screen. "Now, George was quick to admit that CDP didn't sound very classy and that it had just popped into his head as I had described my version of the great idea. But I liked it immediately. And I felt relieved that, if we went with George's name, we wouldn't have to waste time figuring out the perfect name that pleased everybody.

"As I weighed George's proposal, I realized that we're not marketing the great idea and trying to sell it to the crowds. We don't need a beautiful box or a snazzy logo. We're really proposing an almost-stealthy thing here, an initiative that will most likely fly below the radar and only become known when (and if) it produces its first deep people.

"So ever since my visit with George, I've been using the term *CDP*. So have Gail and the staff, and so have some of you. And we're getting used to the sound of it."

Gail joined me in describing how we thought CDP might work over a year's time. We didn't go into detail, but we offered a broad outline of activities that might mark a CDP year: reading, temperament studies, examining the marks of Christian character, identifying spiritual gifts, teaching leadership skills. We emphasized the group-centeredness of everything, the importance of prayer, storytelling, reading and dialogue, shadowing leaders, and linking up with mentoring couples in the congregation.

"Most of you will remember my comment about a teaching hospital sometime back," I said. "It's a place where young would-be doctors come to train under the eye of veteran physicians and surgeons. They get pushed hard, constantly evaluated, given the opportunity to grow. What Gail and I are talking about is a teaching church."

I closed my presentation with a reference back to the words Geoff Handley read at the beginning of the evening: "'You, however, know all about my teaching, my way of life, my purpose, faith, patience, love, endurance, persecutions, sufferings . . .'

"That's what we'd like to make happen in CDP. But we need to see one more thing. Here's Paul in another part of that same letter: 'The things which you have heard me say in the presence of many witnesses [the congregation] entrust to reliable people who will also be qualified to teach others.'

"What he's saying is explosive. It's a ministry strategy that must be a top priority in our church. I want you to dream with me about creating a culture of leadership, a growing number of deepening people. If you'll mandate me to do this, I'll take my best shot, and Gail will be with me—as will the staff—and, with the Holy Spirit's power and guidance, we'll give you a bunch of new leaders in the next few years.

"We'll start first with the CDP initiative. And then we'll begin working on a similar experience for present leaders. And who knows where we might be able to go from there when we have a cadre of people who can do this with or without Gail and me?"

With that I turned the meeting's leadership back to Geoff, who called a fifteen-minute recess and promised a time for questions and discussion.

NOVEMBER 19

Late Evening, the First Fall

From my journal

> *Incredible, absolutely incredible meeting last night with elders, council, and staff. We presented the CDP concept in its present form. Good questions, great support. Handley at his best. Gail sparkled. I felt more excited about what I was presenting than ever. Now we've thrown out the promises. It's time to start delivering.*

GEOFF HANDLEY, MONICA O'DONNELL, AND RICH FISHER got to me as soon as people left their seats to find coffee and visit lavatories. They were delighted with how the presentation had gone. But they reminded me that this was a New England church and that there would be questions if for no other reason than meetings could not end without questions. Of course, I knew that.

Gail was also pleased, but she warned that there was likely to be a few who would test our enthusiasm for the CDP concept.

When Geoff called the meeting back into session, everyone returned to their seats quickly.

"Pastor Mac and Gail have done a great job of summing up for you what is meant when a church decides to move leadership development up the priority list. Our job now is to make sure we understand what's been said but also to remember that neither they nor any of the others who have worked on this have all the answers. At this point they need a sense of direction from us, a gesture that we're behind them and that we'll support them as they take this to the next level. So what questions do you have for them?"

Melba Washington, an elder, was the first to raise her hand.

"Okay, Melba, you're first," Geoff Handley said.

"Pastor, you and Gail did a great job. Thank you. What I want to know is this. You make it sound like if we don't do this, the church will collapse in the next several years. Do you really believe that?"

"Melba, forgive my enthusiasm in an attempt to make a point. But I was trying to get everyone's attention. Nevertheless, the truth is that we have to contemplate a future scenario in which a lot of churches are going to run out of gas . . . or run out of leaders, as the case may be. A great number of the men and women in this room are over fifty—except for you, Melba."

Melba broke out into laughter when I said this, because she was in her sixties.

I went on. "We've done a pretty good job as a church moving into the future. No one can say that we've still got our heads in the twentieth-century clouds. But we have this new generation coming up the pipe. And frankly, they think differently than you and I do.

"Some sociologists call them *emerging adults*. And Melba, these are wonderful younger people, but they have a whole different take on church and faith. They resist highly structured organizations. They say they follow Jesus, but they don't like to subscribe to doctrinal statements. They love community, but they dislike authority. They say they believe in the importance of personal salvation, but sometimes they're not sure how salvation happens.

"We have to think in two ways about these people. First, what are they offering us with their new way of Christian thinking? What can we learn from them? And second, what do they have to learn from us? We are going to have to bring these young adults together with us. And I think CDP is the place to start that generational merger. I can only tell you that if we don't, then you and I better hold on because we're going to be responsible for leading this church until we're ninety-five. Only then can we retire to Florida."

"You're never going to get me to go for Florida, Pastor," Melba said, feigning a sense of repugnance. "I'll die right here in New Hampshire as soon as the frost is out of the ground." Now everyone laughed.

Geoff Handley nodded toward Scott Simmons, a member of the church council.

Scott said, "Pastor, you know that before Dede and I came here, I spent twenty years in the US Army. We had a term we used when we talked battle strategy: *force multiplier*. The term meant taking a soldier or a platoon of soldiers and equipping or training them in such a way that they increased their battle effectiveness four or five times. To put it another way, you have a force multiplier when you don't have to increase the number of troops you have in the field, but by equipping and training them better, you assure that they will accomplish what might have taken a force three times their size to do. That make sense to you?"

"Sure does, Scott. And I think I see where you're going with this," I said.

"Where I'm going is to ask this. Do you see you and Gail giving yourself to this, um . . . CDP . . . as a force multiplier? Is this going to increase *your* effectiveness? And—I suspect I already know your answer—is this going to increase the church's effectiveness to pursue its mission?"

I answered, "Scott, as far as I'm concerned, what you've said nails it. You reallocate some of your time and energy . . . at least I reallocate my time and energy . . . and you invest it in something like CDP, and you upgrade your effectiveness to do ministry many times over. The dream of CDP is all about developing much deeper, more effective leaders who are committed to serving Jesus. We want to get away from just finding people who, we hope, will fill holes in church programs. Think West Point, Scott. Same basic idea."

"Then I'm in," Scott said. "In fact, I'd like to be part of the CDP program."

"Scott, we'll consider you. But don't be disappointed if—"

"Pastor," Geoff Handley interrupted with a grin on his face, "don't go there." Again, more laughter.

Kyle Wood spoke into the laughter. "Geoff . . . Geoff. Have you folks thought about how those people who don't get selected for this program are going to feel? Won't there be some who feel rejected? I mean, there are a whole lot of us who might feel that we'd like to spend a lot of time with Pastor and Gail for a year."

I gestured to Geoff that I would like to respond. "Kyle, you've raised a point that every person who has considered CDP has raised. Truth is, we are not absolutely sure of the answer. All we know—and the parallel may not be totally helpful—is that Jesus picked twelve out of . . . how many? There must have been several hundred or more who were loyalists of some kind.

"But out of those hundreds, only twelve got the nod to get in close to the Master . . . and one of them turned out to be a real disaster.

"CDP, as we've conceived it, begins with *selecting* growable people, not advertising for volunteers. This means a very careful, prayerful, wisdom-centered process of vetting those whom we believe the Holy Spirit has targeted for that moment. If we turn out to be wrong, we'll just have to bite the bullet. But here's where we may have to risk offending someone. And I'm prepared to take that chance."

Adelle Waters, who was sitting next to Gail, turned to her and asked, "Well, if Scott Simmons isn't going to be invited to be a part of CDP"—there was huge laughter—"who is going to be invited to be a part of these groups? Is it going to be all men, married people, or what?"

"Good question, Adelle," Gail said. "We'd anticipate a balance between the genders. And we want single people as well as married couples. And . . . this may surprise some of you . . . we want at least one older couple or older single people. We think that the younger will learn from the older and the older will be inspired by the younger."

"You two plan on shouldering the whole burden of this, Pastor?" Scott Simmons asked.

"Not really," I said. "We'd like to match every unmarried person and every married couple up with mentors from the congregation. That probably means some of you. We think we can train the mentors and then create a way in which all the CDP people meet with their mentoring couple once a month. The mentoring couple would pledge to pray for their people, encourage feedback about how they're doing, and may even bring further insight into what the group is learning.

"Some of you are incredibly busy now, but you might consider the possibility that God would call you to be a mentor to some younger person and that you might want to slip out of other things in order to do this."

There were more questions like these—every one a good question—that followed. Some I tried to answer; others I passed to Gail, especially those on the criteria we were forming for selection. As the discussion moved along, I felt a rush of adrenaline-like excitement in me. It was there because I was feeling even more enthusiastic about the CDP concept, though I hadn't thought that was possible. I really wanted to do this, and I enjoyed selling the idea to our elders. I loved the feeling that, one by one, they were climbing aboard. By the positive nature of their questions, they were saying that they were willing to try something that had never been tried before.

Ten o'clock came quickly, and the questions dwindled to a few that were more about procedures than anything. Finally Geoff said, "Time to bring this conversation to an end. Gordon, you and Gail have been right up on the edge with us. It's been a learning experience for all of us. Thank you."

Then turning to the elders and council members he said, "Are there any of you who want to sum up your feelings in one or two sentences only?"

Joe Geiger, elder, said, "I've been waiting a long time for someone to come up with a breakthrough idea, and I think this is it."

Judy Taylor, another elder, said, "I'd have given anything to have been part of something like this when I was young."

Gilberto Silva, a new elder, chimed in. "My dear sisters and brothers, in my church in Brazil, our pastor started doing this—how do you call it?—this CDP many years ago. He did it just with men. And he picked me." Gilberto looked around the room, and we could see that a tear was forming in his eye. "He selected me . . . and here I am, an elder in your, our, church."

Turning to Geoff, Gilberto said, "Forgive me, Mr. Handley, I am talking more than two sentences."

"Not to worry, Gilberto," Geoff said. "We love to hear your heart speaking."

"I really do hear God saying that this CDP is the way. This is our doorway to the future. And I am thankful that our pastor and his lovely wife, Gail, have this vision. I will promise to help out in any way I can. I'll be a mentor . . . I'll bring Brazilian food over to your house, Mrs. Mac . . . I'll give money if you need it. I am thinking of who it must have been that gave my pastor in Brazil his CDP idea and what a difference it made in my life."

When Gilberto finished, Geoff immediately took charge, and the manner in which he leaned forward told us that he wanted to bring the meeting to a conclusion. Geoff has a way of letting us know that nothing more needs to be said by the group.

"I'm reading approval throughout the room," Geoff said. "Approval that we should encourage our pastor to move ahead to the next phase of CDP. If any of you has a serious objection to this, please talk with me personally. Pastor, where do we go from here?"

I thought for a moment and then said, "Gail and I, with the help of some of you, will make an effort to refine our objectives and the way we're going to pursue them. And we will begin quite quickly to form a list of people that we think God wants to be part of the first group."

Geoff Handley invited Monica O'Donnell to pray.

"Lord Jesus Christ, you who made the first CDP happen with twelve youngish men, we thank you for this special evening. You have been present in this room tonight. I thank you for my brothers and sisters who take our church so seriously and who long to see deeper Christians, more effective leaders, emerge in the coming years. Please give our pastor, Gail, and others much insight as they continue to think about this CDP concept. Protect them from the evil one. I imagine that our spiritual enemy cannot be pleased with an effort like this. Give us, please, safe journeys to our homes and families. We ask this in Jesus' name, amen."

If anything added to the joy of this evening, it was when— as others were leaving—Bruce Bartlett, Claire Dustin, Jason Caldwell, and Rich Fisher gathered around Gail and me and reaffirmed their excitement and support to help making CDP happen.

NOVEMBER 22

The First Fall

To: Pastor Mac
From: Gary Tremley
Subject: Training Program

Pastor MacDonald,
Adelle Waters told my wife, Kathy, about your new leader-
ship training program. We have been looking for something
like this for a long time. As you know, Kathy and I have
struggled in our marriage ever since our children were born.
We've gone to counseling and attended some marriage semi-
nars. But nothing has helped as much as we hoped it would.
But we think that if we could be a part of your group, we
could both benefit from getting exposed to you and Mrs.
Mac. Would you please put us on the list?
Sincerely,
Gary Tremley

On my voice mail

"Gordon, honey, I don't know where you are, but we need
to talk. I just hung up from talking with Patricia Newland,
who heard about CDP from someone on the board and wants
to be part of it. She talked about how depressed she's been

ever since she and Andy broke their engagement. Says that CDP would be the doorway to a fresh start. I told her that we're not that far down the line yet to talk about selection. The only other thing I said to her was that there were other groups in the church more suited to what she was facing. I don't know how we're going to handle this one, but I don't think Patricia is ready for what we've got in mind at all. I can tell that she's going to be very hurt if we tell her that she's not what we're looking for."

Conversation with Joe Geiger in the parking lot

> **JOE**: Hey, Pastor, got a minute? Know you're busy and all but...
>
> **GMAC**: Quite all right, Joe. Whatcha need?
>
> **JOE**: Well, I heard from one of the council guys about this special group you are forming. And I wanted to mention our son, Patrick, to you. He's just dropped out of college . . . sort of discouraged with the workload . . . well, actually—please don't tell him I told you this—he was asked to drop out for a year because of grades. And he's not talking much about it to Millie and me. Kind of gone into a shell. Millie and I think that if John was asked to be a part of your group, it might give him something to do. I don't want to appear that I'm taking of advantage of the fact that I'm on the elder board, but . . .

"OH, BOY, OH BOY, OH BOY," I SAID, AS GAIL AND I SAT OUT on our sunporch that evening. "They said that this would happen . . . that people would come at us, wanting into CDP. It was easy to say we wouldn't take volunteers when CDP was just a piece of paper. But now that we're coming closer to some real action, it's getting sticky. What am I going to tell these people?"

"Tell them the truth . . . just do it lovingly and compassionately. I've seen you speak truthfully to people in the past in a way that people can hear and accept."

"For some of them it's going to be a severe rejection. They'll not see it in any other way. And what accentuates it is that they'll know that we invited others and passed over them," I said.

"Okay, let's put this on our CDP prayer list and ask God to prepare them. And we'll pray that you'll find the right words. You've got several months before the final decisions are made. Maybe some of them will be on to other things, and you'll never have to say another word."

"I wish you were right, but I'm not that confident."

JANUARY AND FEBRUARY

The First Winter

To: Geoff Handley, Monica O'Donnell, Rich Fisher, Pastoral
From: GMAC
Staff, Gail MacDonald
Subject: Mentors

Would you please give thought to the names of older couples
in our church who might consider being mentors to people
in the future CDP group? Obviously, they should be people
of depth who have a heart for being a spiritual father or
mother to younger people.

IN JANUARY AND FEBRUARY I PREACHED SEVERAL TIMES ON
the theme of Christian character and influence. I started using
key words that were beginning to take their place in the CDP
vocabulary. I talked about the concept of cultivation, growability,
influence (my oft-used substitute word for *leadership*), about being
rooted, built-up, and strengthened Christians.

One Sunday I traced the story of Jesus and his way of shaping
his disciples. I talked about the kind of people he picked and
the reasons he might have picked them. I spoke of things that

were obvious to most people: that the people Jesus selected were usually from small towns and backwater regions, that they were tough, maybe even crude at times. I emphasized things like this because our part of the country does not pride itself on being in the center of the universe.

"We tend to think Boston, New York, and Washington are the places where important people come from," I said. "In New Hampshire we only get noticed every four years during the presidential primary. But just maybe it's a place like New Hampshire where God wants to produce a new generation of saints."

On another Sunday I preached on the paragraph in Luke's gospel (the one that Jason Calder's worship team had studied earlier) where there were three wannabe disciples that Jesus apparently discouraged from following him . . . at least for that moment. "It seems to me," I told the congregation, "that all three were good people, well-intentioned, people that were publicly supportive of Jesus and his mission. But for reasons that Jesus never fully explained, he told them no. You could reason that they simply were not ready, maybe not that teachable, that issues in their personal lives needed more attention."

WHEN THE WORSHIP SERVICES ENDED THAT MORNING, I took my place each time at the main entrance to the sanctuary, where I like to greet as many people as I can as they leave.

Among the first to approach me with an outstretched hand was Joe Geiger. "Pastor Mac, I got your message, loud and clear. Forgive the presumption of a father who may love his son too much. I should have thought twice before I suggested Patrick for this group you'll be forming. You're absolutely right. He belongs with another gathering of people. But someday he'll be ready for what you are planning to do. I hope you'll keep your eye out for him."

I hugged Joe Geiger right there in front of everybody. And I whispered in his ear, "I promise to do that."

I was so happy that Joe had understood the situation. And I immediately began to hope that some of the others who'd volunteered themselves for a future CDP experience would come around to see things similarly.

But Patricia Newland didn't.

When I got home from church, Gail said, "Patricia got me off in a corner after second service today. She was crying . . . said she was afraid you'd leave her out when the CDP group was formed. You won't want to hear what else she said."

"Try me," I said.

"She said the Lord spoke to her in a dream the other night and told her that it was his will that she be part of CDP and that when you and I come to understand this, we'll come to her."

"Ooooooh boy."

ON MONDAY MORNING, WHEN I CHECKED MY BLACKBERRY, I found an e-mail from Gary Tremley. It read:

Pastor MacDonald,

Kathy and I heard your sermon today and knew that you were talking to us. I wish you'd had the courage to tell us to our faces that you didn't want people like us in your group instead of doing it in a sermon. We had hoped that we could learn something under your guidance. But it's obvious that you don't think people like us are good enough for your personal attention. So we're going to look for another church where the pastor isn't such an elitist.

Saying good-bye,
Gary Tremley

MID-FEBRUARY

The First Winter

From my journal

> Got an e-mail from Gary Tremley. He was clearly
> angry and felt that I'd rejected him and Kathy and,
> what's worse, done it from the pulpit. Interesting
> how you can preach to several hundred people and
> there are those who think you've designed the entire
> experience just to talk to them. Gary has neither
> answered my e-mails nor returned my phone calls.
> Adelle Waters isn't a lot of help. I think she's
> embarrassed because she suggested to Gary that he
> get in touch with me. But she did apologize to me.
> Seemed to realize that she was out of bounds when
> she originally spoke to Gary and Kathy about CDP.

EVER SINCE THE LATE-FALL ELDERS' MEETING, WHERE THERE
had been a unanimous expression of encouragement for us to
move ahead on the CDP initiative, Gail and I kept working to
refine the idea.

As the weeks of the new year passed, we became committed
to things like these:

- Each CDP group—one a year—would last for about forty weeks and then come to an end.
- Gail and I would team-lead the first couple of groups until we could train others to take our place.
- We would not compromise on selection and requirements for participation.
- Age, marital status, gender, length of time in the faith were not deal-breakers; but "growability" was.
- Our target date for the first CDP group would be early September; the selection process would begin in the spring; actual invitations to participate would be given in June. Our footprint of the year's activities would be complete by June.
- We would pray for one couple to take in our confidence as soon as possible and share the responsibility of forming, even doing some leading of the first CDP group.
- We would try to train a group of older couples to serve as mentors.

Gail and I kept asking ourselves what we believed were the distinguishing marks of deep people. Our list was in a constant state of editing as we studied the Scriptures, read materials on spiritual leadership, and watched people who we considered to be deep.

At this point our list of descriptors went like this:

Deep people:

- demonstrate a consistent loyalty to Jesus and speak of him as their redeemer and Lord;

- have a hunger to keep on growing in every
  aspect of their lives, regardless of age;
- have a clear sense of how a Christian conducts
  him-/herself in the larger world;
- maintain personal relationships that
  appear to be healthy and life-giving;
- are respected because of their wisdom and integrity;
- are aware of how the Holy Spirit has gifted them
  and possess a sense of personal mission or call;
- love to inspire and lead others toward
  personal Christian growth;
- have firm convictions about faith, yet
  are not rigid, pushy, or judgmental;
- are generous with what they have and always
  seem to know just how to serve others;
- are compassionate, the first ones to spot people
  who need counsel or encouragement;
- are people you love to be with because they love
  life and seem to know the best ways to live it; and
- are influential wherever they go.

I gave this list of attributes to a group of church leaders at a breakfast meeting one morning.

"My gosh!" Ken Squires said. "You've described Jesus. Who could ever be like all of these things?"

"That's worried me too, Ken," I said. "But you have to start out with the highest possible standard and then rejoice in the fact that there's such a thing as grace."

Winn Rilkey, the oldest man on our elder board, said, "Oh my . . . have we let a lot of people down!"

"What do you mean, Winn?" I asked.

"Well, do you think we've been leaders like this? When people look at us, do they see these things? I mean, we've given the congregation programs, buildings, all kinds of campaigns. We're always pushing visions of this and that—good stuff, of course—but have we shown them the qualities that are on this list? I'm not sure, frankly."

Judy Taylor said, "Winn, don't be too hard on yourself, or the rest of us, for that matter. I agree with you: this list is a wake-up call. We should have had something like this a long time ago. On the other hand, there's nothing here that I haven't heard before. But seeing it all on one piece of paper . . . well, it's certainly got my attention."

"Well, let me tell you one more little thing that will push your buttons," I said. Everyone became quiet.

"Gail and I have been showing this list to folks whenever we've had a chance. And we've asked them if they've ever seen people who reflect these qualities. And most of them have said yes, they know people like this. But you know what? When we asked them who they were talking about, it turned out that they were all people like you. Like you, Geoff; you, Judy; Winn . . . even you. They rarely ever mentioned someone like myself, who's a preacher, or someone working for a Christian organization. People may admire the 'pros,' but they learn Christian living from you folks, the ones who aren't paid to be deep."

"You planning to produce some people like these, Gordon?" Winn asked pointing to the paper I'd given them.

I laughed. "You make it sound like we heat people up to the boiling point, pour them into molds, and, poof, we have spiritual superstars. The truth? I honestly don't know if we can do this, Winn," I said. "We're in a world now where there is so much that degrades the soul . . . people so busy . . . people so weighted down with pressure . . ." I paused for a moment, trying to gather my thoughts for a more coherent answer. "I am simply not confident

181

that the church—as we presently do church—can produce a lot of these kinds of people. But my conviction is that we'll see the church slowly change if cultivating deep people one by one becomes our number one priority.

"But I do want to clear one thing up. Each of you fits on this list, as far as I'm concerned, and don't forget it. You may not think you embody all of these, but you all do a lot of them well. And I see it constantly. Jesus is clearly in each of your lives. And I'm grateful. So, Winn"—and I looked him in the eye—"the news isn't all that bad."

Monica O'Donnell grabbed the check when the waitress brought it to the table. "This one's mine," she said. "Geoff's always picking these things up when we eat here."

She handed the waitress her debit card and then turned back to me and pointed to the list of spiritual leadership attributes. "Do whatever it takes to produce a few people like these." With that she smiled, stood up, and mimicked an old tune: "I'm late; I'm late for a very important date."

A final sip of coffee and we were all gone.

FEBRUARY 15

The First Winter

To: GMAC
From: Gail
Don't forget to get home early. We have to be in Boston at
Legal's by 5:30 p.m.

ON A TUESDAY EVENING IN FEBRUARY, GAIL AND I DROVE
to Boston and had dinner at Legal Sea Foods with Darrell and
Sandy Lassiter. Darrell is a Massachusetts pastor; he and I were
in the same seminary graduating class and have shared a lot of
life. Our wives are also very close friends, so the four of us try
to connect for an evening every month: they come our way one
time, and the next time we go theirs. I should add that Darrell
has always struggled in his ministry. His church experiences have
been difficult. Mine have been much easier.

As Darrell and I talked about a trip he and Sandy had just
taken to England, I overheard Gail begin to tell Sandy about how
our CDP endeavor was beginning to take shape. Now and then
I'd pick up one of their words or sentences, and I was able to keep
abreast of both conversations.

Suddenly, I heard the women's voices become more excited.
Darrell and I stopped our conversation and looked at them, wondering what they were saying.

"We've decided to do something crazy," Gail said. "Sandy and I are going to drive up to Maine for an overnight at a B&B in Kennebunkport. And we're going to spend two days coming up with a list of biblical leaders and people in Christian history who provide examples of spiritual leadership. We can use it with the CDP group. And you guys"—she said this rather firmly—"cannot come."

"We can come if we want to," Darrell said.

"But you can't," Sandy responded with an exaggerated smirk. "This is a girl thing."

Ten days later, leaving Darrell and me behind, the two women headed up the Maine coast for their little overnight. Several times during the days before they left, Darrell and I suggested that we go with them. But they were both adamant. I think it was Sandy who said to Gail at one point, "Let's not let the professionals spoil our Bible study."

Such piety. Such stubbornness. Such wisdom.

MARCH 13

The First Winter

To: Bruce Bartlett, Claire Dustin, Jason Calder
From: GMAC
Subject: CDP sermon

The elders want me to preach a specific sermon on the CDP
initiative. They think the church has got to be fully aware of
what we're into. I'd like to do it on the first Sunday in April.
Any problems you can think of?
GMAC

THE SUNDAY MORNING ACTIVITIES AT OUR CHURCH HAD
ended, and Gail and I were in our car headed home for lunch and
our traditional Sunday afternoon nap.

"I had an interesting conversation with Rich and Carly Fisher
between services," Gail said.

"About . . . ?"

"Well, they were curious about how things are going in the
CDP initiative, and I told them where we were at this point."

"They seem happy with what you told them?"

"Well, yeah, they seemed very happy with what I told them.
But what I wanted to say to you was that I watched the two of
them carefully as we talked. My sense was that both of them want

terribly to be part of CDP. You should have seen how they lapped up everything I was saying."

"Well, I know Rich—can't speak for Carly—has been gung ho for this ever since the idea first came on the table. But they're both so busy. I mean . . . he's the head of the council, and Carly's almost indispensible to the pantry project—"

Gail interrupted me. "But think about it this way, Gordon. Maybe God is prompting them to take a new step forward in their own growth and, maybe in the future, they will be at the very core of the CDP effort. Your church leaders can always find another chair of the church council, and Carly's wise enough to have been training her successor in the pantry work all along.

"We've been praying for another couple to bring into the formation of this thing, and maybe we've been overlooking the obvious. We've told ourselves that they're too busy doing other things. But what if they're the ones God has prepared to team up with us?"

Gail went on to suggest that we pray specifically about the Fishers for a couple of weeks and then decide if we should approach them.

"Okay," I said, "but don't be surprised if they tell us no. Remember our deal: anyone coming into CDP has to clear their calendar of all priorities in the church and do nothing but CDP for a year. That's asking a lot of them. And besides, how can Rich take this on with all of his responsibilities at school?"

"So who did you talk to this morning?" Gail asked.

"Well, Geoff and Monica asked to talk with me between services. They said that more and more people are hearing about CDP. They think it's time for me to tell the congregation exactly what we want to do. Even if it's going to be a small effort at the beginning, they think that everyone needs to know where it's headed and why you and I may start doing things differently in the near future."

"What did you tell them?" Gail responded.

"Told them I'd do it. Looks like the first Sunday in April might be the best time."

"Are you ready to commit yourself publicly to this?"

"We're in too deep now."

APRIL 3

Sunday, 9:00 Service, the First Spring

To: GMAC
From: Jason Calder
Subject: Worship

GMAC,
All aspects of worship are covered for next Sunday morning.
The only thing you'll have to do is preach. We are all aware
of the pressure you feel to get this one exactly right. So we
wanted to make sure you had nothing else to distract you
from inspiring the congregation to buy into the great idea.
Jason

At 8:55 a.m. on the first Sunday of April, the screen
in our church sanctuary came alive with a second-by-second run-
up to 9 a.m. This was starting time for our first morning worship
service. Some people think this little digital gimmick is cute. I am
not one of them. But that's okay.

At 8:56:30 (I may not care for the digital thing, but I can't stop
looking) Gail and I took our seats in the front row of the sanctuary. At first I felt quite relaxed since my only responsibility was to
preach when sermon time came, and that was (according to the
service script) thirty-eight minutes and thirty seconds off in the

future. All other aspects of worship—singing, praying, Bible reading, a bit of liturgy, meditative moments—were to be led by other pastoral staff members.

At 08:59:59 a.m. the drummer in the praise band got everyone's attention with a direct hit on her drums, and the congregation—clappers and nonclappers both—stood and were soon singing as they were led by Jason Calder.

There followed a time of worship that began loud and ended soft when Bruce Bartlett asked the people to become silent and reflect on the direction their lives had taken during the past week. Was there anything, he asked, that each of us needed to say to God? These wonderful moments of silence provided an opportunity for each of us to mimic the ancient psalmist when he prayed, "Search me, God, and know my heart . . ."

I confess that I didn't do exactly what Bruce asked. As worship had moved along, I gradually became embroiled in a kind of presermon, mental multitasking that overtakes many preachers. Granted: a part of me was reflecting as Bruce asked us to, but the reflection was more about hoping that God would help me communicate well.

At the same time, another part of me began to struggle with doubt about my sermon's introduction. Should I use it or drop it?

A third part of me was attuned to a crying baby (*screeching* might be a more apt word) in the fourth row, whose mother seemed unaware that the infant needed a form of nourishment that only mothers can provide.

It was during that moment of inner turbulence that Gail pressed a note into my hand. The neatness of the handwriting and the length of the note suggested that it had been written before we'd left home to come to church. In her typically sensitive way, Gail had anticipated my need for a final reminder of God's presence before I began to preach.

Honey, I know how important this morning is to you. This great idea of cultivating deep people in our church has been stewing in our hearts for months. You know that I believe it comes from God. I'm prayerful that you'll speak as his messenger, and that you'll trust him to give you the spiritual authority you need. Remember that the elders and council members are behind you all the way. And don't forget that I am your partner in this venture. Preach with conviction and with the anticipation of God's favor. I love you today. GVM

When I read the note, I immediately regained my focus and sense of calm, and as the congregation sang one more song before the sermon, I put my arm around Gail and pulled her closer as a way of expressing my appreciation. She always seemed to have the perfect word that suited the situation.

When the singing had ended and the musicians had cleared the preaching spot of instruments, amplifiers, and music stands, I stepped to the front and asked the people to pray once more. This is what I prayed.

"Heavenly Father, I thank you for the privilege given to me to be a preacher of the Bible. You know that what I have to say to my friends this morning comes from a vision that has been growing in my heart and the hearts of our leaders. I pray that you will give me the ability to describe it well. Be helpful to me, O Lord, and to all who listen. I ask that my voice be the lesser, yours the greater. Amen."

APRIL 3

Sunday Morning, 9:38:35 a.m., the First Spring

From my sermon preparation notes

> *Objective: Get congregation to think about "tomorrow."*
> *Introduce idea of deep people: Who are they? Where*
> *are they to be found? Why are they important? How*
> *do we cultivate them?*

I STARTED THE SERMON THIS WAY. "SOME MONTHS AGO, Rich Fisher, the chair of our church council, gave me a card with these words from the Christian writer Richard Foster: 'The desperate need today is not for a greater number of intelligent people, or gifted people, but . . . for *deep people.*'

"*Deep people!* Many of you have heard me refer to deep people lately. Now you know where I got it from. What impresses me about Foster's statement is that he thinks that the influence of deep people is greater than that of merely gifted or intelligent people. Whoa! Those of us—three or four of us, anyway—who thought we might be gifted or intelligent have just taken a hit.

"Now, I don't think that Richard Foster is degrading intelligence or giftedness at all. Rather, I suspect that he's thinking

191

spiritual priorities. What he may be saying is that intelligence and giftedness alone are not enough to keep an organization or a church going. If any group of Christians wishes to be a pleasure to God, there must be some deep people at the center who know how to hear God speak and how to draw upon his power to do the work Jesus has called us to do.

"Paul was thinking about deep people when he called for Christ-followers in the Colossian church to be rooted, built up, and strengthened. He also called for people who overflowed with gratitude, presumably with praise to God. But let's get past words of definition for a moment and ask what deep people might look like.

"Here are a few ideas. Deep people are loyal to Jesus . . . They're always growing in all aspects of their lives . . . They build strong relationships . . . Others respect them. Additionally, they have a strong sense of purpose . . . They motivate others to move toward Jesus . . . They know what they believe . . . They're generous in the way they give and serve . . . You and I head in their direction when we need encouragement and wisdom . . . And they always seem to be full of joy.

"Now, before I get away from this effort at sketching deep people, please let me offer one more attribute that is very important to me.

"Deep people are influential. Wherever they show up, human beings, institutions, and churches are inspired, renewed, even changed. Think for a moment about a gathering of people—our church, for example—if there were no deep people.

"One day I began to scan through the Bible to see if there was a time when deep people were a scarce commodity. Here's a little line I found in 1 Samuel, chapter 3. 'In those days the word of the LORD was rare; there were not many visions.' Translation: the deep people were missing. Result? No one was hearing a word from God. In another places the biblical writer says of that time, 'Everyone did as he saw fit.'

"What was it like in this period of Israel's history when there were no deep people? *Confusing* and *chaotic* seem apt words to describe things. It was every person for him- or herself. Danger within, and danger without.

"The Irish poet William Butler Yeats visualized these kinds of times when he wrote:

> *Things fall apart; the centre cannot hold;*
> *Mere anarchy is loosed upon the world . . .*
> *The best lack all conviction, while the worst*
> *Are full of passionate intensity.*

"The other day I found myself in a traffic jam at Main and Pleasant Streets. Nothing was moving. Horns were blowing; anxiety was palpable. Then I spotted the problem. The traffic lights weren't working.

"So what was needed? The solution was for someone to get out there and direct traffic. But no one was willing to do this. Everyone, including me, preferred to just sit there and toot car horns. Incidentally, I—being the gentle pastor that I try to be—never blew my horn once. It was all those other guys making the noise." (Congregation: laughter, some hooting.)

"As I sat in my car, I thought to myself that, without deep people, this mess is a picture of what our church could be like in five or ten years. Without them we could be headed toward one big spiritual traffic jam." (Congregation: a faint murmur suggesting agreement.)

"The truth is, men and women, that we've got some challenging days ahead of us in our church. Our congregation is going to need an increasing number of the deepening people Richard

Foster mentions. Without them how are we going to discern what God wants us to do? Without them where do we get our inspiration for growing to be more like Jesus?

"As I have thought about this more and more, I've come to this conclusion. The deep people we will need in the coming years will not just walk through the front door. They will need to be discovered, trained, and challenged into deepening.

"In past years, we've built buildings, hired staff pastors, and launched new programs in the church and beyond it. But discovering and developing deep people may be our church's next great challenge. Over the past months I've been calling it our church's next great idea.

"Now, this great idea—finding and training deep people—is not far from what an ancient Egyptian pharaoh was trying to say when he heard a young Hebrew, Joseph, map out a strategic plan for the country to survive a period of economic downturn. At the top of Joseph's list of action items was the selection of a special kind of person to see the nation through this difficult time.

"Pharaoh, agreeing with Joseph, said, 'Can we find one in whom is the spirit of God?' Pharaoh had smelled out the essence of the great idea. To put my words in his mouth, he is saying, 'Where can we find a deep person . . . someone who understands how to guide our nation through a challenging time?'

"Pharaoh's definition of *deep* and our definition of *deep* might be slightly different. But the man understood the underlying principle. In his world there was a need for someone who was wise, integral, powerful. Not just talented or intelligent. For him, that was someone in whom was the spirit (small *s*) of God. For us, deep people are those in whom is the Holy Spirit (capital *S*) of God.

"I look at all the changes going on in the world today—some good; many not so good—and I know that they are going to impact *every* organization in society, including churches like ours.

Everything we do as a church will soon have to face redesign. We will have to ask ourselves: *Are we still doing what God wants a church to be doing? Are we doing it in the right way? Are we realizing the kinds of results that God desires from us?*

"And how does such a process begin? Well, let me rephrase Pharaoh's question: 'Can *we* find some deep people in whom is the Spirit (capital *S*) of God?' Because when we find them, they will influence what we become and do.

"Let me underscore what I said a few minutes ago. Deep people are not going to magically appear at our front door. We're going to have to cultivate them. And how will we do it? Now, there's a question that's been nagging me for some while.

"Gail and I are moving into the last quarter of our lives. We often think about what the call of God is for men and women who have reached our age. And we've come to this conclusion. God asks us—and many of you—to invest yourselves in cultivating tomorrow's deep people.

"I started this sermon with a quote from Richard Foster about deep people. I'm going to end it with another quote, this one from an Englishman, now with the Lord, Martin Thornton. He said: 'A walloping great congregation is fine and fun, but what most [churches] really need is a couple of saints. The tragedy is that they may well be there in embryo, waiting to be discovered, waiting for sound training, waiting to be emancipated from the cult of the mediocre.'

"So what Foster calls 'deep people,' Thornton calls 'saints.' Even though the word choices are different, the thoughts are identical. Deep people, saints, are 'in embryo' (Thornton's words); they wait to be discovered; they need training; they must be released to God's purposes within this church and beyond it.

"It's clear that Jesus understood this. If you revisit his life while he was here on earth, you'll see that the discovery and training of deep people was his premier passion. Who would ever have labeled those fishermen he invited to follow him as gifted or intelligent? Certainly not me. But Jesus was apparently looking for something more important. He was seeking the potential for depth. And you know what? Once that depth was realized, those men suddenly began to grow and show themselves to be quite intelligent and gifted. *But the depth came first.*

"Here in our church we want to do something similar, and we've given this new venture a name: CDP, Cultivating Deep People. We intend for it to start out very, very small. Most of you will not see any evidence of it at first. But I believe that one day you will see it growing. And when we do, we will all thank God for the deepening people it is producing.

"So then, this is our great new idea: locate and cultivate potentially deep people who will help us walk into tomorrow with faith and great anticipation."

When the sermon ended, the congregation did something it has rarely ever done for a sermon. They applauded.

APRIL 5

The First Spring

From my journal

> *We are into the selection process. Selection, we
> believe, is everything. Make uniformed, un-prayed-about
> decisions, and you pay a severe price later on. And as we
> select the first CDP group, we've got to make sure that
> we have one or two people who might be candidates to
> lead their own CDP group in another year. Gail's totally
> convinced that the Fishers are the ideal choice.*

THE CONVERSATION GAIL AND I HAD ABOUT RICH AND
Carly Fisher was only the first of many others on the same subject: the selection of people for the first CDP group.

Gail (on the phone with GMAC): "I bumped into Sara Stevens
at the car wash a little while ago. She told me about a book she's into,
and I was really impressed with how insightful she was about what
she was reading. I started asking her questions about her spiritual
journey, and it was pretty clear that she's doing a lot of thinking. I'd
like to put her on our CDP list to watch and pray about."

"Sounds good to me," I said.

A few days later I said to Gail, "I ran into Morgan and Larry
Sanger at the mall today."

"And?"

"Well, the first thing I couldn't help but notice is how much they enjoy being together. It shows on their faces when they talk to each other. Too many couples lose a lot of that kind of energy after they've been married for five years."

"You think we've lost our energy?" Gail asked. "And think very carefully about your answer."

"Babe, if we get more energy going in this marriage of ours, I'm going to have a heart attack," I protested.

It was the right answer, and the conversation about the Sangers went on.

"So what else impressed you?" Gail asked.

"Well, when I talked with them, I was impressed with how they responded. They asked great questions. They listened well. I got the feeling that they're a couple with the capability to do something significant with their lives . . . they told me, by the way, that they're going to take a week of vacation time and do a Habitat for Humanity building project. That's pretty impressive for a couple hardly out of their twenties."

"Do you think that we should consider—?"

"That's why I mentioned them."

DURING THE NEXT SIX WEEKS, THERE WERE A LOT OF DIS-cussions like these two. Bruce Bartlett, Claire Dustin, and Jason Calder all approached Gail or me about people in the church who struck them as worthy of consideration.

Claire talked to Gail and me about Lara Anderson. "She's in human resources at the Concord Hospital, and she is a winner. She has a nose for people and how to encourage them. You couldn't ask for anyone more suited to a CDP effort."

Bruce was high on Peter and Olivia Crosby. "I could easily see them heading off to seminary one day. They have real pastoral instincts. I see them praying for people. I see them connecting with newcomers to the church. Just the other day I heard about them spending a whole day helping a Somali family move into an apartment."

And then there was Jason. "Pastor Mac. I've got a couple of thoughts for you. I've been spending time with a guy my age (we're talking twenty-six here) whose name is Damon Marsh. He played hockey for Plymouth State, and now he's a floor manager at Dick's Sporting Goods. He's relatively new in his faith, but he's really taking Jesus seriously. When we talk, he writes down almost everything I say, and he's back to me in a week, reporting the results. If I ask him to help me in a project, he's right there. I see the possibility of 'deep' written all over this guy. He's worth your consideration."

I told Jason that we'd get acquainted with Damon.

"Oh, and my second thought is that you ought to consider Ben and Catherine Jacobs," he said.

"Ben and Catherine? Interesting idea. I'd not thought about—"

"They'll keep things honest. Ben will ask lots of questions and not be content with easy answers. And Catherine? She's one terrific woman. As gracious as they come. You might think about it."

I promised I would.

We also received suggestions from elders and members of the church council. Judy Taylor, for example, a businesswoman who travels a lot, sent me this e-mail:

GMAC,

I have run into Hugo Padilla several times recently at the Southwest counter at Manchester Airport. He seems a remarkable young man. Knowing that you and Gail are in the process of selecting people for CDP, I made it a point to do a quick study on Hugo. My impression? He's personable, gentle, and very believable. In the times I've talked with him, I've noticed how he looks me in the eye and speaks to me with great respect. He loves our church and clearly wants to do more with his life than just dispatch airplanes. You might want to consider him for your CDP group.

Judy

When I studied the names on our vetting list, I was pleased to see how diverse it was. We had singles and marrieds, people in the age range of twenty-five to forty-two. The gender balance was almost equal. Some had grown up in our church; others had come from other parts of the country. It was also interesting to see how many different careers were represented.

Now came the hard part. Like General Marshall had once done with his black book, we had to start making difficult decisions. Who would we select to consider the CDP experience? And who would we drop from the list? The thirty-five names had to be pared down to twenty-five. And, we assumed, the twenty-five would ultimately shrink to thirteen or fourteen.

Again Gail reminded me: this process had to be bathed in prayer.

APRIL 6

The First Spring

To: Rich Fisher, Carly Fisher
From: GMAC
Any chance you guys could join us for dessert on Wednesday evening?

To: GMAC, Carly Fisher
From: Rich Fisher
Time?

IN NEW ENGLAND, APRIL IS THE MONTH WHEN WINTER AND spring fight for control of the landscape. We know that spring is winning the battle when we see the daffodils and the hyacinths make their perennial appearance and begin to decorate the yard with color.

Gail and I were outside looking at the new growth, when Rich and Carly Fisher arrived at our home. The four of us were soon out in the sunporch, eating Gail's lemon meringue pie and bantering about family life, the upcoming Red Sox opener at Fenway, and several challenges Rich was facing at the high school.

After we'd poured a second round of decaf coffee, I raised the subject that had caused us to invite the Fishers to join us that evening. "Gail and I have a proposition for the two of you. And it's about the CDP project."

Immediately, Rich looked at Carly, and I saw her eyes meet his. It was my sense that they'd been anticipating what I was about to say.

"We'd like to ask you to consider being the first people to join the CDP group. We want you to be in this group because we think that, in another year, you could probably lead a group of your own. I'm not sure that we have all that much to teach you. I mean, good grief, you've been giving us ideas from the start. But if you came aboard, the four of us would have the chance to develop this thing together and start laying tracks for the second year."

"So," Gail said, "do you think that this is something we could talk about?"

Rich reached for Carly's hand. She responded with both of hers.

It was Carly who spoke first. "Gordon . . . Gail, you have no idea how much we've hoped that there would be a place for us in the CDP effort. We've prayed about this, and we are fully on board with what's happening . . . and . . . Rich, you talk . . . I'm too emotional."

I thought I saw Rich blink his eyes and then swallow a couple of times before he could speak.

"Gordon, ever since you first spoke to a few of us about the great idea last summer, it's become a vision growing in our hearts. Carly and I decided right at the beginning that we would do everything we could to support and encourage you in this venture. That's what led to that original dream session at our house and why I've kept sending articles and quotes and whatever else in your direction."

"You've been an incredible inspiration to us, both of you," Gail said. "I mean, even the term *deep people* originates with your giving Gordon the Richard Foster quote. You two have been at the root of this idea from the beginning."

"Carly and I decided a long time back that we would support CDP with all of our enthusiasm, but we would not ask to be involved. We'd not push ourselves. But if we were invited to get more deeply involved, we'd pray about it for five more seconds and say yes."

"Five seconds?" I said laughing.

"Well, that's because we've really done all the praying we could do before this. We were just waiting for God to act . . . or, I suppose, not act."

I said, "Let me ask you to think about one or two things before you do your five-second prayer. Rich, you'd need to step away from the council, and Carly, you'd have to back away from the pantry program. We'd really need your complete involvement in the CDP effort. And beyond that is always the possibility that, after this year, you would start your own CDP group. Is any of that a potential deal-breaker?"

"Not really," Carly said. "We've already discussed it. I've got a very capable partner in the pantry who could take over everything, and Rich . . ."

"Well, I'd miss the council a lot," Rich said. "But CDP is much more important. Yeah, I think we understand the implications. Working with the both of you and being part of the first CDP group would be a great opportunity for us."

"What about things at the school, Rich? If we did CDP on Monday nights this first year, would that interfere with school activities?"

"Nope. I wouldn't let it. I'll just give my assistant the word: nothing on my calendar on Monday nights. If we meet on the same night every week, that won't be a problem."

The conversation for the next hour was full of excitement. The ideas, the hopes, the expectations: they abounded in all we talked about.

In the last half hour we had together, we reviewed the thirty names on the CDP vetting list. In the next few days, we would have to reduce it to twenty-five. None of us looked forward to those choices.

After some prayer Rich and Carly finally left us. They promised to let us know their final answer the next day . . . presumably after their five-second prayer.

APRIL 7–20

The First Spring

To: GMAC, Gail MacDonald
From: Carly Fisher
Cc: Rich Fisher
Subject: CDP

We prayed. We talked. We agreed. We're on board. We couldn't
be more thankful.

Carly and Rich

IN THE DAYS THAT FOLLOWED, GAIL AND I (CONSULTING
with the Fishers) trimmed down the list to the twenty-five people
we thought were best suited for this first CDP effort. Our expectation was that only about a dozen of these would finally commit
to the yearlong experience. Soon we were contacting those we'd
selected.

The next Sunday, Gail found Lara Anderson in the visitors'
center at church.

"Lara, this may be a surprise to you, but Gordon and I have an
invitation for you that we'd like you to seriously consider. It concerns what Gordon preached about two weeks ago. We'd like you
to think about spending a year of Monday evenings with a small
group at our home, where we can work through what it means to

be a person of spiritual depth and influence. We're talking about something that's more than just leadership; it's an attempt to explore how a person can be spiritually influential."

"What made you think of me, Mrs. Mac?" Lara asked.

"Glad you asked. We're very much aware of how you're respected by others. Your friends speak of the consistency in the way you live. Others speak of you as a contributor who wants to make a difference with your life. Additionally, we're aware of your reputation at the hospital.

"Lara, we think God has a special interest in seeing you grow and, in the days to come, play a significant role in the life of our church . . . and, perhaps, beyond the church in other settings. And that leads us to believe that a year in the first CDP group would do a lot to help you see more clearly the ways God wants to use you."

"I don't know what to say. I'm thankful, of course. Can I take a few days to . . . ?"

"Of course. We'd like you to come to our home for dinner two weeks from Monday, on May 2. There will be others who have been invited just as I've invited you. We'll talk that night about how CDP will work and what we'd be asking of you. Right now, all you have to do is pray, think about this, and come that night."

Lara thumbed the date into her PDA and said, "Thanks, Mrs. Mac. I can be there."

At about the time Gail was talking with Lara, I found Damon Marsh, the young hockey player whom Jason Calder liked so much.

"Damon, do you recall my sermon on the great idea?"

"Yeah, I was there. You really going to do that?"

"Yes, we are going to do what I was talking about. And you're one of the people we'd like to do it with."

"You can't be serious."

"Damon, I know that you're relatively new to Christian faith. But Jason Calder has talked a lot about you to Gail and me. He's really impressed with your seriousness about following Jesus, and he thinks you have a great ability to build teams and get people organized to get things done. As a result, the two of us have kept sneaking peaks at you around here. We think Jason's right."

"But I've not been around someone like you that much, Pastor Mac. What—?"

"Look, Damon, all I'd like you to do right now is put Monday, May 2, on your calendar and be at our home. We'll introduce you to some terrific people, talk about CDP and how it might work, and then you can make a decision."

BEFORE THE DAY WAS FINISHED, ONE OR BOTH OF US HAD talked to Pete and Olivia Crosby, Hugo Padilla, Sara Stevens, and Morgan and Larry Singer. All of them were surprised, and all of them said they'd be at our home on May 2. In the days that followed, we contacted the rest of the twenty-five people on our list, and most of them also agreed to be there.

Lest you think no one declined, there were three or four who said thanks but no thanks. Among them was Keith Schuler, who said he'd just changed jobs and was sure that he'd be in over his head if he added more commitments to his life. Norm and Bonnie Armstrong confided that they were expecting a baby, and Joe Lewis said that he had promised to coach an indoor soccer team during the next year.

That left two more people on our list: Ben and Catherine Jacobs. On Monday Gail called Catherine and asked if we could schedule a brief telephone conversation some evening that week.

"Great to hear your voices, Pastor, Mrs. Mac," Ben said when we connected on Tuesday night. "What can we do for you?"

"Ben, Catherine, we have a thought for the two of you," Gail said. "We want you to consider joining the first CDP group. You both know what this is all about. You've already made an important contribution or two to the ongoing discussions about it. And now it's time to consider your participation when it starts in the fall."

"Are you sure that we could . . . ?"

"Ben, the answer's yes. We really believe this is the right thing for the both of you. You both have a way of attracting people to the things you believe in. What you say and how you say it impacts others. We think that a CDP group with you both in it would be a great experience. So here's all we want you to do. Pray, talk, and come to our home on Monday, May 2. We'll put the details on the table that evening."

"I'm supposed to work that night at Home Depot," Ben said. "But I think I can trade shifts with somebody else. You okay with this, Cath?"

"Okay? I'm blown out of the water that you're talking to us. But we do have a problem. We've got Zachary, and I don't think you want us bringing him to CDP meetings each week. We're probably not able to afford a sitter every week."

"Catherine, I've already thought about Zachary, and I think I have an idea. Trust me on this. Arrange for a babysitter on May 2, and the expense will be taken care of."

MINUTES AFTER THE CONVERSATION WITH THE JACOBSES, I heard Gail back on the phone.

"Adriana, this is Gail calling. Is Roberto available? I'd like to chat with both of you for a minute."

There was a moment of silence, and then:

"Hi, Roberto. Thanks for getting on the line. I have something I'd like to ask the two of you to consider. Roberto, do you remember at the elders' meeting when you spoke so enthusiastically about the CDP project?" (A bit more silence as Gail listened.)

"I have something for the two of you to think about. And you don't have to respond right away. We have two couples who we really want in CDP. Each has a small child. And they're going to need some financial help to afford a babysitter each Monday night. Now I—" (More silence.)

"That thrills me. I can't tell you what it—"

The phone conversation lasted a few more minutes, and then Gail said good-bye.

"Well, we have the babysitting problem solved. Remember when Roberto Silva said he'd give any money that was needed for CDP? Well, he and Adriana just told me that they would under-write all babysitter costs for the year for the Jacobses and the Crosbys, and for that matter, anyone else who has a child."

MAY 2

Morning, the First Spring

On my voice mail

"Gordon, Monica here on Monday morning. Tom and I are
praying for you and Gail as you face this evening with the
CDP candidates. We're asking the Lord to touch the lives of
each person you've selected so that they will see the significance of the great idea. There are lots of others praying
too. We made sure."

To: GMAC
From: Kelly Martin
Annie Huntoon called. George back in hospital. She says he's
aware of the meeting tomorrow night and wants you to know
he is praying. Annie thinks George is failing.

From my journal

> *Big day. From "great idea" to CDP; from a vision to
> realization. Tonight we do our first test-drive. We're
> getting great support from staff, leaders. Even George
> H is praying although he is probably dying.*

MONDAY, MAY 2, FINALLY ARRIVED. THE MORNING SKIES were clear, and the thermometer said it was already seventy-one degrees outside. I took the first minutes of the morning for a quiet period of personal worship. Then, after brewing some coffee, I went out to the mailbox to get the morning paper, hoping that I wouldn't run into anyone, since I was still in my bathrobe and slippers.

But that was not to be. Hank Soriano, also in his bathrobe, was sitting on his front steps, a coffee mug in his hand.

"Hey, Mac. How's it going?" Hank called out.

"Morning, Hank. Doing great, thanks."

"Looks like you're not going anywhere," Hank said. "Your store closed today?"

"No, no. The store's open. I'm just staying home for a while because we're having a meeting here tonight," I said. "Gotta set up the basement."

"You need help? I've got extra time," Hank said as he came over to where I was standing. He said that he, too, was going to spend the morning at home so he could finish a quarterly sales report for his boss.

"Sure, love it," I said. "Can you come over in about forty-five minutes?"

"No problem. What's the meeting?" Hank asked. You may remember how curious a man Hank is.

"Remember that night when you were over here with all those people who talked about memorable learning experiences? Well, we're taking the next step in that process. We're hosting a bunch of people and asking them to consider being a part of the first learning group. We're calling it CDP—"

"CDP? What's that stand for?"

"Cultivating Deep People. It probably sounds a tad strange to you."

"Yeah . . . never heard that before. What are *deep people*?"

"Well, okay . . . here's the elevator story. Deep people, actually *deepening* people, are men and women who want to take the life and the teachings of Jesus to a new level in their own life experience. They want to influence others to bring Jesus into the center of their lives. The result would be that everyone grows in their personal relationships, the quality of their work lives, and their service in the church and in the community.

"There," I said. "That's about twenty-two floors' worth, Hank. High-speed elevator."

"Twenty-six actually," Hank said. "How about me and Cynthia coming over and helping you serve your guests? There's no game tonight; Sox are traveling. And we're not going anywhere. We could do the dirty work, and you and Gail can relax and enjoy your company."

I was incredulous at Hank's two offers. Unchurched Hank wanted to come over and help me set up the basement and then come back again in the evening with his wife and help serve the dinner?

"You are some kind of friend," I said. "Don't you think you should talk to Cynthia before you commit here?"

"Trust me. Cynthia will be thrilled," Hank responded.

"I'll tell you what," I said. "Let me mention your idea about tonight to Gail and see if she thinks she needs help. When I see you in a little while, I can tell you what she says."

"YOU'VE GOT TO BE KIDDING," GAIL SAID WHEN I TOLD HER about Hank's offer to help that evening.

"I'm serious. Hank said that he and Cynthia would be happy to come over and help you and me serve dinner tonight. I think it's a fun thought myself . . . great possibilities," I said. "Anytime we can get Hank and Cynthia with people from the church is a plus."

"Well, I suppose it would work. You're going to invite them to stay for the after-dinner conversation?"

"Yeah. That wouldn't be a problem for tonight, anyway, and who knows where it will lead?"

THE NIGHT BEFORE, JASON CALDER AND A COUPLE OF HIGH school boys delivered tables, folding chairs, and dinnerware from the church to our garage. It took Hank and me about an hour to carry everything down to the basement and set up the room for the evening dinner.

"Cynthia will call Gail and see what she can do to help," Hank said when I told him that Gail would enjoy having them there that evening.

Later, when I thought over what had transpired between Hank and me early that morning, two insights hit me: first, that Hank Soriano might be a lonely man looking for something worthwhile to do and, second, that God might be opening up the doors to his and Cynthia's lives.

AT 6:30 THAT EVENING, OUR GUESTS BEGAN TO ARRIVE. SINCE the weather had turned cool in the afternoon, someone needed to become the coat-check person. That became Hank Soriano's first task. Then he turned into "bartender," pouring juices and carbonated beverages and making sure people helped themselves to the hors d'oeuvres.

Cynthia was in the kitchen, making the final preparations for the evening dinner.

That left Gail and me free to mill around and engage in casual conversation.

At 7 p.m. I gave a prayer of thanks for the food. Everyone circled the dining room table; filled their plates with pasta, salad, and Italian bread; and headed for the basement.

MAY 2

Later Evening, the First Spring

From my journal

> *Dinner was fabulous. The room was abuzz with*
> *conversation; no one showed any signs of feeling left out.*
> *The Sorianos helped serve and seemed to fit right in. They*
> *are clearly curious about everything that is happening.*

WHEN DINNER AND DESSERT WERE FINISHED, GAIL ASKED the women to clear the tables and the men to rearrange the room into a circle of chairs so our conversation could begin.

Hank and Cynthia Soriano worked as hard as anyone during this transition and then came to me and said, "We've had a great evening, but it's time for us to get out of here."

"No way," I said. "You've come this far into the evening. Why don't you stick around and watch what we're going to do? You may even have some ideas for me when the evening is over."

"Let me check with Cynthia."

A minute later Hank told me the two of them would stay.

Not long after everyone was seated in a circle, our meeting began.

"Gail and I love having you in our home this evening," I said. "You've all met Hank and Cynthia Soriano. They're our friends and neighbors, and they asked if they could help make this evening go as smoothly as possible. Thanks to them, it has. The rest of you know each other from church, so you're not strangers."

For a short while Gail and I introduced the subject of biblical discipleship. We talked about those times in the Scriptures when the older poured his or her life into the younger. We especially emphasized the relation of Jesus to his twelve disciples and how these very ordinary men grew up to be the founders of the greatest movement the world has ever seen.

Then we reached the main point of the evening. Here are some of the highlights of our presentation.

GMAC: "Tonight, as you're all aware, we have a proposal for you. And after we've described it, we're going to ask you to take two weeks to think about whether you want to participate. We're talking about something called the CDP Initiative . . . Cultivating Deep People. It's a name suggested by one of our oldest church members, George Huntoon.

"If you've taken stock of who's here this evening, you've probably noticed that you're a pretty diverse group in terms of age, gender, marital status, cultural background, even what you do for jobs. But there's one thing you all share in common . . . at least as far as Gail and I see things. You are people who have the potential to make a difference in the life of our church and in the life of our community. The key word that Gail and I have kicked around for some months now that describes each of you is *growable* . . . each of you has shown us that you want to mature as Christians and in your ability to influence others."

Then Gail spoke. "We'd like to invite you to our home each Monday night for forty weeks beginning in mid-September. Obviously, we'll have to take a time out for the holidays. But we'll stick as best we can to a forty-week calendar that will end sometime in June. When the forty weeks are over, we will no longer meet as a group. In other words, this will not go on forever.

"Our evenings will begin at 7 p.m. and end at 10:00. Each get-together will be fairly intense, and you're likely to go home at the end of the evening feeling pretty tired. But I think we can promise that you'll not be wasting your time.

"During the year, we'll do a lot of reading and we'll talk about what we're learning. Then a few months into our year, we'll all try writing our life stories.

"Throughout the year we will learn about temperament, biblically defined character, spiritual disciplines, and leadership skills. From time to time, we'll invite guests from our church and outside of our church to talk with us about their journey. We'll also learn how to pray together, and there's no doubt that we'll probably have to support one another when unexpected things come into our lives."

I said, "Gail's told you what you can expect of the CDP experience, but now you need to know what we'd expect of you.

"First, unless you are dying, we'll expect you to be here *every Monday night*. That means purging your calendar of any other events on that evening. Some of you may actually have to go to your bosses and talk with them about this so they won't ask you to do anything on Monday evenings.

"Second, we will always start on time. Promptness is part of the deal. And we need to agree that no one leaves early. We'll be together for the full three hours.

"Third, everyone participates. No one gets a free pass from conversation.

"Fourth, everyone will have a mentor, an older person or couple from the church. They will want to meet with you monthly and ask lots of questions so they can learn what CDP means to you. I suspect that this will become a high point in your month.

"Fifth, Rich and Carly Fisher are teaming up with Gail and me to make this first CDP group work. We have hopes that in another year, they'll be making this same presentation to a group of people just like you.

"Finally, we're going to make every attempt to create a sense of community among us during this next year. We want you to experience what it's like to be a group of people who overcome their differences and generate an authentic love and enjoyment of one another."

THERE WERE QUESTIONS, OF COURSE.

"What if I don't know much about the Bible?" Damon Marsh asked. "Some of you guys seem to know the Bible from one end to another. Won't someone like me slow everyone else down?" We assured Damon that this was not a problem.

"If we became a part of this group, what about some of the other things we're doing at church?" Lara Anderson wanted to know.

"Lara, you'll need to take a hard look at other involvements," Gail answered. "It wouldn't be wise to allow every night of the week to be taken up with activities that are sucking you dry. Gordon and I have discussed this with the elders, and there's strong support from our church leaders that while any of us are involved with CDP, he or she should take a leave from other things—except worship, of course—and major on this experience alone."

This, from Larry Sanger: "Are there people who are going to be envious that we're doing this sort of thing and they didn't get asked?"

"Could be," I said to Larry. "My suggestion? If you're part of the CDP group, just be careful how you talk about it, and maintain the confidentiality of things we might say to each other."

"So if people were to ask me what CDP is for," Ben Jacobs said, "what do I say the overall goal is?"

"How would you answer Ben's question, Rich?" I said, turning to Rich Fisher.

Rich did not hesitate. "Ben, if I were you, I'd simply say that CDP is all about developing a new generation of leaders who will maintain our church's faithfulness to its mission."

We had a few final comments for the group.

"We know we're setting the bar for participation very high," I said. "Most churches and most pastors don't normally do this. So we want you to think and pray—really pray—about what we've invited you to do for the next year. You've got the next few weeks. If you decide that it's not for you, we'd rather you say no now than realize later you were not able to keep the commitments. You don't even have to tell us why you're saying no. Just send Gail or me a text message or a note or stop us when you see us and say, 'I've got to take a pass on CDP.'"

Then Gail said, "The more important things you're likely to learn this coming year will not come from books or videos. They may actually come from observing. Paul used to say—as all rabbis said in his day—'Follow my example.' In other words, watch Gordon and me as something of an example. Notice the way we work as a team. See if you can figure out how we're different from one another. See if we support each other in the best possible way. See how much we enjoy each other. For sure, we're far from perfect, and we'll disappoint you from time to time, but keep watching. And don't be afraid to ask us questions about what you see."

Soon after, Gail and I prayed conversationally. Some of the prayer sounded like this:

> GMAC: Lord, this has been a special evening. Thank you
>   for these friends who've come to be with us.

GAIL: Let them feel assured that we admire them and care that they would continue to grow to be men and women in whom you take great pleasure.

GMAC: Father, I pray that each of them will be able to make clear decisions about their possible involvement in CDP. Let there be no confusion, no misunderstanding.

GAIL: Send everyone to their homes with a gladness for having been together this evening. Give us good rest during the night, and thank you in advance for giving us power to be honorable for Jesus in our work tomorrow. Amen.

Soon, people were getting their coats and sweaters from Cynthia Soriano and heading for their cars. A few stayed to help clean the kitchen. Finally, only the Fishers—Rich and Carly—and the Sorianos were left.

"Incredible evening," Rich said to me. "I think there's the making of a great group here, and I can't wait to see who says the first yes."

"I don't remember when I've ever been among a group of young adults who were so alert," Cynthia Soriano said. "You're so lucky to be able to be involved with them."

Rich and Carly suggested that we get together in a few days to assess our progress and see where we might go from here in the formation of the CDP initiative. And then they left for home, where Aunt Connie was with their boys.

It was clear that Hank and Cynthia wanted to stay until we four were alone. To use an old expression, they seemed *strangely warmed*.

MAY 2

Late, Late Evening, the First Spring

To: Geoff Handley, Monica O'Donnell, Pastoral Staff
From: GMAC
Meeting just ended. Spirit great. Good start. Thanks for
prayers.

"THERE'S PLENTY OF DECAF LEFT FROM DINNER," GAIL SAID
to Hank and Cynthia Soriano and me. "Does anyone want a last
cup?" We all said yes.

Seated in the sunroom, we drank our coffee—we over-
churched and underchurched neighbors—as we talked about the
evening. Hank and Cynthia asked all kinds of questions as they
sought to figure out what made this gathering so different from
any other they'd ever seen before.

"We do this sort of training thing in business all the time,"
Hank said. "Of course, the religious component isn't there, but I
never thought I'd see something like this happening in a church.
You've got to be a lot more serious about what you're into than I
ever imagined. No wonder your sales are up."

A moment later, Hank Soriano asked one more question—
one that I'd never anticipated.

"Hey, if I'm not out of bounds, what would you think about
this? You mentioned that each of these people here tonight would

be assigned some older person to meet with once a month. Is there anyone in your church that would be willing to get together with Cynthia and me like that? I think both Cynthia and me would give our right arms if someone could help us understand how this religious thing works. Who knows? We might even become deep people someday. Whatcha think, Cyn?"

Cynthia nodded her head and said, "That would be nice."

I was astounded. "But you guys don't do church," I said. "You'd really want to get involved with someone like that?"

"Maybe . . . maybe," Cynthia said quietly, "if we did this, we might get to the point where we could consider doing church. You know that elevator story you wrote for Hank last summer? It's still on his desk."

"Yeah. I keep looking at it and saying to myself, 'It would be special to be part of something like that.' So maybe Cynthia's right; this might be a way to get involved . . . let someone help us understand things better."

MAY 6–20

The First Spring

From my journal—four days after the dinner

> George Huntoon is with Jesus. I'm going to miss him.
> But he will always be a reminder to me of the kind of
> younger men and women we're seeking through CDP.

From my journal—ten days after the dinner

> Responses are coming in from the CDP dinner. So
> far, these are the people who have signed on: Ben and
> Catherine Jacobs, Sara Stevens, Damon Marsh, the
> Crosbys, Hugo Padilla, Amy Boyd, Thomas Sanders.
> The Sangers, the McKnights, and Phil Penner have
> declined. We still are waiting to hear from Lara
> Anderson, Matt Cundiff, and Sherry Nordberg.

From my journal—thirteen days after the dinner

> Lara, Sherry, and Matt said yes. Our CDP group is
> formed at fourteen people. Ideal size, Gail says.

ON A MAY EVENING WE INVITED MERCEDES PEREZ TO OUR home for dinner. Naturally much of our conversation centered on the CDP initiative, and we urged her to ask tough questions and offer challenging suggestions.

"Pastor Mac," Mercedes said, "I think that what you and Gail are hoping to do has a kind of revolutionary potential for our church and maybe for others. But I want to remind you that, if you want to make the CDP idea become a core value in the life of our church, you *must* begin to redesign the responsibilities of the lead pastor. From what you've told me, I don't think the elders are moving fast enough on this."

"Could you unpack that for me, Mercedes?" I said.

"Well, right now I'd say that you and everyone else see your job—forgive my business terminology—as the chief preaching officer."

"Okay . . . but what makes you say that?"

"Look at your calendar," Mercedes said. "In terms of your workweek, what one event gets more time than any other?"

"Hm . . . I probably spend about fifteen to eighteen hours in sermon preparation, and then—"

"That's a lot of hours. You must think preaching is pretty important. Now, what's the largest single piece of space in the church building?"

"The worship center, of course."

"And how is it designed?"

"Designed? Well, it has seats that all point forward to the front, where the worship band leads worship and where I preach."

"So what's the message in that, Pastor Mac?" Mercedes asked.

"You must already know the answer," I said. "Save me some time."

"The message," Mercedes said, "is clear. You are a preacher more than anything else. Your investment of time, even the space set aside for preaching, the way you identify yourself: it's mostly about preaching. You are telling us, know it or not, that you believe that preaching is the most important thing you do. So I'm saying that something may need to change . . ."

"Like what?" I asked.

"Like you being less the lead preacher and becoming the lead trainer. Only when people see you spending your biggest amount of time cultivating growable people will they believe that this is your highest priority. You must think about seeing this as I have to see it at the hotel. First and foremost, I am lead trainer; it's the most important thing I do every day. I am the VP for the center, but I make sure nothing ever gets in the way of my involvement in the training process."

"You realize, don't you, Mercedes, that you're fiddling with the way I've looked at things in the church for almost forty years now?"

"Of course, Pastor Mac. I know I fiddle, as you put it. But here's my point. Your most growable people will only give themselves to this process if they see that this CDP is going to be your number one priority. Yours! Not someone else's. So maybe you do a little less preaching in the next year and let people become aware that you're making your greatest investments in the church's future.

"You know what's going to happen? Soon you'll be doing CDP with more than just one group. You'll be launching several groups, and you'll have to be training people around you who can lead those groups. This CDP thing will go viral in a short period of time. I promise you that."

Oh, boy, I thought. I hadn't looked that far ahead. But Mercedes was making sense, and she had the experience to make her point.

Our dinner guest was not through with me.

"I suggest you sit down with the elders and propose that they rewrite your job description—you have one, don't you?—and put training at the top of the priority list. Furthermore, tell them to hold you accountable for how many deepening people you and those who will begin working with you have trained at the end of a year. That will demonstrate to them that some changes are actually happening at the church."

But Mercedes was not yet through.

"Once you have your first CDP group started, it will be time for you to ask who else may need training. Why not your staff? Why not the elders? Tell them that you want to make training 20 percent of all their meeting times. They'll probably fight you at first. But keep working on them. They'll be your next groups. You'll have a CDP staff and CDP elders. There: that's three groups by next year."

Now I fully understood why Mercedes Perez was on her way to being president of her hotel chain. Above all other gifts she had, Mercedes was a visionary.

MAY 16

The First Spring

To: GMAC
From: Darrell Lassiter
Would you be open to getting together in the next few days?
We could meet in Nashua if you're open. Just name the time
& day.

To: Darrell Lassiter
From: GMAC
Starbucks? 5/16? 3 p.m.?

To: GMAC
From: Darrell Lassiter
Thanks. See you then.

WHEN WE WERE SEATED WITH OUR COFFEES, DARRELL
Lassiter, my Massachusetts pastor friend, said to me, "I've been
giving a lot of thought to your great idea."

"We call it CDP now, Darrell. Means Cultivating Deep
People."

"OK . . . CDP . . . Got it. So, I've got some questions . . . mostly
about procedures. But there's one that nags me a bit."

"And that is . . . ?"

"You think any pastor could do what you and Gail are going to try this fall? Look at it this way: the two of you have put in a lot of years. Your congregations have grown; you seem to have left each one happily. So it's not going to be hard for people to want to get next to you and be cultivated . . . as you've been putting it.

"But what about the guy (or gal, for that matter) who pastors this church after you're gone and feels that they've not had this kind of success? How are they going to get the nerve to think they can do this same kind of development?"

"Any other, easier questions?" I asked, trying to buy some time to think of an adequate answer to Darrell's question. I suppose I was trying to lighten things up. My friend had kicked off our conversation with a pretty heavy topic.

"Darrell, look, I'm not totally sure I can answer your question. I know what I think the answer should be . . . what it needs to be."

"What's that?" Darrell asked.

"Well, if the only people who can cultivate others are those who are the most dazzling preachers and those who have led churches to impressive growth—and that's certainly not me, Darrell—pastors like us are in trouble. I know of more than a few pastors out there who've not had the most successful of experiences during their years of ministry. But that doesn't necessarily mean that God hasn't used them.

"One of the most important things to know about pastoring is that the long-term results are never fully known until years and years have passed by. A pastor can stick with a church for a long time and feel as if there are no results. Then, bam! Out of all his effort comes one person—one person, mind you—who becomes an outstanding leader someplace. That's Mordecai in the Bible— virtually a faceless person in the crowd except that he coaches Esther into her role as the rescuer of the Jewish people."

"Good story, but—"

"Let me finish my thought. I'm on a roll now."

"Let 'er roll."

"What I'm saying is that each of us has to do an inventory and ask what we can offer to younger people. And when we know the answer, then we have to figure out how to pass that along. In those places where we lack something to give, we need to find others who can make up for what we don't have and bring them into the mix. That, by the way, is a major reason why I would team up with Gail. She brings all kinds of stuff to the table that I couldn't bring."

Darrell lifted his hand as a signal that he wanted to interrupt. "So what does the Gail-and-Gordon team give together, and what do you give separately?"

"Well, together, we give our home . . . our marriage . . . our love for reading . . . the lifelong lessons we've learned—many the tough way—and our stories."

"And separately?"

"Gail brings a lot of sensitivity and intuition. She brings organizational instincts. She's hospitable; she's incredibly affirming. And she's not afraid to speak the truth."

"You?"

"I guess I'm the dreamer. I ask pretty good questions. I love to break ideas down into parts that people can easily understand. Those are areas where God has given me a bit of a head start."

"But I also hear you saying that you don't have to know everything and do everything perfectly," Darrell said.

"Look, Darrell, I'm not a guy with loads of experience in this. We haven't even done a CDP group yet. But the years have taught me this: people are willing to listen to a man or woman who is truthful about their life experience with Jesus. People will follow after you if you're willing to open your lives to them. Even your weaknesses can become a great strength in the long run if you're a repentant and growing person.

"People want to know where we've struggled . . . They profit from knowing what the struggle taught. They learn when you tell them about how you've had to utterly depend on God. So I don't think a pastor should excuse himself from cultivating people just because he hasn't been a smashing success. He may even be more approachable as a result. If he or she has depth in their lives, the right people will figure that out and blaze a path in their direction."

Darrell and I talked about a number of other things, but I got the feeling that what Darrell was really wanting to know was, could he and Sandy do something like a CDP project together? And so I curled back to the earlier discussion and asked, "Darrell, could I poke you with a rather intrusive question?"

"Yeah, go ahead."

"Were we really talking about you a few minutes ago when we spoke about guys who might feel intimidated by this notion of cultivating deep people?"

"You can tell?"

"Well, let me offer an experimental thought or two, and you tell me where I'm on the wrong track or where I need to bug off. I'm wondering if you and Sandy are tangling over this. Is one of you feeling that the other is not quite up to this challenge?"

"Okay . . . okay . . . Gordon, Sandy told me the other night that she's disappointed in my spiritual life at home and that she questions what I could offer a group of younger people. She thinks you and Gail have hung the moon, that you do everything right . . . and maybe you do. But she compares me to you and . . . well, you know where that leaves things."

"First of all," I said, "Gail and I do not do everything right. There was a time when we, too, struggled to have a healthy spiritual life together. I haven't always been the man she could completely respect.

"But we did work at those things, and more than once I had

to ask her forgiveness for my spiritual disorganization. But we've come a long way, and we don't mind talking about the difficult times when appropriate. We've determined to use our failures . . . to embrace them and be stewards of them for the benefit of others. So if we ever look good to Sandy or to you, it's because there've been some tears along the way and we've dealt with them straight on."

"Thanks. I needed to hear that."

"I have a thought for you," I said. "If you think the two of you have some renewing to do, go home and tell Sandy what's on your mind. Be frank with her: tell her what you think you're hearing her say, where you perceive that she's disappointed in you . . . maybe even the marriage. Why not suggest that the two of you take a week away and assess your lives together? What would a fresh start look like? Don't be afraid to do some repenting if you see that it's appropriate. And by the way, don't be surprised if Sandy opens up and acknowledges some of her own fears and inadequacies. This could be a breakthrough moment for you both."

Darrell thanked me for my candor. An hour later we gave each other a guy-hug in the parking lot, and Darrell said quietly, "You're the only friend with whom I could have had a conversation like this."

"Promise me," I said, "that you'll get back to me with what you decide to do."

Darrell promised.

JUNE 3

The First Spring

To: GMAC
From: Darrell Lassiter
Subject: Advice?

Thanks for our time together. I waited for a day and then suggested to Sandy that we get away for a couple of days and do some thinking about where we want our lives to go from here. She's ready to do this. But we're both a bit nervous about what might come out of this. Any chance we could say some things to each other that would be injurious to the relationship? Or might there be some breakthroughs that would make the second half of our lives a whole lot better? Any advice? Any prayers?

To: Darrell Lassiter
From: GMAC
Subject: Re: Advice?

Quietly remarry Sandy in your heart every day. When you get away, ask her how she needs you to love her. Take good notes when she answers. Repent and forgive. Make those things happen. Start there and get back to me.

ON A FRIDAY AFTERNOON IN JUNE, SOON AFTER THE BLACK-flies exited New England and the mosquitoes showed up, the Fishers and Gail and I drove up to the White Mountains and checked into a B&B that Monica O'Donnell had recommended. We four were hoping to spend twenty-four hours finalizing the footprint of what a year of CDP group experiences might look like.

Gail and I could have worked on this ourselves, but we wanted the Fishers to participate so they could share ownership of the CDP vision.

After getting settled into our rooms, the four of us met for dinner, and our conversation began almost immediately.

"After all these months of dreaming," I said, "I think we've got some solid principles to build on. I've taken the liberty of putting some of this on paper." I passed out file folders containing several pages of ideas—none of which were new to anyone. But I thought it might help if we saw the results of our past discussions all printed out in one presentation.

"The first page is our latest iteration of the CDP purpose: 'CDP: Strengthening and enlarging the core congregation by cultivating growable men and women to be rooted, built up, and strengthened in Christ and to become competent and confident in their call to serve others in his name.'

"I love the two-part concept of being rooted in Christ and in one's call to serve," I said.

Rich responded. "My boss at the high school keeps on talking about *fitness* and *execution*, which always gets people's attention. And what she means by *fitness* is who you are and whether or not you're growing continuously as an educator yourself. *Execution* is what you do and how you do it that impacts others. I think she'd like this purpose statement."

All four of us were in agreement that we had a workable purpose statement. So we went on to the second page, which described the objectives of CDP. Since that first staff discussion, they had been revisited a hundred times (or so it seemed). Any changes were purely cosmetic.

- Identifying growable people
- Folding them into learning communities
  focused on spiritual maturity
- Helping each person discover their
  giftedness and calling
- Pointing them toward leadership opportunities
  in the church or in the larger world

"What do you think will be the hardest of these objectives to achieve?" Gail asked.

For a moment we all studied the objectives in silence. If there was an obvious answer, no one had it on the tip of their tongue.

Finally, Gail said, "Well, I'll tell you what I think . . . it's the second one. Forming a learning community will be very challenging but, if done right, will be incredibly rewarding. In the past we've tended to think of small groups as merely a program in the life of a church. But in the CDP approach we're saying that a learning community of thirteen to fifteen people is the most likely place for people to make major strides forward in their devotion to Christ and an understanding of all that entails. God is more likely to speak into a person's life in that environment than any other."

"Why are you so sure, Gail?" Carly asked.

"Well, take John Wesley. He built the whole Methodist movement on the foundation of learning communities that he called classes. He actually believed that a person was not truly converted to Jesus unless they were connected to a small group where they could acknowledge their sins, give their offerings, and care for one another."

"I'm with Gail," I said. "I don't think a CDP effort would be workable if its members do not become passionate about becoming a learning team."

Carly commented on the third objective, which focused on how people discover their own uniqueness and their ways of influencing others and said to me, "You're thinking about the Myers-Briggs Temperament Indicator here?"

"That's all Gail's thing," I said. "And it's a real *must-do*."

"I'd like to spend the first four weeks—about half of each evening—on temperament," Gail said. "We'll ask everyone to fill out a Myers-Briggs Temperament Indicator before the first meeting. Then, over those first four evenings, we'll learn about the various temperament patterns. When we're finished, I'll show everyone how they originally scored themselves and ask them if they still agree with the results. When everyone's on board, I'll give them name tags that also list their temperament preferences. They'll have a ball comparing their similarities and differences."

"Rich uses the MBTI with the new teachers every year," Carly said. "We've done it together, and now our children have gone through a children's version of the indicator."

"It's made an incredible difference in our marriage and even to our family," Rich said. "Sometimes you find that you love one of your kids but you have a hard time liking them for a while. And usually it's because you're temperamental opposites. And that's good to know."

"So we'll do temperament—or Gail will do it, anyway . . . and we'll really value your input on this, Rich. Then about four months into the year we'll start on personal stories. Temperament helps a person understand a lot about themselves right now, and the story-writing will be a way of helping us learn how we got to the *right now*."

"How are you going to do that?" Rich asked.

"We'll do some teaching on how a story is written," I said. "Then, after we've all spent a month writing, we'll read them aloud—one person each week."

"Oh, wow," Carly said. "Am I going to have to do that? I've never tried doing anything like that before."

"Not to worry, Carly," Gail said. "First of all, Gordon will teach everyone how to do it, and then he and I will take the first two weeks and read our stories. That way everyone will know what a story sounds like. We're confident that if we lead the way in transparency, everyone will follow."

After shared desserts, we left the dining area and settled into overstuffed chairs that were arranged before a huge fireplace. The couple who owned the B&B came in and talked with us for a while and then left us to ourselves.

"During the weeks when we're doing the temperament test, I'm going to take the first hour and use it to teach everyone how to read," I said.

"To read?" Rich asked.

"Yeah, you're the educator, Rich. You'll really like this. I don't think most people know how to read analytically. If they read at all, it's for sensation, for curiosity, perhaps. But few people know how to really *listen* to an author, to understand what he or she is saying. Frankly, I find that a lot of immature Christians struggle with this. They form opinions and judgments prematurely. They don't take the time to know what an author is really trying to say.

"So if people are going to grow deeper, they're going to have to learn how to gain greater insight from what they read. And then we'll want to teach them to dialogue about their reactions to what they're reading.

"Dialogue is different from discussion. Discussion is more or less about the clash of ideas. But dialogue is about forming ideas that none of us foresaw. So we want to teach the group how to listen and then how to cooperate with each other in finding deeper insights, greater truths. That will take a little time, but we'll get there."

"You going to lead it, Gordon?" Carly asked.

"Gail and I will both lead the dialogues for the first few weeks, and then we'll probably ask you two to start doing it. And after a few weeks more, we'll kick it out to others in the group. I think we'll be surprised how quickly they pick it up. You'll know that we've all learned how to dialogue when everyone stops looking toward Gail and me for approval when they say something. When they start talking to each other, you'll know that we're becoming a dialoguing community."

It was getting later into the evening, and we were all beginning to fade. So the four of us joined our hands and prayed. I remember Carly's prayer very specifically:

"Lord," Carly prayed, "as we have talked about our dreams for CDP this evening, I have been reminded several times of those people who greatly invested in, or cultivated, me when I was a girl. My mother; Miss Cummins, my Sunday school teacher; Mr. Canfield, the director of our high school band; and Jenny, our InterVarsity staff worker. In a sense, Lord, every one of those people is written into my soul. I see them in the way I think, the way I talk, the way I have come to believe in you. And now, Father, you've given Rich and me an opportunity to team up with Gordon and Gail and do our own investing and cultivating. I am so grateful. I love the thought that we'll be looking at a dozen or more truly deepening people a year from now . . ."

Minutes later we were headed to our rooms, bone-tired but greatly satisfied to be participants in the formation of CDP, a truly great idea.

JUNE 4

Morning, the First Spring

A handmade card signed by Gail, placed on our breakfast plates the next morning. On the inside Gail printed the comment of a nineteenth-century converted Indian who described his relationship to his bishop.

> "The bishop read the Bible to me daily . . . . The longer I lived with the bishop, the closer I came to him, and found that his life revealed Christ to me . . . his deeds and words made it easier for me to understand the mind and teaching of Christ, about what I read in the Bible. I had a new vision of Christ when I actually saw Christ's life of love, sacrifice, and self-denial in the everyday life of the bishop."
>
> This is what cultivating deep people looks like.
>
> Gail

NEW ENGLAND B&Bs ARE FAMOUS FOR THEIR EXQUISITE breakfasts, and the B&B we'd chosen for an overnight was no exception. We four—Rich and Carly, Gail and I—enjoyed French toast generously garnished with candied walnuts, maple syrup, and other flavorings that only Gail could identify. For me, if the taste is great, identifying the ingredient is unnecessary.

Soon after breakfast and a walk through the garden, which was coming to life, we resumed last night's conversation.

Gail started off by telling Rich and Carly about her time with Sandy Lassiter in March when they'd gone through the Bible and assembled a catalog of provocative leadership biographies. "Our challenge was not in finding enough stories; it was, rather, in selecting the right ones that would illustrate the diverse challenges leaders face. Gordon asked that we limit ourselves to twenty, and that was hard.

"Sandy and I wanted both men and women, and we hoped for examples of younger and older. We also thought it might be wise to include one or two stories where leaders failed so there would be an opportunity to troubleshoot the lives of those who started well and ended poorly."

With that explanation, we began to look over the names that Sandy and Gail produced. They were listed in the rough chronological order that they appeared in the Bible.

Abraham was first. "Abraham didn't lead an organization as such," Gail said. "But Paul called him the 'father of all who believe,' so we decided that his journey out of a pagan culture to the moment where he evidenced his complete trust in God on the mountain qualified him as the leader of the historic movement of faith.

"Joseph, who became the key man in Egypt, was an obvious choice. His struggle to survive, actually thrive, is unparalleled among Bible stories. There would be much for CDP people to chew on as they read Joseph's life together.

"Sandy and I concluded that the most important thing about Joseph was not his public role as a leader but his choice to forgive his brothers and peacefully resolve what could have been an ongoing, generation-by-generation vendetta of vengeance and mayhem."

Moses was third on the list. "Obviously," Gail said, "Moses has to be included because of his extensive preparation for leadership in Egypt and in the desert.

"Then we looped two men together in one spot: Joshua and Caleb. The two of them are kind of bound up together in the story of Israel. They've got a lot to teach."

Gideon made the top twenty. He illustrated the role of growing faith in seemingly hopeless situations. There was Samuel, the first of the great prophets. Along with Moses, Samuel would illustrate the great biblical theme of call and mentoring. Not to be forgotten was the day when Samuel went to the home of Jesse and selected David to be the successor to Saul. That episode, Gail said, would create a lot of opportunity for discussion, as everyone would want to explore what it meant when God said to Samuel, "People look at the outward appearance, but the LORD looks at the heart."

David was chosen, of course. And after him, the women suggested Solomon and Hezekiah, later kings of Israel who became trapped in their fascination with wealth and power.

"The startling truth about Israel's kings," Gail pointed out, "is that almost every one of them came to a bad end, David, maybe, the exception. We could spend an entire year of CDP simply studying the spiritual and character flaws of the kings, and that would be an education in itself. But we decided that these kings were enough to make the point."

The list the women compiled included Isaiah, whom Gail referred to as a prophetic leader. There followed Ezra, Nehemiah, Daniel, and Esther. The first two offered not only an inspirational picture of leadership but an administrative perspective as well. Daniel and Esther were meant to exemplify courage, wisdom, and integrity in dangerous situations.

New Testament leaders included John the Baptizer. "He's a remarkable man," Gail said to us. "The influence of his parents upon him, his ability to show people the power of repentance, and then, most important, his view of his work when it comes to an end and he declares that he must decrease in reputation while Jesus increases. It's an incredible lesson.

"We included Simon Peter, representing the disciples, of course," Gail said. "He alone is worth an entire year of leadership lessons. In the early church we included Stephen, Barnabas, Timothy, and, finally, Paul the strategic thinker, trainer, and theologian."

Rich, Carly, and I each named at least one other biblical person whom we thought should also be on the list. Rich pushed for Elijah; I wanted Aaron to illustrate defective leadership. And Carly simply hoped for more woman leaders. But each time Gail convinced us that she and Sandy had done their homework and had a reason for not including them. Not that they were inferior, she said, but, more often than not, they were similar to someone else whose experience offered more in the way of leadership insight.

We wondered if there wouldn't be room for a group of lesser-known leaders whose lives might be bunched together for analysis. Priscilla and Aquila as cultivators of Apollos in the early church. Why not Moses' brother, Aaron, as a stunning example of weak leadership? And what about Diotrephes as an example to avoid?

"Who in the world is Diotre . . . what's that name?" Carly asked.

"Diotrephes. He's over in Third John," I said. "I love to talk about him occasionally. John said of him, he 'loves to be first.'"

"Doesn't get the servant-leader award, does he?" Rich said.

We now had our lives of blue-ribbon leaders, deep people, from the Bible. During the course of the CDP year, everyone would become quite familiar with them. Where had they come from? What course had they taken toward spiritual depth? What capabilities did they bring to the leadership table? Had they suffered? Failed? What had they learned as a result? And then the bigger questions: How had God used them, and what had been the result? Finally, if we bounced them up to our times, what would they be like today?

JUNE 4

Afternoon, the First Spring

From my journal

> *Wonderful two days with Rich and Carly. Carly's
> parents took their boys for the weekend so they
> could get away with us. Carly said it was the first
> time in months she'd been able to talk adult talk for
> twenty-four straight hours. And it was just that:
> adult talk about our faith in Jesus, our desire to
> cultivate younger people, our dreams for the future
> leaders of our church.*

AS OUR DAY AT THE B&B IN THE WHITE MOUNTAINS PASSED
by—and time seemed to move incredibly fast—the four of us
completed our picture of how the CDP year might look.

"We've got forty meetings, three hours each time," I reminded
the group at one point in the afternoon. "We need a map of sorts
to follow; yet at the same time, Gail and I will try to be sensitive to
where the group is going. We want the Holy Spirit to guide us, and
we'll have to be careful to sense when it would be good to linger
on a topic and when it might be wise to skip past one. Sometimes
we will simply have to throw the evening plan out the window.

"Three out of four weeks, we'll take upward to an hour on

one of these leadership readings. But we're also going to want to include some leaders from the history of the Christian movement who have something to offer in the way of influence."

"Names?" Rich said. "If you're looking for suggestions, I'd love to see us read about St. Francis."

"That's a great one, Rich," I said. "Got any more?"

It wasn't hard for us to produce more names. Carly pushed for Mary Slessor and William and Catherine Booth. Gail, having just read the biographies of both John and Charles Wesley, nominated them. I put St. Patrick's name on the table, and Rich nominated Martin Luther. To these six individuals and couples we eventually added four others: Jonathan and Sarah Edwards, William Wilberforce, William Carey, and George Mueller.

In the middle of the afternoon, we touched on a few other things that we hoped would add to the CDP experience.

"We've got to make sure that prayer is front and center in this group," Gail said with conviction. "I don't care how much you teach a would-be leader . . . if he or she cannot pray for people and do it whenever it's needed, then the rest of what we've taught them doesn't amount to that much. Every CDP evening needs to be marked by prayer. Every person in the group has to get to a point where they are thoroughly at ease addressing God in public prayer. And for some this will take a while."

When the day ended, we decided to conclude our time together with prayer. Shutting the door to the room where we'd been for the past many hours, we sat in a tight circle and prepared ourselves to talk to God.

"Just before we pray," Rich said, breaking the silence, "Carly and I want to thank the two of you for inviting us on this great adventure. You can be sure that we'll knock ourselves out to learn from you, support you, even serve you. Just say the word, and we'll do anything that will help you make the CDP initiative work. Someday we hope to do what you're going to do this coming year. So we'll be watching everything in hopes that we can replicate it . . . and add to it wherever possible."

"Rich," I responded, "Gail and I could never have imagined when the great idea first morphed into CDP that we'd begin a partnership as good as this one is becoming. All we can say is how grateful we are and how much we've come to love the two of you."

Soon after that we prayed.

"Father," Gail prayed, "a year or two ago we could never have dreamed that our church leaders would begin to understand the importance of raising up a new generation of deep people. We could never have imagined that we'd be preparing a plan for this effort with Rich and Carly. How you have surprised us, and how grateful we are for the surprise."

"And Lord," Rich added, "we're struck with how much this great idea is in alignment with Jesus' work with those original twelve. We read over and over again—and never tire of the story—of how their lives were changed, what a difference they made in the world, what powerful people they became . . . We read of these things and dare to think of such possibilities in our time."

"I'm full of gratitude, holy Father," I prayed, "when I think of the people you put in my pathway years ago to begin the process of deepening in me. The affirmations they offered, the rebukes they gave, the insights, the learning experiences, the opportunities . . . all of it floods into my mind in a moment like this, and I'm so touched that you are allowing Gail and me to replicate this process in the life of another generation. Lord, we pledge to give this great idea all we've got. Father, we pray for power, for wisdom, for insight."

Then Carly spoke. "Jesus, I ask that you will give us enormous faith, a vision of what each man and each woman in the CDP group might become because of our investment in them.

Rich and I are so excited to be a part of this. We know that we'll grow as a result of being involved. And we know that the church is going to profit immensely. My heart wants to explode with the anticipation of a few years from now when there might be fifty, sixty, maybe even a hundred deeper people, maybe a lot more, who are equipped to be people of great spiritual influence. Jesus, please give us the power to do this."

Our prayers continued for a while longer as we thought of the group that would be coming together in a few days. We prayed for one another and for our ability to be examples to others, for the continuous support of the leaders as things in the church changed a bit.

And then it came time to say amen. Our bill paid, we said goodbye to the owners of the B&B and promised we'd return soon. Then we headed back home to the great challenge of making CDP come to life.

JUNE–AUGUST

The Second Summer

Handwritten card, via snail mail

Ola, Gordon,

Adriana and I received your note about Mr. and Mrs. Soriano. We would consider it an honor to meet with them. Let us know when they are ready to meet, and we'll invite them to our home for a Brazilian meal and some good bossa nova music. Oh, and let us know how you want to arrange that babysitter fund.

Roberto Silva

IT WAS A WONDERFUL SUMMER IN NEW ENGLAND. GAIL AND I pursued our annual warm-weather objective of downsizing our possessions so that when the truly older years came, we would not be saddled with stuff we didn't need.

We canoed several times on the Pemigewasset River and on some of the lakes in northern Maine. On many evenings, we curled up on the couch in our sunroom and watched as our beloved Red Sox sought another world championship.

In early July we once again returned to Fenway Park as guests of Hank and Cynthia Soriano. It had been just a year since we'd been there last and Hank had popped the elevator-story question. What a distance our friendship had come since then.

245

It was probably about the sixth inning, just before the Red Sox came to bat, when I said to Hank, "Remember back a few weeks ago when you asked about the possibility of meeting with some couple?"

"Yeah . . . I figured you'd forgotten."

"No way I forgot. I just wanted to be careful in selecting someone you might really enjoy meeting."

"Bet you prayed about it too, huh?" Hank said.

I laughed. "Why'd you say that?"

"Hey, come on. I've been listening to you guys. Whenever you have some decision to make, you go into the prayer thing. I've heard Gail talk about how you prayed your way through the selection of the CDP group; so I figure . . ."

"Okay, so now you know one of our secrets. We do pray about a lot of things. And, well . . . we did pray about your question."

"So who did God say would be good for us to meet?"

"If you insist in putting that way, God told me that you should meet Gilberto and Adriana Silva. They're Brazilians. He runs the North American office of a Brazilian company, and I think the four of you would really hit it off. So I'd be glad to introduce you if you're still interested. I told them that you and Cynthia were curious about what's driving the CDP initiative and what it means to be deepening people. So, whenever you're ready, they'd be delighted to get together with you and see where things go."

"Let me talk to Cynthia once more and make sure we're all on the same page."

"The ball's in your court," I said.

An hour later we were exiting from Fenway. The Red Sox had won the game.

IN LATE JULY AND EARLY AUGUST, WE BEGAN TO INVITE each of the CDP people to our home for evening dinner and conversation. The objective: to know each person better and to discern something about their expectations for the coming year.

Matt Cundiff was the first on our list. We learned that he'd been brought up a Roman Catholic and that he'd come to our church with Jason Calder when they were high school kids.

Hugo Padilla, we discovered, came from Texas. He has a wonderful Hispanic sense of humor, and he's very smart. Hugo is the daytime gate manager for Southwest Airlines at the Manchester airport.

Peter and Olivia Crosby are in medical technology. They run an Internet-based business out of a home office that networks with hospitals and clinics who are interested in buying and selling sophisticated medical equipment. They have a three-year-old daughter.

The Jacobses and their son, Zachary, were next, and they were followed by Lara Anderson and Sara Stephens. A few days later we were with Thomas Sanders and Damon Marsh. There were several others after these, and every experience was full of learning.

For example, we learned that

- more than a few had only a superficial knowledge of the Bible;
- busyness and priorities were a perpetual challenge;
- only a few came from stable family backgrounds;
- some struggled to understand the place of prayer or personal worship;
- most of them spent little time with anyone outside of their generation; and
- many thought highly of Jesus but were often embarrassed to be called Christians.

AUGUST 10

The Second Summer

Dear Vince and Ginny,

You are one of a dozen couples Gail and I are writing to ask if you would consider entering into a yearlong relationship with a member of the CDP group that is being formed this year. We imagine a relationship in which you would meet with your "mentee(s)" once a month and talk with them about what they are learning in CDP and how it's helping them grow. We hope that you'd be willing to open yourselves up to them and let them learn something about your long journey of faith. We believe this would be a most unusual and memorable experience for you. If you're willing to consider this, would you meet Gail and me for a luncheon after church on August 21? Please RSVP.

Gail and Gordon MacDonald

YOU WILL FIND THIS HARD TO BELIEVE, BUT ALL TWELVE older married couples who received our letter accepted the invitation. One couple even canceled a weekend getaway to be with us.

When we met with these would-be mentors on that Sunday afternoon, Gail and I and the Fishers talked through our plans for the CDP year and described some of the men and women who were going to be part of this first group.

We went on to explain the role that mentors would play.

"Mentors," I told the group, "will provide a source of older-generational friendship and help reinforce what CDP people would be learning on Monday evenings. Their task is to listen, ask questions, and offer blessing and encouragement whenever possible."

Each mentoring couple would be assigned either a single person or a married couple. The CDP members would take the initiative to contact the mentors and arrange a meeting time each month. We hoped that mentors would entertain their mentees in their homes as frequently as possible and that they would share their lives with their mentees.

There were questions we hoped mentors would ask during every visit, such as:

- What's been happening in CDP
  meetings this past month?
- What do you think you've learned?
- What is God saying to you through
  the CDP experience?
- Where do you think you're deepening
  in your spiritual journey?
- What are you discovering about yourself?

Nothing in the process of building the CDP initiative had come as easily as putting together this group of mentors. Everyone except the O'Donnells were in their sixties, and they seemed eager to mix it up with younger people. Some admitted that they were nervous; nevertheless, they were willing to give CDP mentoring a try.

Carl Klaussen said, "I wish I was more confident that I had anything of value to offer these young people. They seem to be way beyond me in so many ways. But if you say they're interested in my story, then I'll tell it."

When the meeting was over, Monica and Tom O'Donnell approached Gail and me.

"This mentoring thing may need a bit more coordination and follow-up than you're imagining. What if we took this load off your shoulders and made sure the mentoring end of CDP works smoothly? This could be our way of contributing. We could report to Rich and Carly and take a bit of the burden off you two."

I could have kissed the O'Donnells. Gail did.

AUGUST 23

The Second Summer

To: CDP Group
From: GMAC
Subject: Facebook page

We have created a Facebook account called *CDP Group*. Look
it up and click on the group page. Please check it regularly
for pertinent announcements.

Post to CDP Group Facebook page

CDP Group
Our first meeting will be September 12 at 6 p.m. at our
home. Gail's planning for pulled pork sandwiches and
salad. Men bring drinks; women, store-bought dessert.
We have an hour to eat. Then we'll get started with
our meeting. We will be doing two important things:
(1) we'll ask some strange questions; (2) Gail will talk
about temperament.

Please download and print the attached reading
(*The Paul/Timothy Connection*). You'll need to be
acquainted with it before our second meeting.

The Paul/Timothy Connection

MEETING HANK SORIANO AT OUR ADJACENT MAILBOXES ON most mornings during the summer became almost routine. At first I assumed it was a coincidence in timing. Then one day it occurred to me that Hank must be watching for my front door to open. That was his signal to appear and engage me in conversation.

In the moment or two we had together each morning, we'd talk about the Red Sox game the previous night or something important that was on one of our schedules. Occasionally he'd ask about the CDP initiative.

This conversation is a sample.

"So when you having your first meeting with your secret group?"

"Good grief, Hank. It's not a secret group. Where'd you get—"

"Hey, just kidding, Mac. It's the CPR . . . no, the CDP group. So when's it beginning?"

"Monday evening, September 12."

"What's the first time going to be like?"

"Well, we're going to start the group off with a barbecue, and then we'll begin the first meeting with Gail's teaching on temperament."

"Who's going to help get that barbecue ready?" Hank asked.

"Me, I suppose," I said.

"Hey, look. I know that we can't come to the group meeting . . . it's secret and only for the people you picked. I get that. But how about if we come over and help prepare and serve during the barbecue part? Cyn and I will clean things up afterward, and you can get your meeting started. We'll do our thing upstairs and go our way. Wouldn't that help things a bit?"

"Well, to be honest with you, that would be an incredible gift, Hank. But you're a busy man, and Cynthia must have a lot on her plate."

"Trust me. We can always rearrange things. Cyn and I really

enjoy those people of yours. We like being with them whenever it's possible . . . Understand what I'm saying?"

I said that I understood what Hank was saying and told him that I would get back to him.

As I expected, Gail thought Hank's idea was terrific.

A DAY OR TWO LATER I MET WITH BRUCE, CLAIRE, AND Jason for our weekly staff meeting. Bruce and Jason had been gone on vacation, and I had promised that when they returned, I'd give them and Claire an overview of the CDP initiative.

Once again, I reviewed the list of people who would be in the group, careful to thank each of them for the recommendations they'd made during the spring months. We looked over the objectives that had been defined by the staff months before.

I went on to show them the list of leadership case studies we were going to use. And then I summarized our plans to cover temperament, the spiritual disciplines, the traits of Christian character, and the concept of call and spiritual gifting. We talked about the value of the dialogical approach that would be used. I spoke of the importance of prayer, storytelling, and shadowing leaders. Then I finished with a review of the mentoring component.

It was encouraging to sense the enthusiasm of the staff as we talked.

And then Jason Calder spoke. "Pastor Mac . . . Gordon. I don't know if this is the right time, but I do have a question for you."

"Shoot, Jason."

"I would kill to go through an experience like you've just described. We didn't get half that stuff in seminary . . . at least in a way that I could apply it to what I'm doing now. So my question is, and I'm speaking for myself right now, what would it take for you to do something like that with us staff people?"

"I guess I thought you'd probably be too busy," I said. "And sometimes, at least in my experience, we staff people seem to get so familiar with each other that we don't think we have that much to offer each other. So I never assumed that you'd be interested."

"I think you're wrong about that, Gordon," Claire said. "All three of us would love it if you could find a way to walk us through a similar experience."

"Jason and Claire are right on," Bruce said. "We kind of hoped that you might find a way to pull us into this loop of training. Lord knows, we could all use some deepening too. And, frankly, I'll tell you something else that you should know. You've got a bunch of lay leaders who are looking jealously at the CDP group and saying, 'Why just them? Why not us too?' Do you remember Ken Squires's comment last fall when we first introduced the CDP idea? And he's not the only one crying out for spiritual training. You and Gail have whetted a lot of appetites."

"So what are you telling me? Let me hear this clearly."

"The truth is," Claire said, "you've talked so much about cultivating deep people and how important it is for the church, that we've all gotten converted. You've challenged the church to release you to be more of a training pastor, and we've released you as best we know how. You want to train people? . . . Well, here we are."

I was dumbfounded. My fellow staff members were telling me that I'd been keeping my sights too narrow. I had a whole bunch of people on my hands who were hungering to grow. So what was I going to do about it?

This conversation continued for at least another half hour. The message was unmistakable. I was surrounded by people who were getting a vision of a deeper life of faith and service and were looking to me as their leader to help actualize it. When our staff meeting time was over, I could only say to the staff, "I'm blown out of the water by what you've said. I'll give it a lot of thought. I need a few days . . . maybe a lot of days."

SEPTEMBER 12

Morning, the Second Summer

From my journal

> *Interesting meeting with staff last week. They
> surprised me by saying that they covet something like a
> CDP experience. And Bruce says that there are elders
> and council members wondering how they might get in
> on this. If this business of investing in the training of
> others is a new call for Gail and me, we've got to take
> seriously what the staff said. Maybe we have to think
> about three circles of cultivation: CDP (tomorrow's
> leaders), CDP/staff (staff), and CDP/leaders (the
> lay leadership). What if I said to the staff and lay
> leadership, "20 percent of every meeting we will have
> from here on out will be devoted to training"? Would
> they buy into it? What if, in two or three years, we
> made a version of CDP a requirement for every leader?*

SEPTEMBER 12 FINALLY CAME. IT HAD BEEN FOURTEEN
months since the so-called great idea had sprung into being.
Now, of course, we no longer spoke of the "great idea"; we had all
become accustomed to using George Huntoon's name, CDP, to
identify our intention to cultivate deep people.

When I arose that morning, I spent some time in quiet. I lit up my computer and clicked on my "Reflections" file. I was fighting for concentration, and it seemed best to do my praying by typing (does God do e-mails?).

Father, it seems like a decade since the Sorianos and Gail and I went to the ball game and had that crazy conversation about elevator stories. And how long was it after that you moved on Rich Fisher to begin giving me quotes like the one from Richard Foster? I look back and think of the many, many conversations I've had with Gail, with Geoff, Monica, Mercedes, the staff, so many others. Even my Jewish friend, Michael Cohen. How much you have taught us.

I feel a strong call to this CDP idea. You've been gracious to a man like myself. You've put a new dream in my heart just when I thought there would be no more dreams. You've called me to pour my life into younger people wherever they're to be found and whenever they show openness. All I've got is my story, my experience, and what you've taught me from the Scriptures and from remarkable people I've read about and met. In the course of the months, you've given us new words, like *deep* and *deepening*, *cultivate*, *growable*, and *influence*, and they've come alive to us with a freshness of thought.

Thank you, Lord, for giving Gail the same sense of call so that we could share it together. My partnership with her on this has drawn the two of us so close. Then there's our relationship with Rich and Carly; the increasing warmth of our neighbors; the support of the staff people; the mentors. I could not be more thankful, Lord.

And then there's this increasing interest on the part of others in church leadership to enter into a new experience of cultivation. Father, what do I do with that?

And now tonight, we look forward to the first meeting with the CDP group. We've planned and prayed, and now it's in your hands to guide us and provide power wherever we need it. I pray already for what these men and women of the CDP group are going to become. Forgive me if I seem impertinent, but I find myself wanting to pray for them as Jesus prayed for the Twelve in John 17. You've loaned them to Gail and me for a short while. May we be faithful to you in these matters, and may you be pleased with the result.

SEPTEMBER 12

Early Evening, the Second Summer

Pastor MacDonald,

 I know that today is first day of CDP meetings. All morning long I pray for you and Mrs. MacDonald and Mr. and Mrs. Fisher. God give me assurance that this will be wonderful time.

Hana Tchung

AT ABOUT 5:45 P.M. THE CDP PEOPLE BEGAN TO ARRIVE. Everyone had gotten the message about promptness; no one was late. Hank and Cynthia had been with us for about forty-five minutes already, helping us set things up in the backyard. I found myself quietly laughing as I watched the two of them greet each CDP person warmly. The Sorianos had met most of them during the summer, so there were hugs and backslaps. I simply could not believe how much Hank and Cynthia acted as if they belonged in this circle of people.

And then for an instant I was reminded of some of the old saints, like Patrick and Francis, who seemed convinced that the best kind of evangelism began with making people feel welcomed into the community of Christ-followers even if they had yet to believe. Those saints were convinced that the love of Jesus' people could overcome any resistance from the hostile heart. Was that

258

what was happening here? Were Hank and Cynthia being drawn to Jesus without even realizing what was happening to them? If so, it was a wonderful spiritual trick that God was playing on them.

The barbecue dinner was a hit. As instructed, each person had brought his or her bit to contribute to the dinner. And now the 7 p.m. hour neared, and it was time for us to adjourn to the basement and begin our first CDP meeting. Hank and Cynthia insisted that we leave everything on the backyard tables, that they would take care of it all.

GAIL KICKED OFF THE EVENING.

"We're going to begin our time together tonight by going around the circle, each of us saying one sentence. I'd like the sentence to begin with the words, 'Today, I'm thankful for . . .' And I'd like you to complete the sentence by describing one thing that happened in your day for which you are grateful. It can be something that's simple or complex. I'll give everyone a minute to think about the day, and when I think we're ready, I'll begin."

The room became silent, the only noise to be heard coming from upstairs, where Hank and Cynthia Soriano were cleaning our kitchen.

When a few minutes had passed, Gail said, "As I hear the noise upstairs, I'm thankful for Hank and Cynthia and their desire to serve us all this evening."

Damon Marsh followed me. "I'm thankful that I learned today that my mother is cancer-free."

Catherine Jacobs said, "I'm grateful for Aunt Connie and her willingness to take care of our son, Zachary."

Thomas Sanders was next: "I'm thankful for the new contract my company got today that will keep our business alive and well."

Carly Fisher said, "I'm thankful to be in this lovely home that oozes with love and hospitality."

And so the prayers went on until I finished with my expression of thanks. "I'm thankful for all these wonderful men and women who have a desire to walk closer to Jesus. Amen."

Gail then said, "What we just did, in case it hadn't occurred to you, was pray. None of us used religious or sanctimonious words. We simply quieted ourselves and said thanks about things that were important to us or happened to us. These were simple, sentence prayers. Complex prayers are those where we add other items to the prayer menu.

"One of the first things Jesus' disciples asked was that he teach them to pray. They wanted to know how he prayed, why he prayed, and what he said when he prayed. His prayer would be a summary of his major themes. And that's what we'll see as time goes by: how important it is to learn how to pray. Because it's often in our praying that we learn what each other believes, what each other finds to be important. For example, I learned a minute ago that Damon's mother has just gone through a cancer scare. And now I know why Thomas is in such a good mood this evening. You learn those things when you pray together. Right now, the important thing is that every one of us just prayed. We just had our first prayer meeting!"

"Thanks for telling me that," Matt Cundiff said, grinning. "Now I'm really scared. I didn't know I was praying; I don't think I ever prayed out loud before." One or two others signaled agreement with Matt: they hadn't either.

GAIL AND I HAD TALKED MUCH ABOUT THE VERY FIRST THING we wanted the new CDP group to do. Getting acquainted, first impressions were all-important. We decided to use some questions that had worked well in the past whenever we wanted to help a group of strangers become quickly acquainted.

So after the prayer-sentences, I said, "Now that we've prayed, we're going to spend a while on three questions. That means we'll go around the circle three times, each of us answering each question in turn.

"The first question is, what is your major memory of life in the seventh grade?"

I didn't say it, but the question causes many people to reflect on a period of life fraught with emotional perils. Many look back at their seventh-grade year as a time of great disorientation, a period of awkward transformation from childhood to adolescence. It's a way of discovering that, even though we've been strangers, we have a lot in common.

Amy Bishop spoke first: "Right in the middle of my seventh-grade year, my family moved from Oregon to New Hampshire. I had to leave all my friends. In my new school there was no one that was interested in knowing me. All the clique groups were already formed. I was heartbroken."

Thomas Sanders went next. "I just remember that I was in John Glenn Junior High School and that I was the shortest kid in the class. If you're a boy, that's really bad. You don't want to be in the locker room showers when the big guys are around. I can still feel the snap of the towels."

Pete Crosby said, "I've been there; done that. I was pretty small too."

Sara Stephens remembered, "I had my first crush on a boy in the seventh grade. For the longest time I couldn't think of anything else but how to get his attention. And then one day he said something to me that was dirty . . . just plain filthy. I think it was the first time I realized how totally vulnerable I was and how hurt I could get. And I guess there have been other times since where I had a similar experience. But that was the first time."

Lara Anderson said, "Been there, done that too."

Pete Crosby said of his seventh-grade year, "That was the year that my parents told me they were separating. After that I only saw my father a few times a year because my mother moved my brother and me back to where her parents lived."

After we'd gone around the circle, I introduced the second question, which may have seemed even stranger: "When you look back into your childhood, what person or place do you associate with the word *warmth*?"

> **CARLY FISHER**: We had a woodstove in our fireplace, and in the winter, when I came down to breakfast in my pj's, my father always had the fire going strong. I loved to stand with my back to the stove and feel the heat.

> **GAIL**: Warmth for me was coming home from school every afternoon and smelling freshly baked cookies that my mother prepared for my brothers and me. It was her way of saying, "I love you."

> **DAMON MARSH**: I would associate warmth with my mother. My father was an angry man and a drinker. He was what you call a mean drunk, and when he was sober he had no memory of what he'd said or done to us. Thanks to AA he's in recovery now. But in those days all I had was my mother. She was the safest, the warmest place in all my world.

> **LARA ANDERSON**: Warmth for me was my dog, who always slept on the floor by my bed when I was a girl. He was like an alarm clock in the morning. He'd wake me up at almost the same time every morning by jumping up on the bed and licking my face.

> **SHERRY NORDBURG**: Sitting on my dad's lap after dinner each evening. I'd wrap my arms around his neck, and it seemed as if the whole world and I were at peace as long as I was with him.

BEN JACOBS: Sherry, I'd give anything if I could remember one single moment like you just described. There was no warm place or person in my home . . . I can only relate to the word now because of Catherine. She's showed me real warmth. But back then? No warmth whatsoever. Nada.

I asked the third question: "When in your life did you feel closest to God?"

MATT CUNDIFF: I was accused of stealing some money at school when I was in the ninth grade. The nuns, my parents, the priest . . . they all thought I was guilty. And I'd done nothing. Anyway, I was sent home from school, and my mother told me to go to my room and think about whether I had something to confess. So there I was, in my room . . . alone . . . and I had this incredible sense of God's presence. I thought I heard him say, "It's going to be okay." I laid on my bed and actually fell asleep. About an hour later, the phone rang. It was the priest back at school. Another boy had confessed to stealing. He told my mother to bring me back to school. I've never forgotten that God was there when no one else believed me.

HUGO PADILLA: My family was Catholic, too, Matt. We used to go to church every Sunday morning. I remember one day looking up at the statue of Jesus on the cross. And—I was about nine or ten—I felt like Jesus was really alive on that cross and that he was looking straight at me. I had this unbelievable feeling that he knew my name and that he was going to be there for me all my life. I've never forgotten that day.

RICH FISHER: The closest time for me was at an Urbana Missionary Conference. There were eighteen thousand students in the arena, and we began to sing an old Welsh hymn: "Guide Me, O Thou Great Jehovah." The leader asked the instrumentalists not to play, and all those thousands of students began to sing a cappella. The beauty of that hymn and the way we sang it made me feel as if I was in heaven.

THOMAS SANDERS: I went to camp every summer when I was a teenager. And when I was sixteen, I made a decision to become a Christian. I have always remembered how certain I felt that Jesus was right next to me, listening to my prayer to ask him into my life. I've always taken that moment seriously as the starting point of my spiritual journey.

OLIVIA CROSBY: Closest to God . . . When I held our daughter in my arms just after she was born. I couldn't get over how perfect she looked, and I saw God's glory in her.

CATHERINE JACOBS: I felt closest to God the night I met Ben. I had this strong feeling that God was saying to me, "This is the man who will love you all the days of your life. And you will see him grow to be someone you can greatly respect." And God is keeping that promise.

I can't explain it, but when we finished the third round of questions, it was as if there were no strangers in the room. We all knew something about each other that we probably would never have learned any other way.

SEPTEMBER 12

Midevening, the Second Summer

To: Tom and Monica O'Donnell
From: Rich and Carly Fisher
Subject: First CDP group

> Would you please tell all the mentors that the first night has
> been tremendous? We have a great group of people in this
> CDP group, and it's clear to us that God has some plans for
> every one of these men and women.

AFTER A MIDEVENING BREAK FOR REFRESHMENTS, WE
reassembled. For the first four weeks, the second half of the
evening would be Gail's time to teach the Myers-Briggs Temperament Indicator, one of a number of ways of assessing personality
preferences.

Two weeks earlier Gail had asked everyone to complete a
Myers-Briggs Temperament Indicator—a questionnaire designed
to identify personality preferences. When they were returned,
she spent almost an entire day analyzing them. After four weeks,
when she'd finished her teaching on the four sets of preferences,
Gail planned to show everyone the results of their indicators and
ask if they thought theirs was an accurate assessment of who they
saw themselves to be.

"I want you to know how I was led to get interested in the MBTI," Gail said by way of introduction. "In my reading of the Gospels, I was impressed that Jesus was always appropriate in his behavior. He didn't expect people to adapt to him; he adapted to them. If the moment called for him to be quiet and reflective, he was. If the moment required action and people involvement, he jumped right into the middle of things. If the moment needed a visionary, he became that.

"I began to think of the apostle Paul's comment: 'We have the mind of Christ.' And it hit me: if I have the mind of Christ, then I should be appropriate in my attitudes and behaviors too.

"No one should ever hear me say, 'Take me the way I am; I refuse to change.' And so I determined that I would work hard on adapting as Jesus adapted. That meant pushing myself to grow.

"Thirty years ago I signed up for training in the MBTI. And ever since, I've been studying Gordon's personality preferences and mine. And where it's been helpful, I've tried to come alongside others and show them how they could also learn how to adapt to situations as Christ did.

"Now, here's how I'd like us to start. I'd like for you all to pretend that your writing hand is completely disabled. All you've got left is your opposite hand to write with. Now, use that opposite hand to write your name in your notebook."

Everyone, including me, did as she asked and immediately began to exclaim over the clumsiness we felt.

"You've just learned your first lesson about temperament," Gail said. "You have a hand you *prefer* to write with. And if you can't use it, you are forced to write with your *less-preferred* hand. You feel awkward because your less-preferred hand is not developed for writing. It's the same with our temperament.

"In the next few weeks, we're going to learn something about the preferred and less-preferred sides of our personality. And what we're going to learn could change your view of yourselves and of those whom you love the most.

"Effective leaders work from their preferred side of their personalities but are always developing their less-preferred side. If you are working each day in a job that requires you to work out of your less-preferred side, you will experience exhaustion. Wise leaders know when this is happening, and they plan for it.

"Now, this is important for you to hear. Temperament study is not meant to lock us in. It is simply a way of knowing what we do most naturally. Think of it as a baseline for the growth and expansion of your personality. Both Gordon and I have found it useful in understanding ourselves and one another."

For the next hour Gail spoke of extroverts and introverts, the first of the four personality preferences.

Extroverts, she said, get energized by action and engagement with people. They speak or act first, then think. On the other hand, introverts—who sometimes seem to be quiet—get energized from within. Introverts prefer to think first and then act. They aren't shy; they just keep much of what they think to themselves until they are confident of how they want to express it.

Using the Scriptures, Gail said, "Simon Peter was probably an extrovert. And John the beloved disciple was probably an introvert."

People around the circle began to pepper Gail with questions as they saw themselves in her description of personality. I was delighted and amused as I saw the group more and more forget any self-consciousness and dive into this learning experience with Gail.

It was Catherine Jacobs who asked the question that Gail has become accustomed to hearing almost every time the MBTI system is taught.

"Gail, can I ever be different?"

"Oh, by all means, Catherine, so glad you asked what many others are probably wondering," Gail said. "Once we know our centers of strength—or how God has wired us—then we know where we need yet to grow. Gordon's an introvert, for example, but I've watched him develop his extroverted side for years. Most of you would never have dreamed that he's an introvert. That's because he's pushed himself to develop the other side. For all practical purposes he's now able to do both comfortably."

SOON, IT WAS 9:45, TIME TO WIND DOWN THE EVENING. There was a look of protest on almost every face. No one wanted this conversation to end. But we had to keep our covenant with each other: 10 p.m. was going-home time. And we needed to conclude the evening with prayer.

Just as I had asked people to begin the evening with single sentences, I asked them to do the same in the last minutes. This time their sentence was to focus on something that they were thankful they'd experienced during the evening.

> **PETE CROSBY**: I thank you that I've been welcomed into this home.
> **SHERRY NORDBERG**: I thank you for helping me discover that I'm an introvert and that I should not be ashamed of it.
> **MATT**: I thank you for a bunch of new friends.
> **HUGO**: I thank you that Jesus has been in this room tonight.
> **SARA**: I thank you for the joy of learning something new.

The thank-yous went on and on. The last came from Lara Anderson: "I'm thankful that someone cares enough to invite me into a deepening experience."

When we were finished praying, I said a final thing to the group. "I'd like to ask someone to accept the responsibility for coordinating the breakdown of the room at the end of each meeting. It simply means organizing people to make sure that all the furniture is restored to its former position. And then I'm going to ask a second person to do the opposite, by being here five minutes early next Monday and arranging the room for our time together. So who wants to be vice president for restoring things at the end? And who wants to be VP for arranging things at the beginning?"

Thomas Sanders said he would be VP of arrangements, and Sara Stephens volunteered to be VP of restoration.

Minutes later, the room was restored under Sara's supervision, and everyone was on their way out the door. Gail and I walked the Fishers to their car so we could gain a final impression of their thoughts.

"Unbelievable," Rich said. "They were into it within the first ten minutes. There's a real sense of connectedness. They're hungry to learn."

"I just loved Lara's final prayer," Carly said. "She seemed to understand exactly what this is about . . . 'invite me into a deepening experience.'"

We said good night, and as Carly turned on the engine, Rich rolled down the passenger-side window and said, "Good night, rabbis."

As we were walking back to the house, I heard the front door of the Soriano condo open.

"How did the evening go?" Hank asked from his front steps, Cynthia by his side. "We're dying to find out."

Gail and I walked up the driveway to where the Sorianos now stood. I gave a brief description of what had happened and indicated our pleasure at the result. Gail hugged Cynthia and thanked the two of them for what they'd done upstairs.

And then Hank said something I hadn't expected to ever hear from him. "You know, Mac, we were sure it would go well. But just in case you needed some help, we both said a little prayer for you when we got home."

SEPTEMBER 19

The Second Summer

From my journal

*All week long I've been "pestered" by elders, staff,
and others who have wanted to know how the first
CDP meeting went. People are really curious: What did
we do? How well did it go? I find myself anticipating
the moment when we meet again for the second time.
Something in me keeps saying, "I was made for this."*

AT 6:30 P.M. ON THE SECOND MONDAY, THOMAS SANDERS
(VP of arrangements), Hugo Padilla, and Matt Cundiff knocked
on our front door. As Thomas had promised, the three were there
to set up the basement for the meeting scheduled to begin in thirty
minutes.

After prayer, Gail and I planned to begin the evening with our
first Scripture case study, which was entitled "The Paul/Timothy
Connection." The reading had been linked to the new Facebook
group page two weeks before, and when everyone arrived, I saw
that everyone had their own marked-up copy.

Gail started the evening suggesting two rounds of sentence
prayers. "The first time around, we'll express our thanks for
something," she instructed, "and the second time around, we'll

271

say something that we appreciate about who God is or what he does."

When we'd finished praying, I introduced the reading.

"This is going to be the first time we read anything together," I said. "And through the year, we're going to do a lot of reading to each other. So let me talk about how I'd like to see us do it each time.

"First we're going to read the piece out loud even though we committed to reading it before coming here tonight. We'll go around the circle, and each of us will read a paragraph or two before the leader—I'm the leader this time—asks us to pause. At any time, whoever is leading may ask the reader to push the pause button because we need to stop and reflect on what we're hearing. There may be someone who finds reading out loud difficult and wants to slip into it slowly. If so, just say, 'Pass' when it's your turn.

"Now here's the important part. Whether you're reading or listening, look for key words or phrases that the author is using to make his/her point. Always ask yourself, *What is the author trying to say?* None of us should form an opinion about the reading until we are sure we know what the author is saying.

"The kind of conversation I'd like us to have with each other is called *dialogue*. It's a bit different from discussion. When we discuss things, we are tempted to compete with each other. Who's smarter? Who knows more? But dialogue means that we become a combined thinking machine, our hearts and minds all working together in the belief that we can come up with an idea or an insight that none of us could have produced by him- or herself. So think of what we're doing as *cooperative conversation*. We listen to the author, we listen to each other, and then we produce a conclusion *together*.

"Ben . . . I'd like for you to lead off the reading tonight. Just the Acts 16:1–3 segment, where Paul meets Timothy for the first time."

Ben Jacobs began to read. "Paul came to Derbe and then to

Lystra, where a disciple named Timothy lived, whose mother was Jewish and a believer but whose father was a Greek. The believers at Lystra and Iconium spoke well of him. Paul wanted to take him along on the journey, so he circumcised him because of the Jews who lived in that area, for they all knew that his father was a Greek."

Let me record the dialogue we had as if it were a play.

GMAC: Thanks, Ben. First thing we need to do is squeeze this paragraph for anything it can tell us about Timothy and his background. Okay, what information is the author trying to give us?

HUGO PADILLA: That Timothy's from a mixed family? His mother's Jewish, and his father's Greek or Gentile.

OLIVIA CROSBY: He must be youngish because he's identified by his family arrangement.

AMY BOYD: Timothy has a good reputation . . . People seem to like him.

THOMAS SANDERS: And Paul must see some quality in him that makes him want to take Timothy down the road with him.

GMAC: Does Paul's interest in taking Timothy down the road with him, as you put it, Thomas, remind you of anything similar elsewhere in the Bible?

There was no immediate answer.

CARLY FISHER: Well, isn't that what Jesus did? Find people and invite them to go down the road with him?

GMAC: Exactly. Paul's doing what Jesus did. Both were rabbis. You could call this the rabbinical contract. The teacher finds a student with potential and invites him to follow. Timothy is becoming a student of Paul's just as Simon Peter and the others became disciples of the Lord. Remind you of anything else?

HUGO: I think this is exactly what you and Gail are doing to us.

GMAC: Keep that in mind. As Paul saw something in Timothy, don't forget that we've seen something in each of you. Remember when we talked with each of you this summer about CDP? Remember how we told you why you were selected?

WE WORKED OUR WAY THROUGH OTHER SCRIPTURES THAT illuminated the Paul/Timothy connection: Philippians 2:19 and 1 Thessalonians 3:1–5. "What are you hearing in these paragraphs?" I asked. "What does it mean when Paul says of Timothy, 'I have no one else like him who takes a genuine interest in your welfare'?"

AMY: Seems like Timothy's a very caring man. In fact, Paul doesn't think there's anyone quite as compassionate as Timothy.

GMAC: So what kind of competence would you call that?

VARIOUS GROUP MEMBERS: Counselor? Healer? Sympathetic?

GMAC: How about pastor? Could Timothy be a pastoral type?

(Lots of "ums" and "yeses.")

GAIL: So freeze that word *pastor* in your mind. It describes a certain kind of person. Leaving Gordon and me out of this, is there anyone in this circle that strikes you as a *pastor*?

BEN JACOBS: No-brainer . . . Rich Fisher, and Carly too. They're pastors through and through, like Timothy.

GMAC: What makes you say that, Ben?

BEN: When I've been around them, I've never heard either of them talk about themselves. Their first interest is always in how someone else is doing. They are genuinely concerned about you. Seems to me that's a pastor, isn't it?

(Rich, who was sitting next to Ben, whispered a "Thanks," and Carly seemed to struggle with a bit of emotion.)

GMAC: Lara, could you please read 1 Timothy 4:12–16?

LARA ANDERSON: "Don't let anyone look down on you because you are young, but set an example for the believers in speech, in conduct, in love, in faith and in purity . . . Do not neglect your gift, which was given you . . . Watch your life and doctrine closely."

GMAC: So, what's Paul trying to say to Timothy?

THOMAS: That he was to be an example . . . even though he was young?

GMAC: An example of what?

THOMAS: Well, there are five categories here.

GMAC: Let's name them.

SOMEONE: Speech.

GMAC: Meaning?

MATT CUNDIFF: I guess it means the way one talks . . . Whatever comes out of his mouth . . . he's supposed to be an example of the way a Christian talks.

GMAC: What else?

SARA STEPHENS: Love . . . I suppose the way Timothy carried on his personal relationships.

> **RICH FISHER**: Life . . . how he maintained his private life, at the market, spending his money—if he had any—and the way he carried on his daily routines.

THE DIALOGUE WENT ON LIKE THIS FOR THE NEXT THIRTY minutes as we read various paragraphs describing Paul and Timothy and their mentoring relationship. The further we went, the more the group's interest grew. They stopped saying things tentatively as they grew confident that they had something worth offering and that it would be respected. They enjoyed ferreting out fresh insights. It was clear that some of them had never done this before.

There were many questions. Here are a few samples:

- "Aren't Paul and Timothy different in their personality preferences?"
- "Do you think Paul ever worried that Timothy was in over his head?"
- "Why does Paul like to talk about soldiers and athletes and farmers?"

"Let me throw out one idea before we put this paper away for the evening," I said. "When Paul talks about Timothy being an example, and when he talks about himself as an example, like in 'you know all about my teaching, my way of life, my purpose,' he's talking like a rabbi who believed that a lot of truth was best revealed in the actions of the mentor. There were no New Testament Scriptures as we have them today. So people had to learn by watching, studying the senior person, the rabbi. So Paul is talking rabbi-talk. 'Copy me,' he's saying. 'Then someday you, Timothy, can be the rabbi or a pastor—whatever you want to be called.'

"This could be our bottom line for tonight, and it's no small bottom line. *Leaders should conduct themselves in a way that allows others to see Jesus in them. Copy them, and you are copying Jesus.* That, folks, is one of the premier marks of a deepened person."

AFTER A MIDEVENING BREAK FOR REFRESHMENTS, GAIL LED us back into the subject of personality preferences. On this second evening she talked about people whose preferences are called *sensate* or *intuitive*.

"Sensates love detail," Gail said. "They see every tree in the forest. Intuitives, on the other hand, love the big picture. They see only the forest."

Gail asked us to read the story of Jesus' visit to the home of sisters Mary and Martha. She pointed out Martha's irritation that her sister, Mary, simply wanted to sit and listen to Jesus while there was work to be done in the kitchen.

"Martha was the sensate," Gail said. "She wanted to love the Lord by doing something for him, and she thought her sister should be with her, minding the arrangements for dinner. But Mary was the intuitive. The doing and the details were less important to her. She wanted to listen, to think, to learn. That was her way of loving the Lord. Now, both are good women. They're just showing their love out of different preferences.

"Just as Gordon and I are opposites in extraversion and introversion, we are opposites here also. I'm drawn to the details of how a room is decorated. Keeping the checkbook is my job. I wonder if all the birthday cards are going out on time.

"Gordon, on the other hand, is thinking about a book idea or what we're going to do next summer or where the CDP initiative might be three years from now. Details fly right over him."

Again, there followed what seemed to be a million questions as people guessed at their own preference and those of others.

"Gail," Olivia Crosby said, "can I ask you a personal question about this?"

"I'll try to answer, Olivia."

"Can you give me a specific example of where you and Gordon might clash because you're opposites? Because I think Pete and I—"

"Yes, I can. We're clashing right this minute. Gordon is sitting over there having an absolute ball listening to all of you work through this material. As far as he's concerned, time doesn't exist. If he has his way, we'll go on for another hour.

"But I happen to know it's 9:54 p.m., six minutes before 10:00, and we haven't prayed yet so that we can all go home."

"Now, I've finally got you figured out," Olivia Crosby said to Pete with a smile.

Soon people were streaming out the door. Only Sara Stephens and two others stayed behind to restore the basement. And within minutes they, too, were gone.

SEPTEMBER,
OCTOBER, AND
NOVEMBER

The Second Fall

To: GMAC
From: Roberto Silva
Subject: Update on the Sorianos

Olá, Pastor Mac,
We have been with the Sorianos three times. Hank and I
have similar business interests, and it has given us a point
of commonality for friendship. There are many things that
Hank does not understand about following Jesus, but he is
interested because of what he has seen in the lives of those
they've met at your home. We've told them our story of faith
in Jesus, and there have been a lot of questions. We will
keep meeting regularly.

Post to CDP Group Facebook page

CDP Group
For September 26: Read Abraham case study (see link).
Men bring juices; women bring cookies. October 4:

Read Joseph case study. October 11: First 3 chapters of
Oswald Sanders's *Spiritual Leadership*.

Abraham Case Study

THE NEXT FOUR WEEKS OF CDP MEETINGS WENT VERY
smoothly. Gail completed her teaching on personality preferences, describing *thinkers* and *feelers, judgers* and *perceivers*. (This is
all material you can find yourself in a book called *Please Understand
Me* by David Kiersey and Marilyn M. Bates.)

There was great satisfaction for Gail and me as we saw the
group begin to use the material in their relationships with each
other and apply it to other parts of their lives.

THOMAS SANDERS: For the first time I understand
my boss and his way of doing things. We have friction
from time to time, and now I see that most of it stems
from our difference in temperament. He's a big-picture
person (intuitive), and I'm a detail person (sensate). He's
always irritated with me when I start asking nitty-gritty
questions about the projects he wants to launch. And
I get bugged at him when he talks about big ideas but
doesn't count the cost.

HUGO: I think all us Hispanics must be extroverts. My
girlfriend? She's an introvert and wonders why I talk
so much.

LARA: Now I know why growing up with my family
was such a challenge for me. They love to talk—just
talk—about decisions, leave their options open, and
change their minds a dozen times. Me? I want to make
plans, close on decisions, and get on with life. So, now

that I see how we're made differently, I'm going to be more patient with them.

OLIVIA: You know, I never completely understood the Mary and Martha story in the Bible. Now I think I get it. They both thought they were serving Jesus. I know people who fit both descriptions and fall into conflict because no one ever showed them how they were wired.

EACH WEEK THERE WAS A READING. ON THE THIRD MONDAY night, for example, we read through the highlights of the story of Abraham. Gail led the dialogue.

"We want to read through the life of Abraham and see what we could learn about his conversion to the God of the Bible," Gail said. "And before we finish, I'd like for us to be sure we understand why Paul would have said that Abraham is 'the father of all who believe.'"

The reading took us through the moment when Abraham first heard the voice of God call him to leave his pagan homeland. We read about his strange treatment of his wife, Sarah, when he lied to the Egyptians about their relationship. Then there was the story of his nephew, Lot, which provoked a lot of conversation about the differences between the two men. We traced Abraham's doubts and his manipulative actions in trying to father a son. And then finally we reached the pinnacle of the Abraham story: God's call for him to go to the mountain and offer his only son, Isaac, as a sacrifice.

GAIL: So what do you think of this story from beginning to end?

AMY: I've never read the story straight through . . . The man at the beginning and the man at the end are two different people. When the story ends, Abraham is a truly converted man.

GAIL: How so?

AMY: The man at the front end of the story believes God enough to leave his home . . . but the man at the end is ready to give his son back to God. Big difference, I'd say.

DAMON MARSH: Excuse my interruption, Amy, but I was amazed that he'd leave his family, his assets, his whole way of life . . . and he didn't have much of an idea of where he was going. I'd have a rough time doing that. Maybe I hold on to things too tightly.

THOMAS: What do you mean by that, Damon?

DAMON: Well, I've played hockey just about all my life. It's kind of defined me. And now I'm having to think about life without it. Walking away from the ice is the most painful thing I've ever done.

RICH: I know where you're coming from. I felt that way once. It's the same struggle Abraham seemed to have. If he was going to be a man of faith, he had to learn how to hold everything loosely . . . his homeland, even his son.

SHERRY NORDBURG: Could I ask a question?

GAIL: Of course, Sherry.

SHERRY: Well, Abraham really doesn't do well in Egypt, but he's much more responsible in the Lot story where he allows Lot to take the best land and seems to go where God wants him to go . . . away from Sodom and everything. So what does that say?

CARLY: Maybe it means that he's deepening . . . that his faith in God is more mature than it was in Egypt. Hopefully, over this year we'll all do the same.

We talked like this for another thirty minutes and finally came to the mountaintop scene where Abraham's son was on the altar.

GAIL: Let's reread a few lines about Abraham's mountaintop experience with his son. Start with the first lines. Someone want to reread this?

BEN: "Some time later God tested Abraham—"

GAIL: Ben, could you pause there? Key word, anyone?

SEVERAL VOICES: *Tested.*

GAIL: We don't need to go into this for very long, but every deep Christian will tell you that testing is a part of life. Just as Jesus the rabbi tested his disciples regularly, God is testing Abraham here. It's an awful story, but we have to deal with it. Okay, Matt, can you pick up the reading?

MATT CUNDIFF: "Early the next morning, Abraham got up and saddled his donkey—"

GAIL: Sorry, Matt. We'll get through this, but anyone see anything of significance here?

LARA: He got up early and prepared for the trip to the mountain. I think I would have delayed, hoping that God would change his mind.

GAIL: Okay, bingo, Laura. Matt, can you keep us going?

Matt read on about how Abraham and his son, Isaac, climbed the mountain and how, at the top, Abraham began to prepare for the act of sacrifice.

MATT: "Then he reached out his hand and took the knife to slay his son. But the angel of the Lord called out to him from heaven, 'Abraham, Abraham!' 'Here I

GOING DEEP

am,' he replied. 'Do not lay a hand on the boy . . . Now
I know that you fear God.'"

GAIL: What's happening here?

PETE: The angel—or whatever the voice is—says that
Abraham finally fears God. It took all these years for
Abraham to hear those words. He feared God.

GAIL: Sound like a deep person to you?

HUGO: A lot deeper than I'd be.

GAIL: Okay, I have this question. If you were to take
Abraham as the quintessential deep person and ask
God to build into your life as you have seen God build
into Abraham's, what would you pray for?

The answers to Gail's questions sounded like this:

- "Give me the courage to follow you away from places
  I used to think were safe."
- "Help me to be more aware when I'm compromising
  my faith to please others."
- "Give me eyes like Abraham's to see that it's better to
  turn to the hills and avoid the temptations of Sodom."
- "Could I please do a little better than Abraham did when
  it comes to trusting the Lord for things like a son?"
- "May I have the strength to be as obedient as
  Abraham became when the day came to climb that
  mountain."

GAIL: I think God would love to hear those prayers.
They sound like the prayers of deepening people to me.

AS THE WEEKS PASSED, WE STUDIED THE LIVES OF OTHER
biblical heroes. Joseph, for example, became a hero to everyone

284

for his integrity and leadership. But what really stunned the CDP group was the challenge he faced in forgiving his brothers and overcoming his experience of abandonment and rejection by his family.

Everyone enjoyed Moses because they were able to see in detail his deepening as a leader. The business-oriented people took great delight in Moses' organizational skills and in his father-in-law's insights on organizing people. We all learned a lot from Moses' struggle with patience and his pattern of worshipping God.

We studied the prophet Samuel and the day he searched for a new king of Israel. We dialogued about Gideon the faith-builder. And then there was King David, the sinner-saint. David's life forced the CDP group to think carefully about the meaning of repentance and forgiveness as they talked through the reasons for his sin and his tendency to go into denial.

On one of the evenings, we began a reading of Oswald Sanders's classic book *Spiritual Leadership*. Early in the book Sanders wrote, "The true spiritual leader is concerned infinitely more with the service he can render God and his fellow men than with the benefits and pleasures he can extract from life. He aims to put more into life than he takes out of it."

It took the CDP group a long time to get past the implications they sensed in those words.

It wasn't long before Rich and Carly were leading some of the dialogues and doing it just as they'd seen Gail and me do it. Carly surprised me with her ability to tease insights out of people in the circle. Rich was in every sense a leader, and you could see the wealth of experience he'd accumulated in the classroom and in the administrative life of the high school.

Gail and I became more confident with every passing week that the Fishers were the perfect choice for partners in the CDP program and that they would be handling their own CDP group next year better than we could do it.

After we'd finished studying temperament, the group began studying the so-called spiritual disciplines. Gail and I outlined some of the ways the Bible called people to a life of devotion.

We talked, for example, about the principle of Sabbath. "For Israel, Sabbath was the most important day of the week," I said, "and to observe it required backing away from life's routines to refresh oneself in the presence of the Lord. It would be almost impossible for any of us to do it for a full day a week. But how about starting with a half hour each day? Then, later on, maybe an hour?"

For everyone in the CDP group, the Sabbath principle of *spiritual pause* caused more frustration than any subject so far because it spoke to everyone's struggle with busyness. We could only conclude that the Sabbath pause for quietness and worship and hearing God speak was possible if we surrendered some things in life that we truly liked to do. Sabbath, we agreed, could not be added to our schedules. It had to take the place of some things already there. That was not good news to everyone.

We spent time talking about how to read various parts of the Bible and internalize what we were reading. We even looked at the structure of the Bible, its division into Older and New Testaments. One night we reviewed the sections of the New Testament and talked about the purpose of each of the small letters that Paul and the other apostles had written.

Then there was the subject of meditation, or reflection, something more easily understood by the introverts and harder for the extroverts.

We talked about certain kinds of reflective questions that might help a deepening person keep in touch with his or her own heart:

- What events in the past day have had significant meaning to me?

- Was there a time when I felt God speaking to me today?
- Was there anything I did today that troubled me?
- Were thanksgiving and praise on the tip of my tongue today?
- Did I have any sense of God's love today?

Of course, this meant that we got into the discipline of journaling. The group was shocked—just plain shocked!—when Gail and I brought out a bunch of the journals we'd been keeping for forty years. They could not imagine taking time most mornings to describe our impressions of God's voice in our lives.

When the conversation ended, we managed to get everyone to agree to write in a journal every day for two weeks. Then we would take the time to talk about their experience.

Naturally, we spent time on prayer and its place in life. We all agreed it was among the most necessary disciplines for a deepening person. Yet, we all admitted, it was one of the most difficult for most of us to manage.

In early November Gail and I introduced the group to the writings of some of the great spiritual masters of the Christian prayer movement: Augustine, Thomas à Kempis, François Fénelon, and Brigid Herman. We read small selections from each writer.

What was interesting to note was how the prayers of the CDP group began to take on more substantial content each week. As members of the group listened to each other and as they came into contact with unusually deep people from the past, they enlarged their prayers in the group to include new themes and new spiritual interests. Now we were no longer praying sentence prayers; we were expressing more and more of our hearts to the Lord as we gained confidence that he was actually hearing us.

MERCEDES PEREZ WAS OUR FIRST GUEST AT A MONDAY evening CDP gathering. She told her story of faith and described her professional advancement. Mercedes was quite open about the "testings" that she felt were significant in her life journey. The women in the CDP group were obviously filled with admiration as they realized that Mercedes had managed to excel in the business world yet had maintained her devotion to Christ.

Later in the evening, I heard one of our CDP women say to another, "I've seen Mercedes sitting in worship services again and again. It never dawned on me that I should get to know her. She's a gold mine of wisdom."

Among the most important things that Mercedes said to the group was, "This Sabbath principle that Pastor Mac and Gail told you about? It is indispensible. You cannot—trust me on this— cannot live a long and healthy life if you do not know how to say no to certain things and yes to the best things. And you sort out those decisions in your quiet, Sabbath moments, not while you're on the run."

Wilford and Martine Jean-Baptiste visited on another evening. I asked them to talk about what suffering looks like in a country like Haiti. Would they be willing, I asked, to tell the story of their experience in the Haitian earthquake and how they had faced the death of so many of their friends and family members?

Both Wilford and Martine were eloquent, even luminous, as they spoke of the themes of grace and perseverance in their lives. The group hung on every word as the Jean-Baptistes described their sorrow, the necessity of processing their grief, the ways in which God had opened the door for them to come to America and study at Franklin Pierce.

At the end of their story, I invited the group to ask Wilford and Martine questions, and a while later, I suggested prayer for them.

"Could we gather around Wilford and Martine and lay our hands on them as we pray?" Matt Cundiff asked.

Everyone agreed with Matt's idea, so we did as he suggested.

"Sara, Pete, and Damon, could you start us off with very brief prayers that you think would mean something to these two wonderful people? Then if the rest of you have something to say in prayer, you can follow. Carly, I'll ask you to give the ending prayer."

PETE: Lord, these two people are saints. Yes, that's what they are. Thank you for leading them through such difficult moments and bringing them here to our church and our community.

SARA: Heavenly Father, I don't think I ever saw such true joy as I've seen tonight. Pete says they're saints, and I agree. I pray that their joy will never be taken away.

DAMON: God, may I add the word *champion* to saints? They're champions, Lord, not quitters, champions. I'd like to be like that. I never knew there were such incredible people right around us. Make them very, very strong.

Others began to pray: "I think I got a glimpse of Jesus in these two people tonight, Lord. Thank you." "Fill them with your power, Father." "Please restore their stricken country. So many suffering. Maybe you'll call some of us to go there someday."

NOVEMBER 7

The Second Fall

Card to Hana Tchung, via snail mail

Hana,

Your prayers are being answered. CDP is going very, very well. When you are at church, shout louder to God.

Pastor MacDonald

Card to Olivia Crosby, via snail mail

Olivia,

You're greatly loved by all of us; now you're greatly prayed for. You and Pete will not be alone as you walk through this. There are fourteen people who I think, if necessary, would die for you. You will beat this, Olivia.

Gail

Post to CDP Group Facebook page

CDP Group

Please finish reading Sanders by November 7. Question: What does Sanders mean when he says, "The overriding need of the Church . . . is for a leadership that is authoritative, spiritual and sacrificial"? Note his explanation of those words, and ask yourself what it takes to build those qualities into one's life.

ALMOST EVERY MONDAY NIGHT WITH THE CDP GROUP brought some kind of a surprise. Mostly, the surprises were wonderful, exciting. But some were not.

There was the November Monday night, for example, when Damon Marsh called me during the dinner hour and said, "Pastor Mac, I can't make it tonight."

"What's up?" I asked.

"My boss wants me at the store at 7:00 for a special meeting of the managers."

"Damon, we've got a covenant that says that we make Monday nights our priority. Didn't you and your boss—"

"Yeah, we worked it out a long time ago. But tonight is a special meeting . . . I just gotta be there."

"Okay, Damon, I understand. Do what you have to do. We'll miss you. The meeting will be different without you."

ON THAT SAME NIGHT, NEAR THE END OF THE MEETING, THE Crosbys told the group that Olivia might have breast cancer. A week earlier Olivia had detected a growth in her breast. Her doctor had done a biopsy and found the results to be inconclusive. Further tests were necessary, Pete and Olivia said, and she would be seeing a specialist later in the week.

When we prayed for Olivia and Peter that night, almost everyone cried. This is what true community means: when one experiences fear or pain, everyone experiences it.

I was in my office on Tuesday morning when Rich Fisher called me. We often connected for a few minutes the morning after CDP just to compare our impressions of the previous night's meeting. I valued Rich's perspective, and he appeared to value my commentary on why and how Gail and I had done what we did.

In the course of our conversation, I said, "I missed Damon last night. I was under the impression that he'd worked out an agreement with his boss so that he wouldn't have to—"

"Gordon," Rich said, "Damon wasn't at work last night." There was a brief silence, and then Rich said, "We may have a problem."

"What are you saying?"

"I've got a copy of the morning paper right here on my desk," Rich said. "I was reading the sports page just before I called you, and in the hockey section I noticed that the Beavers [our city's club team] played Nashua last night. The game summary says that Damon Marsh scored two goals."

"Must have been a real late-night game then, because Damon was—"

"Gordon, I checked. The game started at 7:30 p.m., and Damon played in all three periods . . . In fact, he scored both his goals in the first ten minutes."

"But Damon said nothing about a game. He told me he had to go back to work."

"I've followed Damon," Rich said, "for the last few years ever since he graduated from here. He played hockey for our school and then for Plymouth State. He was always gung-ho hockey. After Plymouth State, I thought he'd put away his skates, but apparently not last night."

NOVEMBER 8

The Second Fall

BEAVERS SHUT OUT NASHUA 3-0
Damon Marsh, former Plymouth State forward,
scored two first-period goals last night as the
Beavers increased their winning streak to 5 . . .

To: Rich Fisher
From: GMAC
Subject: Damon

Pray. I'm going to have to see Damon before this day is over.

DAMON MARSH HAD LIED TO ME. I MUST HAVE SAT AT MY
desk for thirty minutes trying to sort out what had happened. It
was one thing to miss a Monday night CDP meeting because of a
work situation. But it was another thing to lie about the real reason. How to handle this matter? In the first two months of CDP,
nothing like this had happened.

Finally, I called Gail and told her what I'd learned about
Damon. She was in as much disbelief as I was. "You can't let this
linger," she said. "Damon needs to know as soon as possible that
we're aware of his lie. And we're going to have to make a decision:

do you allow someone to remain in the CDP group when they make a choice like this?"

Soon it was lunchtime. I was scheduled to meet Geoff Handley and Monica O'Donnell at Olive Garden.

I'm not sure I even remember the things Geoff, Monica, and I talked about because I was preoccupied, feeling increasingly angry and sad at the same time about the Damon Marsh thing. I kept my thoughts to myself, but Geoff and Monica must have been aware that their pastor was somewhere else—mentally, anyway—as the lunch conversation went on.

Dick's Sporting Goods is only a block or two away from Olive Garden, so, when the lunch ended, I drove over there and entered the store. I learned that Damon was not due into work until 3:30 p.m. Returning to my car, I called his cell phone.

"Marsh," he answered.

"Damon, Pastor Mac calling."

"Oh, hi, Pastor Mac, what's up?"

"Stopped by the store to see you. They said you're not due in till 3:30. Any chance we could grab a few minutes before you go to work?"

"Sure. I could meet . . . What time's good for you?"

"How about 2:45?"

"Okay. The church or the store or where?"

"Dick's will be good, Damon. I'll be in my car. See you then."

I CALLED RICH FISHER'S OFFICE, AND HE CAME ON THE LINE.

"I'm going to meet Damon at Dick's at 2:45. Is there any chance at all you could—"

"I'll meet you there at 2:30," Rich said.

When I called Gail and told her what was going to happen, she said she'd call Carly and that the two women would pray for us.

AT 2:30, I RETURNED TO DICK'S PARKING LOT AND MET Rich.

"You don't have to say a thing, Rich. Just listen and tell me what you heard later."

A few minutes later, Damon Marsh pulled in beside my pickup. I motioned to him to join me in my car. Rich had moved to the backseat.

"Sorry you couldn't be there last night, Damon. We wanted—"

"Sorry I wasn't there too. Boss calls these meetings sometimes at the last minute, and—"

"Damon. Let's look each other in the eye and speak truth. The sports page this morning says you scored two goals last night in the Beavers game. I'm also noticing a bruise on your cheek that wasn't there on Sunday. Looks like a high stick to me. Do we have some facts wrong, Damon?"

There was a long silence as Damon stared out the windshield of my car.

Then he said, "I scrimmage a lot with the Beaver team, to keep up my game and all that. Yesterday morning the coach called and asked if I could play for the team last night. One of the guys was—"

"Damon, Rich and I don't need to know all that. What we need to know is why you lied. There was no store meeting, was there?"

"No, there wasn't. I just knew that telling you that I was going to skip the CDP meeting because of a hockey game wouldn't fly. So I took the easiest way out. Sometimes I wonder if I'm addicted to hockey. When the coach called yesterday morning, I just couldn't say no. And so I called you . . . and . . . I'm sorry. I'm really sorry. I wouldn't hurt you guys for anything. I just screwed up. It will never happen again."

The three of us talked for a little while longer until I felt there was nothing more to say except to bring closure to what had happened.

"Damon, many of us have lied to someone somewhere along the way. And then we discovered that it's one of the worst of betrayals. You've got my forgiveness. Let's put this behind us and remember the lesson that's been learned. You made a commitment for Monday nights. Do you still want to keep it?"

"Absolutely. I love every one of those guys. When the game was over last night, I didn't hear anything anyone was saying about my play. I just felt horrible because I knew where I was supposed to be and that I'd lied to you. All I could do was hope that no one would find out. I swore to myself that I'd never do it again."

Rich and I prayed for Damon and spoke in our prayers about fresh starts. Then we got out of the car and gave him a hug before he left us to go into work.

After Damon was gone, I said to Rich, "That's the way we have to handle things when we commit to cultivating deep people. Respectful, loving confrontation, rebuke, grace. He'll be a better man because of what he's learned. But man, this has really squashed my spirit. I'm shot."

NOVEMBER 10

The Second Fall

On my voice mail

> "Hey, GMAC, Soriano here. Any chance you and Gail have a few moments tonight? Cynthia and I would like to come over if it's possible."

DURING THE FALL, HANK AND CYNTHIA SORIANO HAD BEEN present in Sunday worship from time to time. They usually sat near the rear of the worship center.

Over the past few weeks, our contact with our neighbors had been minimal. Mailbox conversations were rare in the colder mornings. Hank had taken several business trips, and Cynthia had been spending several days at a time with her aged mother in Rhode Island.

On my end, I was deep into CDP activities, and there were many conversations with Geoff Handley and Bruce Bartlett about readjusting my responsibilities as senior pastor. Church life was always busy, and there were lots of people who needed pastoral attention.

When I got Hank's voice mail, I texted him immediately that we'd be home that night and if they wanted to come over around 8 p.m., we'd have some coffee and apple pie that Gail had made.

"Do you think anything's wrong?" Gail asked me when I got home that evening. "Maybe they want to tell us that they've tried church and found it not to their liking."

"Let's wait and try not to jump to conclusions." And so we waited. But secretly I shared Gail's concern.

At 8 p.m. exactly that night, the Sorianos were at our front door. We didn't realize how much we had missed the more frequent contact of the summer and early fall months until we saw them in our home. There's something about Hank Soriano that I really love.

Soon we were seated, eating apple pie and drinking coffee. "So what's happening? You strike oil or something?" I asked.

"No oil. But maybe something just as good," Hank said.

"Just as good? Don't keep us guessing."

"Well, you probably know that we've been getting together with the Silvas. Five or six times now. They're really incredible people. Some of your real 'deep people.' I've rarely met a guy like Roberto in all my life. And Cyn—"

"I think the same about Adriana," Cynthia said. "The two of them . . . they just drip with the joy of the Lord."

"The joy of what?" I asked.

Gail sat forward in her chair. This wasn't language we were used to hearing from the Sorianos.

"The joy of the Lord . . . you know . . . Oh, come on. Tell them, Hank," Cynthia said.

"Okay. Ahh . . ." Hank exhaled loudly as if he were trying to get the nerve to say something big. "Last night we were with Roberto and Adriana, and Adriana asked us if we had ever considered becoming followers of Jesus. Over the past weeks they've had us reading the stories of Jesus in the Bible. Then they get us to come over and talk about what we've learned. And I'll tell you, they've been great, very patient, helping us understand what Jesus-following means. Understand what I'm saying?

"Both Cyn and me have been interested because we've met so many people right here in this house who have impressed us. We like being with them. And Roberto and Adriana finally explained to us what we were seeing. All these people we like so much and want to know better, they have one thing in common. They've all, Roberto said—one way or another—organized their lives around Jesus.

"Those words made sense to Cyn and me. We've been organizing things at work all our lives. But what we've never done before or after we got married was think about how you organize yourself. So the Silvas asked us if we'd like to become part of this group of people we like so much by making the same choice they've made.

"So when they asked us if we'd like to make the choice, I looked at Cyn . . . she looked at me . . . and we decided right there, yeah . . . we would. So last night we said prayers to Jesus with Roberto and Adriana, and I guess we're Jesus fans now. Understand what I'm saying?"

Jesus-following? Jesus fans? When had I ever heard anyone describe their initial conversion experience with terms like that? But I certainly did understand what Hank was saying.

Gail went around the table to where Cynthia was sitting and hugged her tightly. Hank and me? We exchanged high fives.

All I could say to my neighbor was, "Welcome to the community. Welcome, welcome, welcome. You're my neighbor, my friend, and my spiritual brother."

There were tears all over my face. I couldn't restrain them. My neighbor, Hank Soriano, the guy who used to think I was "president" of the church, had just told me that he'd decided, along with his wife, to become a Christian . . . well, a Jesus fan. He got it!

A moment later, Hank said, "So do you think that we could

get considered for the second CDP team when you select people next year? This year we'll simply help you out any way we can."

WHEN GAIL AND I WENT TO BED THAT NIGHT, OUR HEARTS felt as if they were exploding. We had joy because Hank and Cynthia were going down the road as new followers of Jesus. But we also had sorrow because Peter and Olivia Crosby might be in serious trouble—there was no news yet.

These four people—the Sorianos and Crosbys—they were our people, our sons and daughters in faith. When you give your hearts to people like these, their joy becomes your joy; their sorrow becomes your sorrow.

NOVEMBER 11

The Second Fall

To: Geoff Hanley, Monica O'Donnell, Pastoral Staff, Rich
Fisher
From: GMAC
Cc: Carly Fisher
Subject: News

The Sorianos came over to our home last night. They told
us that they've made a decision to follow Jesus. The Silvas
have been meeting with them each week, and the other night
Hank and Cynthia decided they wanted to be followers of the
Lord. A big part of the reason? What they have seen in the
people (CDP group, mentors, etc.) who have been in and out
of our home for the past months. I think that's the way a
lot of evangelism is going to be done in the future. A loving
community radiates the love of Christ. Others are drawn to it.

To: Rich Fisher, Carly Fisher
From: GMAC

I think Gail and I need to get away for a few days in December.
So we're going to place CDP in your laps on 12/5. We'll ask the
Sorianos to have the house open and refreshments ready. I'll
remind Thomas and Lara about furniture arrangements.

IT WAS ABOUT THIS TIME THAT I SUGGESTED TO GAIL THAT we should plan to get away to warmer weather for a few days. The week of December 5, almost three weeks away, seemed just right, I said, since Christmas would be two weeks away. We'd done no serious vacationing during the summer, I said, and it might be good for us to drop out for just a short while.

"That means we're going to be gone for a CDP meeting?" Gail said.

"Yeah, we are."

"But that's an important Monday night."

"Right . . . it's important. But it's also important that we go away. Not just for ourselves, but for Rich and Carly. This will be their first opportunity to lead an entire CDP evening on their own. And it will be good for both them and the group if we're not there.

"I was thinking about Michael Cohen's description of the rabbinical contract the other day. He made the point that a rabbi sometimes intentionally separated from his learners so they could discover what they'd learned and what they could do when he wasn't there. Rich and Carly are gaining confidence that they can partner in leading their own CDP group next year. So in the words of Jesus, 'It is good for them that we go away.'"

"So that's your rationalization for getting a little vacation," Gail teased.

"Call it the voice of Gordon the rabbi," I said with exaggerated pomposity.

THE NEXT MONDAY, NOVEMBER 11, THE CDP GROUP MET at 6 p.m. Over the weekend Cynthia Soriano had told Gail that she'd enjoy making a kettle of New England clam chowder, some homemade Italian bread, and a salad, if anyone wanted to come early. When we placed a message on the Facebook group page, everyone but the Crosbys responded within hours, saying they would be there.

Pete Crosby phoned to say that he and Olivia would not be there until 7 p.m. because they were scheduled to see Olivia's doctor and learn the results of her latest tests.

When we gathered to give thanks for the food, you could tell that everyone was mindful that Pete and Olivia were conferring with the doctor at that very minute. Lara Anderson asked if we could pray for them. As I listened to each of the prayers that followed, I was startled by the spiritual maturity evidenced in what was said. In just a matter of weeks, young men and women who had at one time felt awkward about praying were now confident that God was hearing them and would respond.

At one point there was a few seconds of silence, and I heard Cynthia Soriano clear her throat and begin to pray. Apparently, she and Hank had come from the kitchen and joined us.

"Dear God," Cynthia prayed, "I have been where Olivia is at. I've known the fear she must be facing . . . such terrible fear. Please, God, give Olivia courage. And help her husband, Peter, to be strong for her."

Then followed Hank's voice, not brash, not arrogant, but humble. "And Jesus, I've been where Pete is at. I know how difficult it is"—his voice cracked—"to try to be strong for your wife, whom you love, when you're worried as hell . . . I mean, heck. You help them, Jesus. You can do this."

You could sense that everyone was touched by the simplicity and straightforwardness of what Hank and Cynthia had said.

When we finished, I went over to the corner of the room where Hank and Cynthia were standing and said quietly, "After we've eaten, is there any chance you might want to tell everyone what happened to the two of you last week?"

Hank stared at me for a moment. Then he turned to Cynthia

and said, "That something you . . . ?" Cynthia nodded vigorously. Hank then looked back at me and said, "Yeah, I can do that."

A half hour later, I asked for quiet. "We need to thank Hank and Cynthia for this incredible supper." Everyone cheered. "And the Sorianos also have something they want to say to you," I added.

Hank stood up. "Mac . . . I mean Pastor Mac . . . thought maybe you'd be interested to hear about something that Cynthia and I did the other night. We've had a lot of wonderful experiences in these years we've been married. But one of our best experiences has been getting to know Gail and Gordon and, because of them, meeting all of you.

"We've never been with any people quite like all of you. You're full of excitement . . . you like each other . . . you want to be deep people. As time has gone by, we've found ourselves saying that we'd like to be part of a group of people like you. A couple of months ago, Mac introduced us to Roberto and Adriana Silva, and we've been getting together with them, kind of like our own private CDP meeting. And the other night when we were with them again, we prayed and told Jesus that we'd like to be followers, if he'd have us, and—"

Hank never got to finish his sentence because all around him people exploded into cheers and applause. There were hugs and backslaps all around as people in the CDP group gathered around Hank and Cynthia to express their excitement that the Sorianos were part of our spiritual family.

While all this was going on, the cell phone in my pocket began to vibrate. Pete Crosby's name blinked on the screen. I stepped out of the room, away from the noise, and answered, "Hi Pete. What can you tell me?"

"It's benign, Pastor Mac," Pete said. "It's benign! Olivia will have day surgery in a couple of weeks, and this thing will be over and done with. We can't wait to get to your house and share the good news with all of you."

"Pete, I'm thrilled. You two get here as soon as you can. The clam chowder is still hot, and your friends are waiting for you."

I went into the living room and told everyone what I'd just learned. If anything, the noise of genuine joy increased. And in the middle of the praise were Hank and Cynthia Soriano. They were as excited as anyone.

NOVEMBER 15

The Second Fall

To: Rich Fisher, Carly Fisher
From: GMAC
Any chance we could get together in the next week or so
and review the first three months of CDP?

To: Gail MacDonald
From: Carly Fisher
Rich and I would love it if you and Gordon could join us for
dinner on Tuesday, November 22. Possible?

To: Carly Fisher
From: Gail MacDonald
Possible! What can I bring?

"I'M GOING TO HAVE LUNCH AT THE HOSPITAL TODAY WITH
Lara Anderson," Gail told me at breakfast the morning after our
weekly CDP meeting.

"What's up?" I asked.

"She wants to talk to me about her work life and some of the
challenges she faces at the hospital. So we're getting together.
What's on your plate?"

"Oh . . . staff meeting this morning. I have a couple of

meetings in the afternoon that I'd love to dodge but can't. Then elders for dinner and a meeting at six. I'll be home around nine thirty."

I ARRIVED BACK HOME A LITTLE AFTER 9 P.M. GAIL WAS waiting for me, and we watched the evening news together. (We usually TiVo the news each evening in case we're gone during the news hour.) After we'd watched the headline portion of the news, we switched off the TV so we could talk about our days. Gail insisted I go first.

I told her about my weekly staff conference with Bruce, Claire, and Jason. We'd taken the first sixty minutes for what we were now calling CDP-Staff.

I should tell you that when Jason and the others told me back in September that they would love to experience something similar to what we were going to do on Monday nights, I took their idea seriously. Early in October we'd begun allocating sixty minutes at the beginning of every staff meeting to cover issues of spiritual growth and leadership competency.

This morning had been our fifth CDP-Staff experience. We'd read through the same biblical material on Abraham's conversion that the CDP group had done earlier. It led us to review the Hank and Cynthia Soriano story and how their commitment to Christ a few days earlier was the result of being drawn into the community of Christians: friendship with neighbors, exposure to the CDP group and others, and finally, a more specific encounter with the Silvas. It seemed clear to us that this was going to be the way of evangelism in the future: inviting people into the company of Christians and letting them observe the love of Christ for themselves. The Holy Spirit would make their time of commitment clear.

Gail wanted to know about the elders' meeting, and I simply

told her that it was mostly about routine church business: financial reports and a presentation by the people in our children's ministry. Overall morale was good, it seemed. Geoff Handley had asked me to say a few words about the CDP group, and I was able to tell them some thrilling stories about prayer and the way the group was forming a tight sense of community.

And what had Gail's day been like? I wanted to know.

"I had the most incredible time with Lara at the hospital," she said. "Over lunch she shared what the group has come to mean to her. The emphasis on prayer has touched her deeply. And the readings have brought her heart and her mind to life again. She's watching and learning from how we ask questions. And she's excited to see how we get people working together as a group. I can tell you this: Lara is deepening by leaps and bounds.

"We spent much of the time talking about her job and its daily challenges. She enjoys the people she works with, and it's clear that they have a lot of respect for her.

"After lunch I met Lara's boss and her assistant," Gail continued. "Then we toured the hospital, and, once again, I got a chance to see how much she's appreciated. What occurred to me was that I was beginning to see Lara in a whole new light by coming to her world, where she's the expert. When she's at our house or at the church, we're the experts, if you know what I mean. But there, at the hospital, it was different."

"Funny we've not thought about this before," I said. "You know how important it is to me to visit church leaders where they work. Perhaps we ought to do the same for the CDP group. What if, over the next several weeks, we tried to visit each CDP person where they work? I could do the men, you the women."

We agreed to try and make it happen.

OVER THE NEXT COUPLE OF WEEKS, GAIL AND I SCHEDULED times (usually lunches) with members of the CDP group. My first get-together was with Hugo Padilla. He had to get permission from his boss at Southwest Airlines for me to visit. Even the TSA got into the process because I had to go through security to reach some of the places where Hugo works.

Hugo's fluency in both English and Spanish put him in a unique position at Southwest. He managed all gate activity, and all gate agents reported to him. Hugo was the first to be summoned if there was any problem or situation that was outside the normal routines. Because his mother tongue was Spanish, he was the go-to guy when there were Hispanic passengers in need of assistance. And the list of Hugo's responsibilities did not stop there.

While I was there, I watched Hugo intervene in a couple of situations with passengers who were upset. In a short time he resolved their complaints to the satisfaction of everyone. Later, I told Hugo how much I admired his capability to gain people's confidence and put them at ease.

Gail visited Amy Boyd (buyer for Macy's), Sherry Nordberg (city library), and Sara Stephens (development person for our public radio station). A day after being with Hugo Padilla, I met with Damon Marsh (at Dick's), Pete and Olivia Crosby (at their MedTech office at home), and Thomas Sanders (software development at TMC Solutions).

Gail and I came away from these experiences with similar impressions:

- Our CDP people were under a lot of pressure every day—far more than we could ever have imagined. Daily, it seemed the message they received was to work harder, longer, better . . . for less.

- Our CDP people were highly respected
by their working colleagues.
- Our relationship with each member of the group
immediately changed when they knew that we
were aware of what they were doing every day.
Conversely, we had a greater sensitivity about
what cultivating and deepening meant in their
lives . . . not just how it worked in church but
beyond the church in their larger world.

THE TUESDAY BEFORE THANKSGIVING, GAIL AND I WENT TO
Rich and Carly's home for dinner. The four of us hoped to evaluate the progress of the CDP group and to think through the next couple of months.

Their boys, Jacob and Caleb, ate with us and then left the table to do their homework. We adults adjourned to the living room to talk.

"Let's start with what the two of you have experienced over the first eleven weeks," I said to Rich and Carly.

Typical of Rich's systematic ways, he immediately reached for a notebook, where he'd recorded comments in anticipation of my question. "Carly and I spent some time talking last night after the meeting . . . and here's what we came up with."

The best way to show you how Rich and Carly think is to record their comments in the order I remember them.

RICH: Selection was exactly what you both said it would
be: *everything*. We've not faced some of the typical
problems most groups seem to have where one person
can't get along with another or another person doesn't
want to stick with the disciplines. So the selection thing:
that's been an important learning experience for us. The

temperament teaching? Indispensible. It's been amazing to us to see how much easier it is to connect with each other when you know something about how we're all wired.

CARLY: We both agreed that the emphasis on dialogue has made a tremendous difference in getting people to think and work together. I wish we could teach this to everyone in the church. Lots of us never learn to listen to one another and then participate in creating ideas and insights that are bigger and better than ones we might have created ourselves.

RICH: The readings from the Bible and other sources are making a huge difference in our understanding of how God wants to build us into deeper people.

And community. I've been doing group work at school for years. But I'm watching people come together on a whole new level. All kinds of things are happening that cause us to love and value each other. Things like the Olivia Crosby scare, the Soriano story, even doing little team jobs like setting up and down each week. Everything we do seems to be one more lesson in building a sense of community.

CARLY: Prayer. We're all learning how to pray on a whole new level. Everyone's learning how to pray for each other, and they're learning how to make prayer a start-up event of each day. I remember last summer when Gail said prayer would be the main event.

We're beginning to hear how much each CDP member is enjoying their mentors. They've all had at least two meetings, and the word we're getting back is that everyone's loving the experience. Once again, the generations are learning how to talk with each other.

RICH: You'd be interested to know that we've had two meetings with our mentors, Russ and Gretchen Milner. Our boys love them. Russ had them down to one of his Burger Kings the other day, and they got to make their own hamburgers. And we're finding that they have a lot to say to us about spiritual leadership. They've suffered, you know. Gretchen went through depression. Russ had a serious prostate surgery. And they've given us a lot of insight into how those experiences have deepened them.

"One thing more," Carly said. "We want you to know that we're having the time of our lives. We're learning what it takes to cultivate deepening people. I can only dream about the difference these guys are going to make in the coming years. You can see them coming alive more and more every week."

"I forgot one something," Rich said. "I've thought a lot about the Damon Marsh thing. I learned something by watching you confront Damon. You did it pointedly, but lovingly and respectfully. And then I appreciated the fact that we gave him a way back. I still worry about Damon, but I think it was the right thing to do when we gave him grace.

"So where do we go from here?" Rich asked.

"We've just about finished with an overview of spiritual disciplines," Gail said, "and we'll want to move toward a study of some of the unique marks of Christian character during the next eight to ten weeks. But the big thing coming is storytelling."

We'd talked about storytelling with Rich and Carly back in the summer. And now the time was coming.

"How do you see that working?" Rich asked.

"Next week, we'll introduce the concept of life story and do some teaching on how everyone can write their own autobiography," I said. "I've brought a list of guidelines to give you both that the others will get next Monday. Could you guys work up a schedule for everyone to read their stories?"

"Are you confident that everyone can do this?" Carly asked.

"Well, to be honest, we've never tried it before, and I'm sure that some will struggle with the idea when they hear about it for the first time. But Gail and I will be available to coach anyone who needs some help to get started. And, most important, the two of us will be the first readers. Gail will read her story the first night, and I'll go second. Then we'd like for the two of you to be third and fourth. That way everyone will have had a month of stories, and they'll have a good idea of what storytelling sounds like. You both up to this?"

Rich and Carly agreed.

NOVEMBER 28

The Second Fall

From my journal

> *It's not been the best of weeks. I fear that we've had*
> *our first serious setback in CDP. We may have lost*
> *Damon Marsh. The disappointment that Jesus must*
> *have felt about Peter in his moment of great failure and*
> *the sense of loss that Paul must have experienced over*
> *Demas is suddenly very real to me.*

WHEN THE CDP GROUP GATHERED IN OUR BASEMENT ON the last Monday night in November, Damon Marsh was missing. This time he had not called Gail or me.

"I know where he is," Rich said quietly to me a few minutes before we were to begin.

Rich took out his iPhone. The Beavers' website was on his screen. One flick of Rich's finger brought up the team's schedule. As I looked down at the screen, I saw the news. Tonight, at 7:30 p.m.—just thirty-two minutes from now—the Beavers were to face off against Keene at our city arena. Then Rich flicked his finger again, and a news item said that "former Plymouth State hockey player Damon Marsh will be starting in the place of injured forward Tom Bergeron."

IT WAS AN IMPULSIVE DECISION, BUT I DECIDED TO FOLLOW my instincts. I went to Rich and said, "You lead the reading tonight. I need to go down to the arena and see if I can find Damon Marsh. I'll be back by break time."

As I backed out of our driveway, I imagined the day Jesus went to the shores of Galilee to find Simon Peter, who'd decided to return to fishing. I reminded myself that Jesus did not berate Peter or focus on his most recent failure. Rather, he prepared a breakfast for him and his friends and found ways to let the faltering disciple know that he was loved. Were my feelings about Damon similar to Jesus' feelings about Simon Peter?

One cannot be a cultivator of deepening people and wallow in self-pity if one of them decides to go in a different direction. You don't love that person any less, and you don't give up on them too quickly. But there does come a time when you have to release them to their own choices.

BY 7:15 P.M. I HAD BOUGHT A TICKET AND WAS IN THE arena. The Beavers do not draw National Hockey League crowds, so it was easy to make my way down to rinkside, where both teams were warming up, skating in circles at their respective ends of the ice.

Almost immediately I saw Damon, a number 9 on his jersey. He was skating with another team member, and the two were so involved in conversation that he skated right past the place where I was standing without noticing me. I watched as he moved behind the goal and around the circle a second time. Again, when he came by again, it was as if I were invisible.

It was during the third circling that Damon spotted me. Slowly he skated across the ice to where I was standing and scraped to a halt, his hockey stick in both hands.

In his uniform and pads and wearing his skates, Damon

appeared to be a much larger man than the one who had come to our home for the last eleven Monday nights. Seconds—seeming like an hour—passed as we stood just looking at one another. Embarrassment—shame, maybe?—was written all over his face. Clearly, it had not occurred to him that I might care enough to come after him.

Finally, Damon spoke. "I had to make a choice, Pastor Mac. I was going to call you, but I put off the call until it was too late. Here's the way it is. Thanks for giving me a chance in CDP. But I have to be here. I love playing this game more than anything. Sorry." Then without giving me a chance to say a word, Damon Marsh skated off.

I WAS BACK AT THE CONDO BY 8 P.M. BUT SAT OUT IN THE car by myself for fifteen minutes, thinking about what had just transpired. I fought off the temptation to feel sorry for myself. What was far more important was Damon Marsh's choice. It might make all the difference in his future. But he wasn't thinking *future*. He was seizing hold of the *now* and not considering the consequences.

Inside, the CDP group (minus one now) had spent a good hour on the reading from the book of Isaiah. Rich had started things with a brief prayer time and then said to Ben Jacobs, "Ben, you've watched us do this for a while now. You lead the dialogue tonight. Pretend I'm not here."

Apparently Ben did an incredible job. Later that night, when we were getting ready for bed, Gail described his confident demeanor. "He did it exactly as he's seen you and me do it. He made sure that everyone was into the flow of things. And when we finished, we all knew what was important about Isaiah's role in the coming of the Messiah. He mentioned to the group that of all the people we've studied so far, Isaiah was the one he connected with most intimately."

WHEN THE MIDEVENING BREAK WAS OVER AND THE GROUP was back together again, I told them where I'd been and, without going into detail, said that Damon had decided to drop out of CDP to play hockey with the Beavers. I stressed the fact that Damon's choice should not cause any of us to love him less. We should always keep the door open with the hope that Damon would want to return. Nevertheless, it now appeared that Damon Marsh—having loved hockey more than the CDP group—would no longer be among us on Monday nights.

FOR THE REST OF THE EVENING, WE INTRODUCED THE GROUP to the idea of storytelling. "You're about to face your biggest challenge so far in CDP," Gail told them. "Over the next several weeks we're going to write our stories."

"My story?" Hugo Padilla said. "I have no story. I don't remember much of anything about my younger days."

"Trust me, Hugo," I said. "You will."

Gail passed out an article we'd written that described how a person might begin to write their story.

Start by blocking your life off into five year increments: 0–5, 5–10, etc. Then identify some basic pieces of information that ought to go into each block. This will invigorate the memory:

- Where did you live during those years?
- Where did you go to school? Or where did you work?
- What were the significant deaths, births, life-shifting events?

Then give greater attention to each block, with these four questions in mind:

- Who were the 5 *people* (at the most) who were most influential in your life during that block of time (either positively or negatively)?
- What were the 3–5 critical *events* in each block that marked or changed your life forever (again, either positively or negatively)?
- What were the key *ideas* (3–5) that guided your life during that block of time?
- What was your *perception of God* in that period of your life?

The article went on to say:

A story is not useful if it doesn't include the things we've learned the hard way: failures, doubts, fears, wounds. It should reveal the formative influences that have made us the way we are.

The truth is that writing one's story will take some time. It probably will not be done in an hour, not even in one evening. But it is likely to be a very significant experience because most people have never taken the time or effort to put their lives into one comprehensive narrative. Sometimes the attempt brings insight that was never there before. And sometimes some pain is rediscovered.

Many in the circle became quieter and quieter as we talked. For some, the struggle had to do with their feeling that they were not good writers. For others, it was the fear of going back and dredging up memories they'd buried deep in their hearts.

"Look, Gail or I will meet with any of you who are having a tough time with this. We'll coach you all the way. I promise you that this will be one of the most memorable experiences in your spiritual journey. And, by the way, when story-reading time comes several weeks from now, we'll do one story a week. Gail and I will be the first two in line."

The prayer time that night reflected both sadness (Damon) and anxiety (story-writing).

SHERRY: Lord, we really love Damon. Please speak into his life and help him sort out what his priorities should be.

HUGO: And Father, help him to see that choices really count, that we live sometimes for years to come with the consequences of decisions made today.

CATHERINE: Father, you know that I'm petrified by this story thing. Give me courage and the ability to do this well.

MATT: And God, I've never written anything in my life . . . nothing like this, anyway. I pray for lots of help . . . that Pastor Mac, oh God, will be there when I need him—did you hear that, Pastor Mac?

You don't normally hear laughter during a prayer time. But Matt's aside caused it that night.

OLIVIA: Dear Father, I'm like Catherine and Matt: scared of this project. There've been some difficult moments in my past that I'd rather keep inside. So I need help too, Lord—did you hear that, Gail?

More laughter.

BEN: Lord Jesus, you know all our stories. I already know what storytelling can mean. There were godly men who told me their stories when I was terribly mixed up. And they gave me a safe place to tell mine. What a difference for me, Lord. What a difference . . . So give my dear brothers and sisters who I love so much a lot of courage and a lot of perseverance. I just imagine what we're going to learn about you and about ourselves in the next few months.

When we said amen, I looked at Gail and she at me. We both knew what the other was thinking: Ben Jacobs understood how to speak into the fears of others. He was deepening before our eyes.

DECEMBER 1

The Second Fall

Post to CDP Group Facebook Page

CDP Group
Gail and I will be away from you on December 5. Rich
and Carly will be leading the meeting. Please bring your
Ezra reading (*Spiritual Leader/Organizational Leader*)
and your two-week journals. Also, you will be meeting
two extraordinary people, Samuel and Ramya Anand,
who will be there to tell their story.

To: Geoff Handley
From: GMAC
Subject: —

Thanks for pushing Gail and me to come down here. We're
having a great time, getting some rest, missing all of you.
You're a wonderful friend and leader, Geoff.

GAIL AND I SPENT THE FIRST WEEK OF DECEMBER IN
Florida. The weather was ideal, and we had a chance to sit out
in the sun, talk, read books, and do a lot of walking. Some might
have the impression that we are always absorbed in church work.

But the fact is that we know how to break away and have lots of fun together.

During a walk we began talking about Damon Marsh. "I am so troubled about Damon," Gail said. "What did we miss when we selected him?"

"Perhaps we need to remind ourselves that just because a person drops out doesn't mean that a mistake was made," I said. "Unless you think that Jesus made a mistake with Judas."

At another time we talked about how much our love for the group had grown.

"You know," I said, "there are times when I'm sitting with the CDP group on Monday night, and I feel as if I'm having the greatest church experience of my life. I have this sense that what's going on is exactly what Jesus wanted his followers to experience. I'm getting to know every person in that circle. I know their names, where they've come from. What they do all week, their dreams, their fears . . . and I feel as if they are working to know me. It's more than just a community; it's a kind of spiritual family."

"Are you going to be able to say good-bye to these kids?" Gail asked me. I picked up on Gail's use of the word *kids*. It was a term of endearment, showing the way she felt toward these men and women, our spiritual children.

"You know, it's really going to be difficult. I remember how much I grieved when our two left home. In some ways I'm going to have a similar grief when these guys go. And I suspect I'm going to want to find excuses to keep the group meeting with us."

"But you can't do that," Gail said.

"Why not?"

"Because Michael Cohen told you that good rabbis *go away*."

"Well, Rabbi Cohen must not have known how difficult this may be."

DECEMBER 5

The Second Fall

Postcard from Florida to Connie Peterson

Connie,

    Gordon and I are in Florida, absorbing the sun. But that doesn't mean that our hearts aren't in New England. As we prayed for the CDP group today, we found it hard to get past Ben and Catherine's names. We've come to love them. Ben's pastoral spirit is so obvious. It's clear that the entire CDP group looks to the two of them as inspirational figures. To think that it all began with your decision to invite your nephew to come and live with you when he was in trouble. How proud you must be, and how grateful we are for you.

Love,

Gail

Card to Hana Tchung, via snail mail

Hana,

    Keep shouting! It's working. Those CDP people you're praying for are deepening.

GMAC

On Monday night, December 5, Gail and I went to an early movie on our Florida vacation. But as we sat in the theater, I noticed that Gail kept stealing glances at her watch. She was obviously thinking of the CDP meeting soon to begin.

"Hey," I whispered, "concentrate on the movie."

"I can't. I just feel so guilty that we're not there," Gail whispered. "I really miss everybody."

"Try to remember that we're giving Rich and Carly a chance to lead without us being around. It will probably be the best night of the year."

And it probably was.

Later the Fishers would tell us how everyone dove into the life of Ezra and became impressed with Ezra's ability to discern God's guidance while, at the same time, using sound management principles to lead a crowd of people back to Jerusalem, where they could begin to restore the spiritual life of the city.

As expected, Samuel and Ramya Anand spent the second hour of the evening telling the story of their Christian lives and how they had come to dearly love each other despite the fact that their marriage had been arranged by their families in the traditional ways of India. The group had lots of questions for them.

Then in the third hour, as had been planned, the group talked about their experiences in writing down their spiritual reflections in experimental journals. Some loved the experiences; some admitted that they had a difficult time. But all were eager to talk about how they could develop journaling as a regular discipline.

At about 9 p.m., while the CDP meeting was still going, my cell phone buzzed.

"Soriano here." I heard the familiar Bostonian accent of my neighbor and increasingly good friend, Hank.

"Can't get away from you, can we?" I said with a chuckle. "So, how are you and Cynthia?"

"Great . . . Cyn's on the line. Can you put your phone on speaker so Gail can hear?"

"Sure." We were in our car, huddling close so that we could hear Hank's voice on the phone.

"Great time going on over at your house," he said. "We made a batch of cannolis and took them over for the halftime. When we got there, they were just finishing up whatever they were reading together, and we fed them. Then Sam and Ram Anand—how do you pronounce their names?"

"For heaven's sake, Hank," Cynthia said. "It's *not* Sam and Ram . . . it's Samuel and Ramya. Get it right for once."

By now Gail and I were working hard to suppress our laughter at these two dear people, new members in the family of God, as they tried to adjust to new ways of looking at life.

"Well, you know who I'm talking about," Hank went on. "Anyway, they're terrific people. Remind me of Roberto and Adriana . . . they really have their faith nailed down. So, they're there with the group. We didn't hang around. We just cleaned up and left."

The four of us talked for a few more minutes and then said good-bye.

"You know," I said, "I'm glad I'm here, but to be honest, I'm homesick when I hear Hank and Cynthia's voices. It's so renewing to me to hear their fresh impressions of things that I often begin to take for granted. You can't afford not to have people like the Sorianos in your circle of friendship."

At 10:45, the phone rang again. It was Rich and Carly Fisher. I'd made them promise to call us no matter how late.

"Tonight was better than any dream session I've ever been a part of," Rich said. "You would have been so proud of Carly. She led most of the first hour of dialogue, and everyone . . . well, it was like throwing red meat to dogs. Everyone wanted in on the action."

"What about the Anands?" Gail asked.

"The group hung on every one of their words. They have a love for Jesus that's infectious. We were all blown away. Thanks for letting us do this. It beats anything we've ever done before."

"So next year you guys will be ready to do this on your own?" Gail said.

"In a word, *yes*. We can't wait," Carly answered.

Before we went to sleep that night, Gail and I hugged tightly and said a whole pile of thank-yous to God. For the Fishers, for the Sorianos, for the Anands, for the elders and their support of CDP, for our own partnership and the way God had led us into this experience.

And then we finished by praying for Damon Marsh.

DECEMBER 12

The Second Fall

To: GMAC
From: Michael Cohen
Subject: Talmidim

How are your talmidim doing?

To: Michael Cohen
From: GMAC
Subject: Re: Talmidim

Rabbi Michael, it's going great. I think it may be time to invite you and Esther to meet the group. You willing to consider that?
Rabbi GMAC

To: GMAC
From: Michael Cohen
Subject: Re: Re: Talmidim

Let me know when.

OUR LAST CDP MEETING FOR THE CALENDAR YEAR OCCURRED on Monday, December 12. We read through the pertinent scriptures that narrated the story of John the Baptist, and we paid particular attention to his view of his own call to service in John 3:23–36. The group talked about his sense of stewardship: that his success was a gift from God. We took note of his sense of personal identity: that he knew he was not the Christ. There was his awareness of purpose: to introduce Christ to the world. And finally, his passion: that Jesus might grow (increase) in recognition and that he might diminish.

"His story is counterintuitive," Ben Jacobs had said. "We're taught by culture to go for the gold ring at all costs, to grab the spotlight, to climb to the top of the heap. But this guy, John, is going the other direction. And then Jesus calls him the greatest of all the prophets. Boy, is he ever a deep person."

FOLLOWING "HALFTIME" (AS HANK SORIANO CALLED IT), we talked about our stories. Everyone was making their first efforts at writing, and some were excited; others, daunted. There were lots of comments and questions: among them some very important ones:

- "If I really tell my story the way it should be told, there are some things I'd not want to get out of this room."
- "I'm finding it painful to write my story. There are things that I guess I've buried. Now I'm having to face them."
- "I'm beginning to realize that my story changes with age. Some of the facts are the same, but my understanding of the facts seems to change as I get older."

- "I've never looked back long enough to realize how many people loved me and went out of their way to help me grow up."

It was about 9:35 that evening, just as we were getting ready to go to our final prayer time, that my cell phone vibrated. Normally, we ignored phones during a CDP meeting, but for some reason I felt compelled to take a look to see who was calling at this time of night. It was Jason Calder.

I slipped from the room and hit the talk button.

"Yeah, Jason. What's up?"

"Gordon, I wouldn't have bothered you if I wasn't sure you'd want to know this. Damon Marsh was severely injured in a hockey game tonight over in Portsmouth."

"What happened?"

"Apparently the game got real rough. Someone took a run at Damon and slammed him into the boards, and they're worried that he's got a spinal cord injury and may be paralyzed. His father is at the hospital . . . says they may airlift him to Mass General in Boston. He wanted me to know, because he said they need prayers badly. He sounded pretty desperate."

After I'd hung up from the call from Jason, I stood in shock for a moment. My last meeting with Damon had been rinkside at the arena. Then, he'd looked big, imposing, ready to take on the world. Now, I imagined him in an emergency room: unable to move, scared, wondering what happened.

I rejoined the group, broke into the conversation, and told everyone what I'd just learned about Damon. Several people began to cry. Others just sat in stunned silence.

Then Lara Anderson spoke. "Okay. This is what I'm thinking. Gordon and Gail brought us together to learn what it means to be deepening people. So we need to ask what deep people do in a moment like this. Damon may have left us for something else that he preferred to do at the moment, but that doesn't mean we left Damon. So let's ask ourselves what we should be doing. What do you guys think?"

The group immediately swung into a dialogue mode.

CATHERINE JACOBS: Well, we should pray, obviously.

THOMAS SANDERS: We should do everything we can think of to move in Damon's direction and let him know that he's got a dozen or more people who are there for him.

AMY BOYD: I'll get in touch with Martin and Kate Lane. They've been Damon's mentors, and they've kept seeing him even though he dropped CDP team meetings. They'll want to know.

PETE CROSBY: Occurs to me that if they fly Damon to Boston, his parents are going to need to stay down there for a while. Maybe we could chip in, get some others to join us, and pay for the first three or four nights in a hotel so they don't have to drive back up here to sleep.

BEN JACOBS: I'll set up a Facebook page tonight, and we'll publish daily bulletins on Damon's progress. We can make a wall for people to write in with their prayers and notes of encouragement.

There was a time in my pastoral ministry when Gail and I would have taken the initiative to come up with these ideas and make them happen. Now neither one of us had to say a word or lift a finger. The CDP group had become a team. They knew how to dialogue together, organize everything, and make something happen. This was leadership.

From that moment forth, I began to refer to these wonderful spiritual sons and daughters of ours not as the CDP group but, rather, the *CDP team.*

When we went to prayer, Ben Jacobs said, "How would all of you feel if we knelt while we prayed? I'd just feel good about doing that."

There was a concert of agreement, and in a second we were all on our knees, praying for our prodigal friend who was in real trouble.

ABOUT THE TIME WE FINISHED, MY CELL PHONE RANG AGAIN. It was Jason again. He'd heard from Damon's father and learned that a Medevac helicopter team was preparing to move Damon to Massachusetts General Hospital in Boston for immediate surgery.

When everyone was gone, I called Hank Soriano.

"Hank, sorry to bother you so late at night, but I figured you would want to know what we've learned in the last hour." I told him about Damon and the fact that he was being moved to Boston. His father and, presumably, his mother would be following in a car.

"This night's going to be hell for them," Hank said. "Anyone going to be there to sit with them?"

"Not that I know of," I said.

"Wanna go down there?"

"Yeah," I said. "I really do. He's my spiritual son, Hank. He may have run away from home, but he's still a spiritual son."

"I'll drive you."

"Don't you have to work in the morning?"

"That's why I've got a laptop and a cell phone. I don't go to work; the work goes to me."

Just as I ended the call with Hank, my phone began ringing again. It was Martin Lane, Damon's mentor.

"Amy Boyd just called to tell us about Damon's injury. I'd like to go down to MGH and stay there for a while. I'm sure—"

"Martin, Hank Soriano and I are just leaving my home. Want to come with us?"

"I can meet you in ten minutes at the Walmart parking lot. I'll leave my car there."

AT 1 A.M., HANK SORIANO, MARTIN LANE, AND I DROVE into the parking garage at Massachusetts General Hospital. We got there just minutes after Damon's mother and father arrived. Even though the Marshes had been divorced for several years, Damon's injury reunited them, at least for this night.

The five of us spent the night in one of the hospital's reception areas. Occasionally, someone brought us an update on the progress of Damon's surgery. Each time I would pray a prayer of thanks, if the news was good—or a prayer of intercession, if the news was discouraging. The Marshes seemed to be grateful for three men they'd never met before.

DECEMBER 31

The Second Winter

To: Geoff Handley
From: GMAC
Subject: CDP-Elders

After the first of the year, I'd love to meet and talk with you about where we want CDP-Elders to go in the coming year. We've got ten or twelve shots per year with the elders if we set aside one hour during each monthly meeting for training. Then we might want to think of a weekend retreat. I'd be interested in what themes you think would be helpful.

To: GMAC
From: Geoff Handley
Subject: Re: CDP-Elders

I look forward to our meeting. Themes that immediately come to mind? Biblical leaders (like the studies you're doing on Monday nights), how elders can do less management stuff and more pastoral work with the people, and what you refer to as dialogue. I don't think many of us are very good at that.

On the afternoon of December 31, Damon Marsh's father called Jason Calder to say that Damon had begun to recover a small amount of movement and feeling in his extremities. It appeared that the paralysis was losing its grip.

The orthopedic surgeons were amazed, one even going as far as to use the word *miracle* in his comments. A few hours later in the day, they began to talk about the possibility that Damon might walk again and possibly, over time, resume a reasonably normal life. But they were quick to add that he would never play hockey again.

When the news went out on the Damon Marsh Facebook page, it seemed as if the whole church—the whole city, in fact—began to cheer.

Within an hour, even though it was New Year's Eve, members of the CDP team began to make plans to get together that evening. The word went out on Facebook, by texting, and the old-fashioned way: phone calls.

Ben and Catherine Jacobs insisted on hosting the gathering at their apartment. By 5 p.m., every CDP team member who was in town indicated they would be there. At first I pushed for the meeting to be at our home, but Gail felt that it was important for the Jacobses to host this one, even though all of us would need a shoehorn to fit in their place.

When Gail and I arrived at the Jacobses' home that evening, we saw Hank and Cynthia getting out of their car down the street. Catherine had called and located them just as they were about to go to Boston to celebrate New Year's Eve at their favorite restaurant, Legal's. Having been invited, they canceled their reservation for the evening and, typical of them, began putting food together to take to the CDP gathering.

When we were all there, we knelt once again, this time

offering prayers of thanksgiving. Everyone prayed. Everyone! Each member of the CDP team, Gail and me, Hank and Cynthia. Everyone! Then we ate good food and simply hung out together.

JANUARY 2

The Second Winter

Post to CDP Group Facebook Page

CDP Group
No meeting tonight. Gail and I will be in Boston today to see Damon Marsh. We'll post an update here when we get back this evening.

TWO DAYS LATER GAIL AND I DROVE TO BOSTON TO SEE Damon. It was our fourth visit to his hospital room. When we walked in, we found him alone. Many of the sophisticated medical devices that had been in play during past visits were now gone or turned off. Damon was gathering strength and was continuing to regain the use of his limbs.

His face lit up when he saw us. He took Gail's hand and, as best as he could, drew it to his lips and kissed her fingers. When I came near his bed, he grabbed my hand with a surprisingly strong grip and tried to draw me close. It seemed a gesture of great affection.

Soon, Gail and I were seated on either side of Damon's bed, listening to Damon describe for us all he remembered about the past three weeks. He had no memory of the hockey game or of the moment when he had been blindsided by the Portsmouth player. His first post-accident memories were of his father and

336

mother telling him about the outpouring of love from people in our city. But, he said, the most important memory was of the messages he got from various CDP team members. He could not believe that, after what he'd done, they wanted to be there for him in his worst hour.

"And you, Pastor Mac: my father said you came that first night with Hank and Mr. Lane. Dad said the three of you spent the whole night with him and my mom while I was in surgery. And here you are again. You guys are always coming to where I am."

Damon's mouth was dry, and he asked if I could help him drink some water through a straw. When he'd had enough, he continued what he wanted to say.

"I can remember the night you came to the arena just before that game began. I was so torn. I wanted to be with you and the CDP people, but the game . . . I just couldn't let it go. So I skated away and never thought I'd ever see the two of you again. But you're here . . ."

Damon struggled with some tears for a moment, and then he went on. "You know, I dumped the CDP group for a hockey team. But when I ended up here, I hardly heard a word from the team. But the CDP group hasn't stopped sending me cards, making phone calls, finding all sorts of ways to let me know that I'm still one of them."

"Damon, do you want to come back?" Gail asked.

"I want to come back so bad. Can you come back if you've walked away? I mean, I lied to you that first time, and then I ditched you at the arena."

"Well, Damon, the answer to your question is yes. That's what Christian love is all about. Lots of people walked away from Jesus. I can remember walking away at times myself. Now, I don't know if anybody has ever skated away from Jesus, but lots of us have walked, even run away. And thankfully, a lot have come back."

"Apparently you're going to spend a few months in rehab," Gail said, "and we're going to do our best to keep you in the loop. But if you're sure you really want to, we'll begin to think about your being a part of a CDP team next fall. That's something to think about. In the meantime, all your CDP team brothers and sisters from this year have every intention of keeping in close touch with you."

When we left Damon's bedside and headed for our car, I found myself mulling over the tough lessons Damon was learning. There are those of us who learn the hard way. And now it was Damon's turn.

I asked Gail if she remembered the night that Wilford Jean-Baptiste had been at our home and had described his most poignant moments of learning. "I learn from Mr. Experience," Wilford had said. "I must figure it out for *myself* . . . and that not really all *bad*. Young people today get too much too easy. There are things that you learn *best* the hard way. You fail. And you fail again. And then, three, four, six failure times later, you figure out how to do something the right way. *And you never forget it.*"

Damon would never forget.

JANUARY 9

The Second Winter

From my journal

> *I have been working on the story of my life, which
> I'll be reading to the CDP team in the next few days.
> Because I'm something of a writer, the actual exer-
> cise of writing the story has not been that difficult.
> In fact, I've rather enjoyed the exercise. Enjoyed it
> except for the places where I have to reveal some
> of the dark sides of my life. I would prefer to bury
> some things in the past, but that would be dishonest.
> If Gail and I are going to lead the way in showing
> how God's grace works in the difficult moments as
> well as in the better ones, I've got to open my life
> to the CDP team and trust that their reaction will be
> that of deepening people.*

ON THE SECOND MONDAY IN JANUARY, FOUR MONTHS AFTER
we'd had our first CDP team meeting, we began a season of
storytelling.

The guidelines were simple. Each person wrote his or her
story, and on a designated night they read it to the group. It was
agreed that if, for any reason, someone missed an evening (there

are such things as the flu, you understand), then we would wait a week and push the schedule ahead. Reason? We felt it important that everyone hear every story.

We arranged a dinner at 6 p.m. on that first evening of story-telling. Rabbi Michael Cohen and his wife, Esther, joined us for the hour. As usual, Hank and Cynthia were there to help prepare the food and serve it. Although they were not part of the CDP team meetings, everyone considered them part of the extended family by now.

When the Cohens arrived, the entire CDP team was there to greet them. Gail had name tags for all of us so our guests would not have to struggle with names. I asked Michael if there was an appropriate Jewish prayer for a meal like the one we were about to eat, and he said yes, and he would offer the prayer if I wanted . . . which I did.

We all became quiet, and the rabbi raised his hands and prayed: "Blessed are you, HaShem, our God, King of the universe, by whose word everything comes to be."

Then Michael told us that there was a longer prayer to be said at the end of the meal. "If you will permit me at the end of our eating, I shall say that prayer."

For the next half hour we ate. Then, at the end of the meal, Michael once again prayed. "Blessed is the Lord our God, Sovereign of the universe, who sustains the entire world with goodness, kindness, and mercy. God gives food to all creatures, for God's mercy is everlasting. Through God's abundant goodness we have not lacked sustenance, and may we not lack sustenance forever, for the sake of God's great name. God sustains all, does good to all, and provides food for all the creatures whom God has created. Blessed is the Lord our God, who provides food for all."

Then it was time for our meeting to begin. This time, with the Cohens and the Sorianos as guests, there were nineteen of us, a very tight fit.

"Michael, could you give us some thoughts on the way a rabbi's disciples were taught in ancient times?" I asked.

Michael was eloquent. He named a few of the great rabbis of the past—Hillel, Shammai, and, some centuries later, Maimonides. But he focused mainly on their disciples, how they learned and what was expected of them since they followed such great mentors. Michael went on to talk about the power of the rabbinical contract: *instruction, imitation*, and *examination*. What he said and how he said it was important because he was speaking out of Jewish culture.

When he neared the end of his presentation, Michael spoke of the painful moment when the rabbi and his disciple separated from one another. "The goal of the rabbi was to produce some, as my friends Gordon and Gail say, 'deep people.' But once a disciple came near to deepness, the rabbi had to send him off, because if he did not go his own way, he could not hope to remain deep. Depth, you see, does not come from staying under the umbrella of the rabbi-teacher. It comes when you take what you have been taught, plant it in your own heart, and then go off to serve and teach other people. So must it be with all of you someday."

The room was quiet when Michael Cohen said these words. Everyone knew that five months from now, they would no longer be coming to our home each Monday night. During these past months, being together every Monday evening had become a routine part of everyone's week. None of us could imagine a time when it would be different. So Michael's words were a sober reminder to us all: this learning community we enjoyed so much was only temporary. The CDP team would, in a sense, lose its spiritual mother and father. Similarly, we would lose our spiritual sons and daughters. Who would grieve the most?

WHEN MICHAEL AND ESTHER LEFT US THAT EVENING, EVERYone gave them an affectionate good-bye. We had all thoroughly enjoyed the two of them and hoped that they would come back sometime. When I walked the Cohens to their car, Michael told me, "I have learned much tonight, friend. I've seen something in those people in your home that moves me greatly. I see love in their eyes; I hear love in their voices. You and Gail are doing well. You are indeed like rabbis."

THAT NIGHT, AFTER THE COHENS HAD LEFT AND THE Sorianos had retreated to the kitchen to clean up, I read the story of my life to the CDP team. It took me almost thirty-five minutes to read my twelve pages. And why not? Mine is a long life, twice as long as almost anyone else's in the room.

My story began with my childhood: its blessed moments and its sadness. I told about the years when I left home to go to boarding school and then on to the university. I described the night I made a deliberate decision to follow Jesus and what the results were.

Then I wrote of how I'd met Gail and the difference she'd made in my life. There were the names of a few of the men and women who served in my life as mentors and the gifts of insight they'd offered. I did not withhold the catalog of my many failures, even one that, many years ago, had been terribly injurious to the marriage Gail and I share.

I tried describing my sense of call from God to be a pastor and, later on, to be an encourager, something like a spiritual father, to younger people. As I came toward the end, there were some places where I became emotional and I had to pause until the threat of tears subsided. In the last minutes, I told of how we'd come to this wonderful New Hampshire church and how much we loved serving the people and watching them grow in their faith.

When I was through reading, the group affirmed me appreciatively. It's possible that they had not expected me to be so transparent. I welcomed their questions, and for twenty minutes they peppered me with queries about the various stages in my life.

Finally, Gail said, "We're going to do for Gordon what we'll be doing for all of you when it's your turn. We're going to put him in the middle of the room and gather around and pray for him, all of us."

And they did. Thomas Sanders put a chair in the middle, and I sat down. The CDP team crowded around me, and I felt their hands on my head, my shoulders and back, on my knees and feet. And then I spent almost thirty minutes listening to the prayers of our spiritual children. I could not record those prayers and put them in this book. They are simply too sacred to repeat.

JANUARY AND
FEBRUARY

The Second Winter

Handwritten note, found on my car seat

Gordon,

    I just want you to know how much it means to me that we're a partnership. I'm thinking about the CDP team today. Their lives are changing before our eyes. The Holy Spirit is doing marvelous things in these spiritual sons and daughters of ours. In fact, we may be seeing a turn-around toward deepening in our entire church leadership, elders, staff, mentors. Let's keep believing that this is exactly what God wants us to be doing.

Love you,
Gail

THE MONDAY NIGHTS OF JANUARY AND FEBRUARY PASSED quickly. Each week there was an hour of storytelling, questions, teaching, and a prayer time. And every week you could feel the group becoming more bonded. Much of the bonding came from the stories themselves. Each story contained humor, drama, success, and failure.

344

Some men described occasions when they failed, were humiliated, or totally lost confidence in themselves. A couple of the women spoke of sexual abuse. There were stories about broken family relationships, shattered dreams, physical illnesses.

Then there were the breakthrough stories of conversion to the saving way of Jesus, of falling in and out of love, of memorable events that sometimes sounded a lot like miracles. We learned about the moments when people had reached new levels of maturity, learned lessons the hard way, discovered the kindness of God.

There were many tears. Sometimes we listened to the storyteller of the week with incredulity. How had we known this person for so long and yet not been in touch with the suffering they had faced? How, we often asked, did this person survive what he or she was describing?

We came to realize that every one of us had suffered in some way or another. And we hated to admit it, but we were forced to face the fact that affliction did more to help people grow deep than anything else. The very thing one feared the most—suffering— often brought about the greatest deepening. In that crucible, we experienced the love of Jesus and the clearing out of things that are detrimental to spiritual deepening.

I came to see in those many weeks that storytelling does more to bring a group of people together than almost anything else. You can do all the Bible studies you want, but nothing creates community like the sharing of stories. And relatively few people are willing to do that until they have had time to trust one another and know that their story will be received in love and grace.

"I could never have told my story if we'd done this during the first weeks we met," Amy Boyd said.

"Without this experience, I think I'd have gone through life thinking that I was the only one who came out of a totally broken family," Ben Jacobs said after he had finished reading his story.

For one of the first times, Ben had spoken of the day when, at the age of twelve, a trusted man in his childhood church tried to assault him during a ride home from a church function. Before he read his story to the CDP team, Ben had only confided this horrific memory to a couple of men in our church and to the therapist who had helped him work through those memories.

Sara Stephens wrote of the heartbreak of an engagement that was broken a week before the wedding date. Before she was finished, every woman in the room was in tears. The men expressed frustration as they tried to understand how a guy could do that to a woman like Sara.

Rich and Carly Fisher both told magnificent stories that, in part, described their early struggle to put their marriage on a sure footing.

Sherry Nordberg had the most difficult time. As the most introverted member of the CDP team, she was terrified of putting her story on paper. More than once she met with Gail and sought advice about how to express thoughts she'd secreted away for so long. And when the night came for her to read, she started haltingly but managed to gather strength as she felt the encouragement of the people in the circle. Two or three times she wept as she spoke of the hurt of being misunderstood when she found it difficult to put her inner thoughts into words others would understand.

There was a very special moment during Sherry's reading when Olivia Crosby, who was sitting next to Sherry, put her arm around her and pulled her close. From that point forward Sherry read with great courage. *Remember this moment*, I said to myself, *when it comes time to talk about Olivia's spiritual gifts.*

DURING THE SAME WEEKS THAT WE WERE READING OUR stories, we also studied the gifts of the Holy Spirit. We were moving from the subject of depth of character and Christlikeness to the depth of the servanthood lifestyle. We read excerpts from Brother Lawrence's *The Practice of the Presence of God*, where he spoke of turning the most menial of tasks into acts of worship.

Reflecting on his work in a monastery kitchen, Lawrence said, "I turn over my little omelet in the pan for the love of God. When it is finished, if I have nothing to do, I prostrate myself on the ground and adore my God, from whom came the grace to make it. After that, I get up, more content than a king."

"It's not really occurred to me that one can turn the smallest events of the day into an act of worship," Matt Cundiff said. "I've always thought that God was interested only in things you did when you were involved in church programs. Silly me."

"What he's saying," Thomas Sanders added, "is that there's a sacred element to everything a person does. So all of my work is to be done with the idea that God might use it in one way or another. Listen to this."

Thomas took his notebook and searched its pages for a moment. Then he said, "We read this in Oswald Sanders's book. Remember? 'Towels and dishes and sandals, all the ordinary sordid things of our lives, reveal more quickly than anything what we are made of. It takes God Almighty Incarnate in us to do the meanest duty as it ought to be done.'"

There was a collective "Wow" spoken around the circle.

When Thomas was through, Carly Fisher spoke. "We've spent the last many weeks talking about Christian character and the notion that God wants to speak through what we are. Now we're saying that God wants to speak through what we do and how we do it. That's a challenge for a mother of boys. So much of my life over the past few years has been made up of meaningless, repetitive activities. Kind of like turning an omelet in a pan. But Lawrence is saying that those repetitive activities are as important to God as the moment when Gordon preaches on Sunday morning. Have I got this right?"

A number of people in the circle wanted to respond to Carly's idea and finally concluded that she was onto something they all needed to think about in the coming days. Most of them had never contemplated the meaning of a life in which every task, every activity, contained the seeds of servanthood in the name of Jesus.

"THERE'S A LOT OF SPACE GIVEN IN THE NEW TESTAMENT to the topic of giftedness," Gail said to the CDP team one evening. "When we use the word *gift*, we're talking about something that goes beyond everyday skills or talents.

"We use the word *gift* when we think we see someone doing something that can only be explained by God's hand upon their lives. It's a capability of some kind that brings a kind of richness to the people around that person and points them to Jesus. And when we see someone working out of their giftedness, utilizing that capability, we all feel that we're seeing God alive and acting in that person.

"Now here's a little thought for you," Gail went on. "When someone reveals a talent, we applaud. But when someone reveals a gift, we affirm. Affirmation means that we celebrate not how good a person is, but how great God is in using that person. So we affirm someone by saying, 'I want you to know that I see the hand of God on you when you do that.'"

We looked at the comments Paul made about spiritual gifts to the Roman, Corinthian, and Ephesian Christians. In some passages the list of gifts looked like specific abilities. In another place the gifts sounded like positions of authority and influence in the church: evangelists, pastors, teachers.

The leadership case study for that evening was about Barnabas. As we read the sections in the book of Acts that pertained to his life and involvement with people, we asked ourselves what Barnabas's gifts might be.

"I love this man," Ben Jacobs said. "I would do anything to have his gifts."

"You do have them, Ben," Gail said. "Anyone see Barnabas in Ben?"

Matt Cundiff spoke up. "Well, the first thing we know about Barnabas is his name. It means 'encouragement.' The people who knew him nicknamed him *encouragement*. I think they must have done that because wherever he went, he had this way of lifting people up, giving them hope, helping them find a kind of joy.

"Ben's like that," Matt went on. "I rarely ever see him thinking about himself. He's always encouraging people."

"Matt's right," Pete Crosby said. "I see encouragement in Ben all the time. He must have phoned me every day for two weeks during Olivia's cancer scare. He wanted to know if there was any news. He often prayed for me right over the phone. He kept assuring me that he had confidence in God that this was going to work out. I always felt a new surge of hope when Ben got in touch."

Three or four others told Ben Jacobs stories where they, too, had experienced Ben's soft but clear way of pressing courage into them. Ben sat quietly, listening to everything that was being said. I could tell that he was embarrassed, but I could also tell that he was absorbing these comments. There had to be a sense in which this man, who had come out of such a painful background, was becoming aware that God was building him into a new and different person. And the group was giving evidence to that.

Barnabas, the group decided, was a truly gifted people person. He not only encouraged people but he gave to people, he connected people, he willingly took a backseat in favor of other people, and he believed in restoring people.

"That's an incredible man," Amy Boyd said. "Where would the early church have been without Barnabas?"

We listed other gifts Paul wrote about: hospitality, serving, leading, giving, caring. And we agreed that these were just the beginning. Perhaps the Bible did not list all the possible gifts; perhaps God wished that his people would observe one another and see the many and varied ways in which we could uniquely serve him and one another.

"Watch each other in the coming weeks; look for evidences of gifts," Gail said. "There will be a night when we'll talk about what we've observed."

Having said this, Gail turned in my direction and began to tap on her wristwatch. I knew the meaning of the message instantly. We were approaching 10 p.m.

But I was not the only person to see Gail's signal. Others picked up on it, too, and began to laugh.

"We're onto the two of you," Thomas Sanders said. "Gail's the timekeeper, Mrs. Structure. And Gordon is Mr. Process, who never wants anything to end. So we've got Gail to thank that things get done according to schedule . . ."

"And we've got Gordon to thank for the enthusiasm of the moment," Rich Fisher said. "You need both. That's why they're a team."

After everyone had left, Gail said to me, "They're watching everything, aren't they?"

"Everything!" I said. "It had better be worth watching."

MARCH 1

The Second Winter

To: GMAC
From: Tom and Monica O'Donnell
Subject: CDP Mentors

We entertained the CDP mentors last night for dinner. They spent the entire evening sharing their experiences. We can tell you that we've got a ten out of ten going in this effort. A few sample comments from mentors:

- "We've been doing this for six months now. Both Millie and I have come to think that our evening with Amy Boyd is the high point of the month. She's becoming a daughter to us."
- "We love Pete and Olivia. We were among the first people they told when the cancer scare happened. I (Alice) was able to be there for Olivia since I went through a similar experience ten years ago."
- "Our Matt Cundiff is deepening. We see it every time we're with him. He tells us everything he's learning, and it's making us grow too."
- "Tell me: why weren't we doing this mentoring thing twenty years ago? Where was my mentor when I was that age?"

- "Even though Damon Marsh had to step away from the CDP team, we have remained his mentors. Now Damon is joining us for dinner every couple of weeks, and we're pleased at his spiritual growth. He's recovering nicely from his hockey injury, and he talks quite openly about what he's learned. He'll be ready for CDP next year, and we'll be there for him."

I RAN INTO KEN AND MARY ANN SQUIRES AT STAPLES, AND we talked awhile.

"Gordon, I can't tell you how much we're enjoying the mentoring relationship we have with Ben and Catherine Jacobs," Mary Ann said. "This young man is nothing like what anyone remembers when he first came to live at Connie Peterson's."

Ken said, "You know, the word that comes to mind when I think of him is *godly*. And Catherine is just like him. The two of them are becoming everything you meant when you first used the term *deep people*. Our times with them each month are incredible. Catherine told us the other night about the evening when everyone called Ben the ideal encourager. And we can see it with our own eyes. Ben speaks so caringly about the group. It's amazing to me how he's gone out of his way to know something about every person. And the two of them are passionate about praying for people. I tell you, they are pastoral material. It won't be long before you're going to want this couple sitting with people who are struggling or suffering or whatever . . . They know how to get into people's lives. He was telling me about Damon Marsh the other night, and—"

"Damon Marsh?" I interrupted Ken.

"Yeah. Ben meets with Damon every week. Now that Damon is more mobile, Ben picks him up on Saturday morning, and they eat breakfast together at Friendly's. Ben walks him through the CDP material from the previous Monday night. I tell you, Ben's determined to build in that young man's life."

"So Damon's got Martin and Kate Lane mentoring him, and he's got Ben Jacobs teaching him. I didn't know."

"You can't know everything, Gordon," Mary Ann said. "But what you should know is that there's a whole team of people beginning to come together under the CDP flag. You and Gail have got the CDP team itself. The elders are getting used to monthly training. And your staff is talking about what a difference it's making for them. And then don't forget us mentors. Every one of us is growing through our contacts with our mentees. To top it all off, people are becoming Christ-followers. The Silvas had us over for dinner the other night, and they had the Sorianos there. Hank and Cynthia told us how they've committed themselves to Jesus, and how they've been so involved with the CDP team. They know more about what's going on than we do."

When I returned to the church office, Kelly Martin handed me a light blue envelope, the kind that contains a large greeting card. When I opened it, the front of the card simply read: *Thank You.*

Inside was a handwritten note from Monica O'Donnell.

Remember that conversation we had about fifteen months ago in the parking lot at Friendly's? In case you've forgotten, it was the one in which I urged you to *partner* with Gail in the CDP initiative. I told you that it would send a powerful message to the men in our church. Well, you partnered, and one man I know of got the message—my man, Tom. I can't tell you how much it has meant to me that he and I are working together as partners in this mentoring program. Tom is growing. And we are beginning to discover how to affirm each other's gifts.

"Affirm; don't applaud." That's what Sherry Nordberg, our mentee, has taught us. We may be deepening as individuals. And so is our marriage.

Gratefully,

Monica

MARCH 5

The Second Winter

Post to CDP Group Facebook page

> **CDP Group**
> Please be prepared on Monday evening for two
> assignments. First, I will be making biographical
> recommendations. Each of you will be receiving a
> biography of some great Christian leader out of the
> past (men get men; women get women) for you to
> study. Then, over the next two months, we're going
> to invite each of you to shadow Gordon and me for an
> entire Sunday morning. More on Monday.

Voice mail for Bruce Bartlett

"Bruce, this is Gordon. Would you keep a special eye on Ben
Jacobs? I'm getting strong vibes that this guy is headed in
the direction of strong spiritual leadership. Ken and Mary
Ann Squires—they're Ben and Catherine's mentors—see the
Jacobses as terrific candidates for a pastoral care ministry
someday. I'd love it if he could shadow you someday when
he has a day off from his job at the Home Depot. Thanks."

To: GMAC
From: Bruce Bartlett
I've got a call into Ben now. Thanks.

It was a beautiful Monday morning, the kind where New Englanders actually begin to believe in spring again. When I went out to the mailbox to get my *New York Times*, Hank Soriano just happened to come out to get his paper at the same time. Yes, I think he was waiting for me.

"Met the Squires the other night," Hank told me. "Roberto and Adriana had them and us over for dinner. Great time; we really hit it off. Ken and I and our wives are going to spend next weekend on a Salvation Army project together. We're going to take a bunch of neighborhood children up to a camp for the weekend. Good chance for these kids to get away and play and hear a little bit about Jesus. You know much about this guy named Daniel in the Bible? Ken wants me to tell the kids about him on Sunday morning. Think of it . . . I'm going to be a preacher, just like you, Mac. So ask the group tonight to pray for Cyn and me. I tell ya, this is all real new stuff for me."

That Monday evening the CDP team spent the first half of the evening on the subject of God's call. What does it mean to be called by God? How would one know if they were being called? And what do you do about it?

We'd asked Rich and Carly Fisher to lead the discussion on call that evening, and they were ready to go when we finished a brief circle of prayer.

Carly led us through several scriptural accounts of men and women who experienced a call from God: Noah, Mary the mother of Jesus, Jeremiah, Esther, and Jonah—the man who resisted his call.

"For some of you the call will become very clear one day if it hasn't already," Carly said to the group. For others of you there is likely to be a simple sense of affection for some particular function in life, and whenever you're doing that thing, you'll feel this 'aha' in your heart. You hear yourself saying, 'This is what I was made for.'"

"I had that aha feeling this last Saturday morning," Ben Jacobs said.

"Want to talk about it, Ben?" Carly said.

"Well, just that I've been meeting with a guy for breakfast for a few weeks now. And I found myself automatically asking him questions that got him to open up his life to me. In fact, at one point he said, 'No one's ever asked me these kinds of questions before.' Then I realized that I wasn't just asking questions in order to ask questions. I really was interested in hearing this guy's heart. And he trusted me with his answers. And something inside of me said just what you said a moment ago: 'Ben, you were made for moments like this.'"

I was probably the only one in the room who knew that Ben Jacobs was talking about his times with Damon Marsh, and I noticed that he was wise enough not to say who he'd been with.

AFTER THE BREAK IN THE MIDDLE OF THE EVENING, LARA Anderson read her story. She told of how she'd grown up in a stable small-town family. Her life, it seemed, was trouble-free. Until her sixteenth birthday.

"I ran with three girlfriends who did everything together," she read to us. "And doing everything together included drinking too much one night. There was no designated driver when we got into a car to drive home. We hadn't gone a mile down the road when the girl who was driving lost control, and we crashed head-on into a tree. The girl up front in the passenger seat died instantly. The girl who was driving lost a leg. The EMTs had to cut the third girl and me out of the backseat, and I spent a month in the hospital and six months in rehab after that.

"I've never really gotten past that night," Lara said. "Although I was only one of four, I feel responsible for what happened. I have blamed myself . . ." Suddenly, Lara broke down and began to sob. After a minute, she handed her paper to Sherry Nordburg and said, "Can you finish this for me?"

Sherry picked up where Lara left off and read for a few minutes. When Lara had composed herself, she took the paper back and continued reading to the end. Then she wept again.

The entire CDP team seemed to connect with the pain in Lara's voice. Several of the women moved to where she was seated and tried to hug her.

After several moments, Rich Fisher put the prayer chair in the middle of the room and asked Lara if they could pray for her. And the next minutes were filled with an incredible force of prayer:

"Father, give our dear sister, Lara, an ability to lay these terrible memories at your feet. And help her to know how much she is loved in this group."

"Jesus, you know all about this kind of suffering. Give Lara an ability to move her pain along to a place where she can use it for the good of others."

"Lord, God, while I cannot explain why one girl died in that accident, I could not be more thankful that you spared Lara's life and gave her a story that will always remain with us."

Gail closed the time of prayer. "Father, I've followed Lara around the hospital and have seen how much she's loved there. Now I know why. You took her terrible suffering and used it in her life to make her a genuinely compassionate woman. We hate the thought that there was an accident, that a young girl died. But we love what you have brought out of it in Lara's life. She's now our wonderful Lara, who knows the hospital world from the inside out and can bring a word of hope to anyone wherever it's needed. We thank you, Lord."

OUR EVENING ENDED WITH EVERYONE LEAVING, A BIOGRA-phy in their hands and a date when they were to spend a Sunday morning, one by one, with Gail and me.

MARCH 12

The Second Winter

To: GMAC, Gail MacDonald
From: Tom and Monica O'Donnell
Subject: Mentor Retreat?

The mentors met together at our house last evening. We had a great time. We invited Rich and Carly to share their impressions of CDP, and they thrilled us. We are wondering about the possibility of a mentor retreat in May. Thirty-six hours to share what we've all learned about mentoring and to pray for our mentees. Any thoughts?

To: Tom and Monica O'Donnell
From: GMAC
Subject: Re: Mentor Retreat?

To resurrect an old term: I think it's a great idea.

To: Matt Cundiff
From: GMAC
Hi, Matt. Reminding you to meet us in the front lobby tomorrow morning at 8 a.m. Come with your ears and eyes wide open.

MATT CUNDIFF WAS THE FIRST TO JOIN GAIL AND ME FOR A Sunday morning "shadowing." We found each other in the lobby right at 8 a.m.

"Matt, here's what we'd like you to do. Stay on my shoulder or on Gail's and just listen to every conversation. We'll introduce you if it's the natural thing to do. And if there's any moment where we need privacy, we'll give you a nod to step away for a moment. But we want you to watch everything during the morning and be able to describe your experience to the group tomorrow night."

"OKAY, MATT," I SAID ON MONDAY EVENING, WHEN THE meeting began and we had prayed. "Tell the group what you saw yesterday."

"I have to tell you guys, that was quite an experience!" Matt said. "First, I never realized how different church is when you're on the front row. I've always sat in the balcony. You see all sorts of things you never saw before. And, I should add, you see worship in a new way too.

"There are people coming at Gordon and Gail all the time. Every one of them has a comment or a question. And the questions range from, 'What do I say to my dying mother?' to, 'Why did they decide to paint the women's room pink?' If you're Gordon or Gail, or anyone else in leadership, you've got to be ready to dignify every person no matter what.

"And then there are those people who are . . . how can I say this? . . . are kind of off the wall. It's obvious that they just want attention, and you have to know how to treat them with respect, but not let them dominate your time, because they'll take every minute you're willing to give them.

"I don't want to embarrass Gail, but I was really impressed with the ways she was there for Gordon. Once or twice he didn't know a name of someone, and she found a way to give it to him without anyone noticing. I saw how she encouraged him before he got up to preach. And then I saw just how much prayer means to people who come to the front. They really need people who can pray for them. And I saw how many of them went away with lighter hearts . . . just because someone gave them a blessing. And I wondered what it would take for me to do that. Then it occurred to me that this is exactly what Gordon and Gail have been preparing us to do each week when we pull out the prayer chair and pray for each other."

ONE OF THE MAIN TOPICS OF THE EVENING WAS THE THEME of biography. Rich was scheduled to present a study on St. Francis. You could tell instantly that his reading of Francis's life lit him up. Within a half hour virtually everyone in the group was ready to go out and buy the same book to learn for themselves how Francis had battled the religious hierarchy so that he could engage with the poor and not get bogged down by bureaucracy.

I had the feeling that the younger people in the group were quick to see the possibility that Francis could become a hero for Christians in the twenty-first century. They loved the fact that Francis had a high view of creation, that he clamored for peace when others were quick to want to go to war, and that he preferred the company of lepers to the company of kings.

Rich invited dialogue on whether or not a St. Francis-type would be heard in today's world. He challenged us all to ask ourselves whether we'd be willing to buy into Francis's view of disciplined poverty in order to identify with the poor and disadvantaged. Rich wouldn't let anyone romanticize Francis. He had his blind spots, and we talked about them. By the time we were finished, Rich had impressed upon us that being a spiritual leader can exact a high cost.

At the end of the evening, Hugo Padilla summarized the CDP team's mood rather well: "Jesus said that his followers had to share his cross in order to follow. And so Francis took him seriously. Until this year I don't think any of us minded following Jesus. We just didn't know that there was a cross involved."

MAY 19

The Second Spring

To: GMAC
From: Ben Jacobs
Have an idea. Could I bring Damon Marsh to our May 19 evening? If you're reluctant, I'll understand. But if you're open, I'd like to make it happen.

To: Ben Jacobs
From: GMAC
Am in mtg. Love idea. Do it. Surprise everybody.

To: GMAC, Gail MacDonald
From: Tom and Monica O'Donnell
We are on mentor retreat. Only one couple missing.
Incredible time. This is a bunch of renewed people.
Mentoring agrees with us. More when we get home.

OUR CDP YEAR WAS BEGINNING TO HEAD TOWARD ITS conclusion. Each week Gail and I reminded the group that we were coming toward the final week and that after that we'd have individual meetings to talk about what each of them might do with their experiences.

Monday night, May 19, was a night to remember. We invited

everyone for dinner—and, yes, the Sorianos were there to help with both the food prep and cleanup. Everyone was present at 6 p.m., except Ben Jacobs. When people asked Catherine where Ben was, she simply said he'd be coming later.

Then, just as the dinner ended, everyone heard the front door upstairs open and shut. Down the stairs came Ben, and right behind him was Damon Marsh.

There was a dead silence for just a few seconds as people took this all in, and then there were cheers. Damon stood there a step or two above Ben and took in the force of the welcome. And then the tears came.

When everything quieted, Ben spoke, Damon standing at his side.

"This is one of my most special friends," Ben said as he pointed to Damon. "We've spent a few months getting to know each other, and I can tell you that Damon is a deepening person."

With that, Ben stepped aside and motioned to Damon.

Damon said, "I can't tell all of you enough times how much your ways of supporting me have meant to my family and myself. I've had great doctors and PT people, but the greatest thing I've had has been your love and prayers. It's a miracle that I'm here and can even walk down those stairs without any assistance."

After we were all seated, Damon asked if he could say one more thing.

"I need to say one very painful thing to all of you. Many months ago, I was the phony on the CDP team. I made the commitment to be a part of this group, and then I broke my promise. And I did it in the worst possible way. I lied to Pastor Mac, and I lied to all of you. The fact is that I had something almost like an addiction. I couldn't say no to hockey, and I almost lost the finest friends a guy could have. So even though I've said it to several of you before, I want to say it again: I am so very sorry. I have learned much from my own sin and even more from your forgiveness. And Pastor Mac and Gail have told me that there will be a place for me in next year's CDP team."

Again, everyone in the room cheered. Off in the corner I saw Hank and Cynthia Soriano standing. Suddenly, Hank spoke out, "You'll be on the same CDP team with Cyn and me, Damon. Understand what I'm saying?"

And then Rich Fisher said, "And, Damon, you know what? You and Hank and Cynthia will be in the group that Carly and I will be leading. Get that?" More cheers.

Everyone insisted that Damon remain for the evening, and he gladly accepted the invitation.

JUNE 4

The Second Summer

From my journal

> Tonight is our next-to-last CDP team meeting. One
> more to go after this, but that one will be at the
> church with a much larger group of people. I have
> a feeling that the meeting this evening will have enor-
> mous implications for some of the group. I know
> that Gail and I are going to have a hard time adjust-
> ing to Monday nights this summer without the CDP
> team being here. But saying the rabbinical good-bye is
> essential. As Michael Cohen put it: there will be no
> deep people if they are not sent on their way.

ON MONDAY NIGHT, JUNE 4, MEMBERS OF THE CDP TEAM
arrived at our home for our last official meeting. For the thirty-
ninth time, Thomas Sanders had a team on hand to rearrange the
basement.

As people arrived, there were a lot of comments about what
it was going to be like to have a free Monday or two later in
the month. But there was no sense that this was eagerly anticipated. Rather, there was a hint of uneasiness in the air as all of us
contemplated life after CDP.

As we had done at the beginning of almost every other Monday night, we began with prayer, now a flow of expressions of praise, appreciation, and worship.

"Here's what we're going to do tonight," I said when we finished. "Each of you is going to be in the proverbial spotlight for a few minutes while the rest of us talk about what we think just might be your core spiritual giftedness. Don't be surprised if you hear some things about yourself tonight that you never thought of."

"Remember, we're not necessarily talking about talents," Gail added. "We're more interested in what we see in a person when we believe God's hand is upon them. The benefit of this exercise will be in hearing what a dozen other people have been observing about us. And remember, we *affirm*, not . . . ?"

"Applaud," everyone answered.

"Thomas," I said. "We have to start somewhere, and you might as well be first."

For several minutes the group talked about their appreciation for Thomas Sanders and the ways in which he'd contributed to our journey together throughout the year. Finally, Pete Crosby summed up what everybody was saying. "Thomas, we all see you as an organizer. Whenever the group has needed to get something done, you've been among the very first to act. You've got a way of getting people to work as a team. I remember the very first meeting when we hardly knew each other. Gordon asked for a volunteer to set up the circle of chairs each week. You took the job immediately, and I can't remember coming here during these months that you didn't already have people working to arrange the room exactly as Gail and Gordon wanted it. Small thing. But the way you've done it says something about the gift that God has given you. People like to work under your guidance, Thomas."

Olivia Crosby was next. Once again the conversation among group members began while Olivia listened. Several remembered times over the course of the year when Olivia had approached them to say that she sensed they were discouraged or disappointed about something. They talked about her cheerful ways and her quickness to pray for people. And, someone added, Olivia always checked up afterward to see how they were doing.

"You are one of the most intuitive, discerning people I've ever met," Lara Anderson said to Olivia. "You'd be the first person I'd go to if I needed prayer."

Then there was Hugo Padilla. Two or three told funny stories about Hugo and his ways of brightening up the room with humor and enthusiasm.

"We just love you to death, Hugo," Amy Boyd said. "You're always the most optimistic person in the room. I can think of several times when some of us began to disagree about something and were on the verge of real irritability. Immediately you jumped into action and found ways to bring us back together. You're not only a problem solver; you're a peacemaker."

When it was Sara Stephens's turn, everyone began kidding her about her enthusiastic personality. All through the year, Sara was among the very first to leap at new topics and to exclaim over things she was learning.

"Sara has never seen anything she couldn't sell," Pete Crosby said. "She convinces people all day long to give to public radio, and then she comes here and convinces us all that CDP is the greatest thing since sliced bread. Sara, I'm going to bet that you end up being an evangelist. Who could ever say no to Jesus after you've made the introduction? If you're excited about something, the whole world seems to get the message real quick."

After a few more Sara stories, the group moved to Carly Fisher.

"Carly," Olivia Crosby said, "you are such a woman of God.

You never let us forget the importance of prayer and you never stop reminding us that if we forget our dependence on God, things will go flat on us. I think you have the gift of wisdom. You see things that a lot of us don't see at first. And when we listen to you, we come to understandings that we would never have come to by ourselves. You're the first friend I turn to when it comes to getting a broader perspective on what's happening.

Let me mention just a couple more. There was Sherry Nordburg, our introverted librarian. When the group came to her, there were comments about her quietness. Sherry was usually among the last to speak when we dialogued as a group. In the early days of the CDP team, some people had wondered if Sherry would ever say much. But as the year had gone by, she had become more and more vocal. Still, compared to Amy Boyd or Sara Stephens, Sherry was quiet.

"Sherry, I have to tell you," Hugo Padilla said, "I couldn't figure you out when we first began together. Then as the weeks went by, I realized that you were a deep well of thought and insight. You were always watching us and intuiting what we might need, whether it was a Kleenex when we were sneezing or a pen because we didn't have anything to write with. My guess is that your spiritual gift is what Paul called *serving*, or *service*. I think I also see the gift of mercy, maybe even hospitality. You seem to love helping make other people comfortable, providing what they need, supporting them when they have to get something done. And I just want to say thank you. You've been a servant to me many times."

Let me tell you what the group concluded when we got to Rich Fisher. Almost everyone had something to say about their respect for Rich. And I was not surprised at what I heard.

"Everyone knows that Rich is an educator," Pete Crosby said. "He knows how to simplify ideas and explain them so that we can all understand better. If he and Carly lead a CDP team this next year, it's going to be incredible. They will take everything we've done this year, find ways to improve upon it, and cultivate a whole new group of deepening people. What one of them can't do, the other one can. You guys are a great team."

Just as Gail and I had anticipated, the evening became more and more sacred. More than a few cried as we sat in the circle and heard their friends describe them in terms of their growth and gifting. I had the feeling that, in one or two instances, people had never heard anyone talk that openly about them and do it in such an affirming way.

It was almost 10:30 before the meeting ended. Even Gail lost track of the time. None of us wanted to go anywhere.

Finally, since it was mine to do, I ended the evening with this comment: "We'll see you all at the church next Monday at 6:30 p.m. The elders and their wives are planning a big dinner for us and our mentors. And they're going to be asking everybody to talk about what CDP has meant. So think of next Monday evening as part of the rabbi's examination time.

"And I've never kicked you out of the house before, but it's late and we're exhausted. We really need to get to bed. So do you mind hustling on your way, and Gail and I will take care of cleaning up tomorrow morning?"

Respecting my wishes, everyone was soon out the door. Minutes after we'd closed the front door for the last time, Gail and I turned out the lights and fell into bed. I suspect we were both asleep in fifteen minutes.

An hour later—about midnight, I woke up thinking I heard voices. Then I heard a peal of laughter. What was that noise coming from? I realized it was coming from the front of our house, under a streetlight. I lifted the window quietly, wondering what was going on. And I heard familiar voices.

I recognized several of the voices and realized that they were CDP team people who simply didn't want to say good night and go home. They were enjoying one another too much. And then I heard one more voice among the group. The Boston accent was unmistakable. I knew I was hearing the voice of Hank Soriano when I heard the words, "Understand what I'm saying?"

JUNE 11

The Second Spring

To: GMAC, Gail MacDonald, CDP Team, CDP Mentors
From: Geoff Handley
Subject: Dinner on June 11

The elders and their wives would like to invite all of you
to join us for dinner on June 11, 6:30 p.m., at the church.
Please dress casually, but come prepared to talk about what
God has been saying into your lives.

ONE MORNING SEVERAL WEEKS BEFORE THE LAST CDP TEAM
meeting at our home, I joined Geoff Handley, Monica O'Donnell,
Rich Fisher, and Bruce Bartlett for a breakfast at Friendly's. We
were seated at the same table we'd been at almost two years
before when I'd first spoken of my dream of a group of newly
trained (deepened) leaders for our church.

"Gordon," Geoff Handley said after we'd given our orders to the
waitress, "we have an idea for you. We'd like to throw a dinner for
the CDP team and provide them a chance to tell us what they think
this year of CDP has meant to them. Would this be okay with you?"

I said that I thought it was a terrific idea.

"We'd like to invite all the mentors too. And anyone else that
you think needs to be included."

After a minute I said, "Yeah, I can think of a few I'd like to see there." I told Monica that I'd e-mail the names by the end of the day.

"So June 11 it is," Geoff Handley said. "Business adjourned."

The rest of our breakfast was taken up with CDP stories. Rich and I spoke of funny moments on Monday evenings when the laughter could hardly be stopped. Bruce described the responses of the staff to the 20 percent training rule that affected the agenda of each staff meeting. And Geoff and Monica shared the reactions of the elders, who were becoming increasingly responsive to the teaching component of every elders' meeting.

At the end of breakfast, we all agreed: we'd come a long way in two years.

WHEN GAIL AND I ENTERED THE COMMONS ON THE EVEning of June 11, we were amazed at how the room had been transformed to a place of beauty. It had changed from a coffee bar to a banquet hall.

There was soft background music, dimmed lights, and round tables set and decorated with an artistic flair. The elders and their spouses had clearly gone out of the way to send the signal that this was a very important night, not to be forgotten.

Each table had place cards so that everyone knew where to sit. One CDP team member was assigned per table. With them: their mentoring couple. Others at each table were elders and council members (with spouses) and members of the pastoral staff.

As I moved among the tables I also saw the names of some of the most precious people in Gail's life and mine. At one table were place cards for Hank and Cynthia Soriano. At another table I saw the names of Rabbi Michael and Esther Cohen. And at still a third and fourth table, I saw the names of Mercedes Perez, Hana Tchung, and Wilfred and Martine Jean-Baptiste. At the table reserved for Ben and Catherine and their mentors was a name card for Damon Marsh and his mentors, Martin and Kate Lane.

Before long, everyone was seated. The invocation was given by Jason Calder, and we all began to eat a sumptuous meal.

After eating, Gail and I wandered among the tables. We overheard conversations about leaders in church history—Wilberforce, Wesley, Patrick, Slessor, and William and Catherine Booth. In other places the conversation was about temperament and who was similar to whom. I started laughing when I neared the table where Hank and Cynthia Soriano were sitting because I heard Hank saying to the group, "So we're at Fenway, and I asked Gordon what his church's elevator story was, and he said, 'What's an elevator story?'" Even I thought it was funny.

After the dessert and the clearing of tables, Geoff Handley and Monica O'Donnell went to the microphone. Geoff spoke first. "This is a very special night for the elders. We want to celebrate a great idea that you now know as CDP—Cultivating Deep People. It took us two years to get to this moment, and none of us would have ever imagined that it would look like this. We think we've discovered together a new way of doing church ministry. The CDP concept of small groups of people becoming learning teams and helping each other grow has great, great promise."

Then Monica spoke. "We're grateful to all of you who are mentors and who have walked with the CDP team through this year. In the next few minutes we would like to hear from each member of the CDP team. Speaking first and then introducing the rest of the CDP team are Rich and Carly Fisher."

"You know something?" I whispered to Gail. "If this was a year ago, they would have asked Rich to do this. But now somebody's getting the message: we do this as partners, and that's exactly what Rich and Carly are."

Let me give you a condensed version of what was said:

CARLY: This has been one of the most significant years of our lives. We have watched a group of men and women become deepening people. And I can tell you that I've watched my husband deepen over these months as we have met regularly as a little community of learners every Monday night.

RICH: If anyone has been deepened this year, it's Carly and me. I always thought we had a good marriage, but after this year, we have come to love each other more than ever. Tonight is the fortieth night the CDP team has been together. We started the journey learning something about who we were. We continued learning about Christian character and the nature of biblical godliness. We heard each other's stories. We studied how God gives spiritual gifts and leadership skills to his people. And we did a lot of learning about leaders in the Bible and in the history of the Christian movement.

CARLY: Among the most important things we learned was how to sustain ourselves spiritually. A deep person knows how to listen to his or her own heart, how to hear God speak in various ways, and where to go when he or she needs wisdom and encouragement. We'd like to introduce you to the CDP team, even though you have probably met all of them many times before. As we call out their names, Rich and I would like them to come to the front and tell you one thing that has been important to them. The first is Matt Cundiff. Matt?

MATT: In all my life, no one ever came to me and told me that they saw something special enough in me to make them want to invest in my future. No one!

When Pastor Mac approached me last summer about CDP, I was blown out of the water. I had no idea how much this year would change my life.

LARA: I know that Pastor Mac and Gail want us to talk about the things we read over the year or something like that, but, for me, the most memorable thing about being in their home was watching the two of them working together. Hang around them for a while, and you discover that they're very different people—temperamental opposites, as Gail puts it. But they've learned how to work together as partners. Watching how they've done that has given me a lot of hope about my own future.

PETE AND OLIVIA: Don't ever believe the critic who says that people in a church don't know how to care for each other. We went through a terrible moment during the CDP year, and we experienced what it was like to be surrounded by a community of brothers and sisters. We've seen real care close up. And we've learned this year how Christ-oriented caring works. We've dedicated ourselves to becoming people who will always want to come alongside when God prompts us with the word that someone's in trouble.

THOMAS: I've always been a loudmouth. I've talked too much and, if the truth was told, had little that was substantial to say. This year I learned how to listen and how to speak a bit more humbly. I don't have to have the last or the loudest word. I know how to add my voice to the voices of others and come to insights that God wants to give us together.

SHERRY: I've been the quiet one in the group. Quiet because I never thought I had much of value to say. But the CDP team taught me that God has things to say through me. They made me feel confident that I was not in CDP by mistake. I will always be introverted, I suppose, but I'm no longer afraid to speak out of my heart.

HUGO: I learned to read this year. I mean really, really read with understanding. I learned to listen to authors and study biblical characters with the assumption that each of them had something to teach me.

SARA: While I agree with everything else that's been said, I want to say something about what it's like as a single woman who came out of a broken family to be welcomed into the kind of home Pastor Mac and Gail have. The way Gail has decorated her home—pictures on the wall, the modesty of the furnishings, the warmth of the color. Their home just pulls you in and says, "You're safe and valued here." I learned much about hospitality and how God can use our homes to provide a place for deepening.

AMY: I received so much from the guests that came to our CDP team meetings and opened their lives to us. Some of you came and told your stories. You made me love our church more than ever because I got to see you outside the church building and get a sense of who you are and what you believe in. I loved getting to know Mr. and Mrs. Soriano as they came over from their house again and again and made sure we were well fed. I'm thrilled to see Rabbi and Mrs. Cohen here tonight because I will never forget their visit and the things they taught us about learning. And Mercedes Perez gave me a great sense of how a woman can be a leader not just in church but in the world of business. Mr. and Mrs. Anand? We have never heard a story of love like yours. And the Jean-Baptistes: what can you say about them? They are 100 percent joy and love. We're all different in some way because of these people.

Next up was Damon Marsh.

Damon Marsh? I thought to myself. *Had Rich and Carly planned for him to speak?* I was astounded, and my heart was pounding through my chest as Damon walked slowly with the aid of a cane to the microphone.

Damon stood silently for a minute, and then he began. "In the world of running, there is a term that indicates that a runner failed to finish a race. The term is DNF, and it stands for *did not finish*. I am the one who didn't finish this year. I dropped out, something like a few of the disciples-gone-AWOL in the Bible. I know about Judas Iscariot, Jesus' disciple, and about Demas, Paul's disciple. In both cases, they didn't finish. But I'm most attracted to Simon Peter because, although he dropped out for a moment, he did, in fact, finish. And he finished well.

"So I want to say this. The DNF beside my name is about to be erased. Pastor Mac and Gail have made it plain to me that I'm going to have a second chance to join a CDP team, starting in September. I've learned that this is what one calls *grace*. All these who have just spoken are deepening people because they finished. I'm deepening in another way. I didn't finish, and God's using my experience to teach me."

When Damon started back to his seat, I got up from my chair and hugged him as tightly as I could. And we both wept.

That left Ben and Catherine Jacobs.

CATHERINE: Thank you, all of you, for giving me my husband. Thank you, Aunt Connie, for taking a young and deeply hurting Ben Jacobs into your home. And thank you, all of you church leaders, for standing behind CDP. I've watched my husband become a deepened man this year. We are on a journey together that is headed somewhere exciting. Like Abraham's journey toward faith—I hope I say this right, Rabbi Cohen—we, too, are on a journey of faith. We've learned a very important thing in our CDP team: that God wants us to be fully submitted to his purposes. And that's where we are headed tonight: to becoming fully submitted.

BEN: Catherine has said it all, I think. This church saved my life . . . no, I guess God did through you. I came here a total mess six years ago. Russ Milner and Ernie Yost, they latched on to me and wouldn't let go. Now I've become a husband, a father, and a friend to many of you in this community. I know we're supposed to make Jesus proud, and I want to do that. But I want to make all of you proud too. I am your son in the Lord.

THERE WERE COMMENTS FROM A COUPLE OF THE MENTORS who spoke of what it meant to have CDP members in their homes over the year. They admitted to some fear when the year began, but, they said, they had become convinced of the importance of mixing it up with younger people.

One of them said, "My best friends are my age. Nothing surprising about that. But I learned this year that if you want to stay young, if you want your life to mean something, get into the world of people younger than yourself. Listen to them; tell them your story; give dignity to their questions; cheer them on. You'll have something worthwhile to do for a lifetime."

THEN THE FINAL MOMENTS OF THE EVENING WERE GIVEN TO Gail and me. As we went to the front of the commons, the CDP team, followed by others, gave us a warm round of applause that was a bit embarrassing. When they finally became quiet, Gail and I spoke.

> **GORDON**: There's a thousand thanks to give for what has happened this year. But I want to say a public thank-you to Hana Tchung. She has prayed twice a week every one of these forty weeks for Gail and me and the CDP team. I have got to believe that Hana deserves a gold medal for her part.
>
> **GAIL**: The elders made a big decision when they relieved Gordon of certain responsibilities so that he and I could major on training initiative. CDP simply wouldn't have happened without their support. We now have a dozen men and women whom we see God preparing for positions of influence in and beyond the life of our church. And they are simply the beginning of what we think will be many, many more.
>
> **GORDON**: Among the most important conversations I had when the so-called great idea started coming to life were the ones I had with Rich. Rich was the one who gave me the idea to talk about deep people. There followed many conversations with both Rich and Carly as we planned and prayed together.
>
> The pastoral staff—Bruce, Claire, Jason—have been behind the CDP initiative from day one. I cannot tell you how many conversations I enjoyed with them as we dreamed together about what a difference something like CDP could be for our church.
>
> Rabbi Cohen gave me a wonderful gift when he

talked to me about the rabbinical contract and gave me so much insight on how Jesus trained his talmidim. Thank you, Michael. And Mercedes Perez. We garnered some great ideas from what I learned when I visited the Northeast Center. Then there are Hank and Cynthia Soriano, our neighbors and friends. Most of you will never know how many ways they served behind the scenes and made what we did in our home a possibility. And to the rest of you: your questions, your encouragement, your prayers are simply the greatest gift you could have given.

GAIL: If it's thanks we're giving, then both Gordon and I want to give a public thanksgiving to God, who put this great idea into our hearts and into the hearts of many of you. In the final analysis, CDP is not about any of us. It's been God's from the beginning. We all—the team, the mentors, Gordon and me—we are his to be used. We have had the guidance of God's Spirit throughout this process. If there has been accomplishment, the credit belongs to him.

We love you, CDP team. We'll look forward to conversations with each of you this summer as we think about where you go from here. We're not going to let you go. We've got too much love invested in you. And whether or not you end up using your giftedness in the church or in something beyond the church, our prayer is it will be done in Jesus' name.

SOON AFTER, THE EVENING ENDED WITH A BEAUTIFUL BENEdiction from Claire Dustin. There were a lot of hugs, expressions of thanks, and pictures taken.

Michael and Esther Cohen came over to thank Gail and me for

being included. It was clear that Michael was greatly touched by what he'd heard and seen. "Maybe . . . maybe, my friend, Gordon, you can help me start a CDP group of my own."

A half hour later, Gail and I were headed home. During the ten-minute drive, we rehearsed the evening and what it had meant to us. "I was reading through my journal this morning," I said to Gail. "I came across a reference to that moment two summers back when I thought I'd heard God speak: *'You must pray for an idea that will keep your elevator story honest.'* You know, that's when this whole thing started . . . unless, of course, you want to go further back to our night at Fenway with the Sorianos."

When we drove into our driveway, who should be sitting on our front steps but Hank and Cynthia?

"Don't worry. No problems," Hank said when we approached them.

"We just wanted to be the last guys to say thanks tonight," Cynthia added.

"I want you to know that this has been the most important year of my life," Hank said. "Cyn and I became a part of a community of people like we thought we'd never meet. We've become Christ-followers. We're excited about where our lives may head in this new journey. After all, we've probably got gifts like all the other guys. Next year we'll figure out what they are."

With that, the Sorianos began to walk away toward their home. Then, suddenly, Hank turned around and said, "Oh, by the way. The company just gave me four tickets to one of the Red Sox–Yankee games in July. We need to get that night on our calendars. Understand what I'm saying?"

REFERENCES

Brother Lawrence (1611–1691). *The Practice of the Presence of God.*
Brewster, MA: Paraclete Press, reprint 2010.

Foster, Richard. *Celebration of Discipline.* New York: HarperCollins,
1988. (emphasis added)

Kiersey, David and Bates, Marilyn M. *Please Understand Me.* Del Mar,
CA: Prometheus Nemesis, 1984.

Larabee, Eric. *Commander in Chief: Franklin Delano Roosevelt, His
Lieutenants, and Their War.* Annapolis, MD: Naval Institute Press,
2004.

MacDonald, Gordon. *Who Stole My Church? What to Do When the
Church You Love Tries to Enter the 21st Century.* Nashville: Thomas
Nelson, 2008.

Sanders, Oswald. *Spiritual Leadership.* Chicago: Moody, orig. 1967,
reprint 1994.

Sangster, W. E. *Doctor Sangster.* London: Epworth Press, 1962, 109.

Thornton, Martin. *Spiritual Direction.* Boston: Cowley Publications, 1984.

West Point, the US Military Academy. "Mission." http://www
.militarynewcomers.com/WESTPOINT/resources/04_miss.html.

Yeats, William Butler (1865–1939). "The Second Coming." Lines 2–3,
6–7. Available at http://www.online-literature.com/donne/780/.

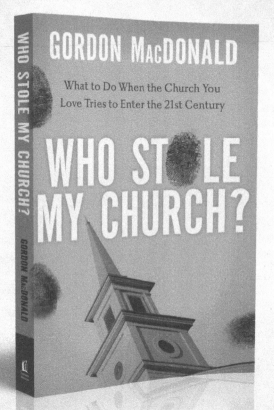